Step by Step
to College and Career Success

Fourth Edition

Step by Step
to College
and Career
Success

John N. Gardner

President, John N. Gardner Institute for Excellence in Undergraduate Education
Brevard, North Carolina

Distinguished Professor Emeritus, Library and Information Science
Senior Fellow, National Resource Center for The First-Year Experience
and Students in Transition
University of South Carolina, Columbia

Betsy O. Barefoot

Vice President and Senior Scholar
John N. Gardner Institute for Excellence in Undergraduate Education
Brevard, North Carolina

Bedford/St. Martin's

Boston | New York

For Bedford/St. Martin's

Executive Editor: Carrie Brandon
Developmental Editors: Julie Kelly and Martha Bustin
Senior Production Editor: Christina Horn
Production Supervisor: Andrew Ensor
Marketing Manager: Christina Shea
Editorial Assistant: Nicholas Murphy
Production Assistant: Alexis Biasell
Copyeditor: Susan Zorn
Indexer: Jake Kawatski
Senior Art Director: Anna Palchik
Text and Cover Design: TODA (The Office of Design and Architecture)
Cover Art: Photograph by Jonathan Stark
Composition: Greg Johnson, Textbook Perfect
Printing and Binding: RR Donnelley and Sons

President: Joan E. Feinberg
Editorial Director: Denise B. Wydra
Editor in Chief: Karen S. Henry
Director of Marketing: Karen R. Soeltz
Director of Production: Susan W. Brown
Associate Director, Editorial Production: Elise S. Kaiser
Managing Editor: Elizabeth M. Schaaf

Library of Congress Control Number: 2010928942

Copyright © 2011, 2010, 2008, 2006 by Bedford/St. Martin's

Manufactured in the United States of America.

5 4 3 2 1
f e d c b

For information, write: Bedford/St. Martin's, 75 Arlington Street, Boston, MA 02116 (617-399-4000)

ISBN: 978-0-312-63801-6

Acknowledgments

All photographs by Jonathan Stark except as noted. Page 33: © Digital Vision/Getty Images; page 41: Banana Stock/Superstock; page 50: The Advertising Archives; page 68: © David Fischer/Getty Images; page 143: Anderson Ross/Blend Images/Punchstock.

Brief Contents

Contents

13

Staying Healthy   158

Feedback

Letters to the Editors of *Step by Step*

Read what instructors are saying about *Step by Step to College and Career Success*. Have some feedback of your own? We would love to hear from you. Please email us at collegesuccess@bedfordstmartins.com.

"I am truly enjoying using this book, and the students are actually answering the questions in it. The online videos are terrific."

Jennifer Rockwood
University of Toledo

"This text is direct and to the point with specific advice in every area that is important to college success. The material is easily read and immediately relevant to every student. The special boxed features such as Where to Go for Help provide easy access to helpful information."

Judy Lynch
Kansas State University

"[*Step by Step to College and Career Success* contains] compressed, efficient information, which is helpful to the fast paced program we offer (10 weeks as opposed to 18). It has some of the same core concepts for each general topic area that I have found very helpful to offer students for college success."

Evelyn Dufner
International Academy of Design and Technology

"*Step by Step to College and Career Success* effectively addresses transitional issues, academic success skills, and considerations about exploring future careers. These are important topics for all first-year students. In addition, the textbook is not only informational; it is also direct and to the point in its delivery."

Dorothy Ward
University of Texas at El Paso

"I like that the book is inclusive in the topics, language, tone, and target audience. It is written to embrace a broad range of experiences. I also like the self-assessments that come with the beginning of each chapter."

Carrie McLean
North Carolina State University

"[*Step by Step to College and Career Success* is] an up-to-date, hip book for first-year students that realistically looks at life as a college student."

Lynn Burgess
Tallahassee Community College

"[*Step by Step to College and Career Success* is] concise, to the point, relevant, [and offers] great coverage of important topics for all college students."

Patricia Santoianni
Sinclair Community College

"This text is a succinct volume with information on all the traditional student success topics. The Building Your Portfolio activities are excellent applications of the topics."

Patsy Krech
The University of Memphis

Preface

What does it mean to be a successful college student? Because today's students are more varied than ever before in terms of backgrounds, goals, and resources, the answer is not always obvious.

Many students in college are seeking not only high academic performance but also practical tools for career advancement—or help succeeding at the jobs they have right now. Students might be entering college directly from high school, they might be entering after taking time off to work or to explore alternatives to college, or they might be taking classes while still working. Students at community colleges might plan to transfer to four-year institutions, or they might be working toward an associate's degree or certificate. At all institutions, many more students today are "nontraditional," whether that means older than eighteen or balancing the responsibilities of work and family care with the demands of school. We have more students in our classrooms whose first language is not English. And many students today are the first in their families to attend college—so they might be unfamiliar with the conventions of higher education in the United States.

Given this variety of students and goals, there might not be a single definition of college success—but clearly, there is a greater need than ever for a course and a text that can support students and teachers in the college success course.

One thing is true these days of almost all students—of most of us, in fact. We have less time available for sustained reading, and our expectations have been transformed by the visual quality of digital media. Many college students will be more easily engaged by a book—and will more easily digest its contents—if it is succinct and to the point, especially if presented in a visually dynamic manner. Even our education cycles have been speeded up: The material that used to be covered in a full year is now often treated in shorter courses lasting sixteen weeks, ten weeks, or even fewer.

We created *Step by Step* to provide an accessible book that would be useful to all students, whatever their backgrounds or their educational goals. We've pared away extras and have focused on the most crucial skills and the most important choices that students have to make. *Step by Step* is a convenient tool kit that covers a wide variety of topics in a format that will encourage its use. The coverage of each topic is concise, and the design makes it easy for students to find and understand the material. Our intention has been to create a book that can serve as both the text for a wide-ranging course and as a reliable reference for students in classes with a condensed syllabus.

For schools and instructors who want more in-depth coverage in a more traditional format, we publish two other titles. *Your College Experience,* Ninth Edition, addresses the whole student, with chapters not only on academic skills and critical thinking, but also on managing money, relationships, wellness, and choosing a career (ISBN-13: 978-0-312-68862-2). *Your College Experience,* Concise Ninth Edition, focuses on academic topics and now has expanded coverage of writing, speaking, the library, research, and information literacy (ISBN-13: 978-0-312-63799-6).

New to the Fourth Edition

Bedford/St. Martin's Commitment to Development and Design

Every sentence and paragraph of this book has been edited with care to ensure that it is concise and to the point. The book's new provocative design is similarly streamlined and functional and offers a modular organization, which makes the book easier for students to read and use as a reference.

New Chapters on Topics Relevant to Today's Students

- **A new chapter on money management** outlines important strategies from how to create a budget and cut costs to how to obtain and keep financial aid.

- **A new chapter on technology in college** covers such topics as navigating learning management systems and online course registration, understanding information literacy, and conducting electronic research.

Expanded Coverage of Topics Critical to College Success

- **A new section on emotional intelligence** discusses what emotional intelligence is, why everyone should understand it, and why it matters in college.

- **A completely revised critical-thinking chapter** makes this complex but crucial topic easier to teach and learn. The revised chapter includes advice on becoming a critical thinker, avoiding logical fallacies, thinking critically about arguments, and evaluating sources.

- **Expanded coverage of diversity:** At the request of users, we have broadened our coverage and devoted an entire chapter to this important topic. It discusses various issues from understanding diversity to embracing diversity on campus.

New End-of-Chapter Exercises to Help Students Assess What They've Learned

Every chapter ends with a collection of exercises. A one-minute paper prompt is a quick and easy assessment tool that will help alert you when students don't understand what was said or discussed in class. Short-answer questions ask students to reflect on chapter material and its relevance to their academic and personal lives both now and in the future. Fully revised Building Your Portfolio exercises help students assemble a collection of their own work.

Resources for Instructors

For more information about instructor resources and to request a copy, visit **bedfordstmartins.com/ stepbystep/catalog**.

The **Instructor's Manual and Test Bank**, revised by Julie Alexander-Hamilton of the John N. Gardner Institute for Excellence in Undergraduate Education, includes chapter objectives, teaching suggestions, additional exercises, test questions, a list of common concerns of first-year students, an introduction to the first-year experience course, a sample lesson plan for each chapter, and various case studies relevant to the topics covered. Available in print and online.

The **Computerized Test Bank** includes a mix of fresh, carefully crafted multiple-choice, fill-in-the-blank, and short-answer questions. The questions appear in Microsoft Word format and in easy-to-use test bank software that allows instructors to add, edit, resequence, and print questions and answers. Instructors can also export questions into a variety of formats, including WebCT and Blackboard.

Ideas and Conversations: A Collection of Interviews about Teaching College Success, a film directed by Peter Berkow and produced by Bedford/St. Martin's, features interviews with instructors and administrators involved in the College Success course. Meet your colleagues and hear their tips for teaching this course and getting students engaged. The film is available both online and on DVD.

French Fries Are Not Vegetables and Other College Lessons: A Documentary on the First Year of College follows five students through their first year in college as they live through this crucial transition. Gritty and honest, the film looks at this transition from the student's perspective. Available on DVD and free to all adopters.

The **Custom with Care program** allows Bedford/St. Martin's Custom Publishing to offer the highest-quality books and media created in consultation with publishing professionals committed to the discipline. Make *Step by Step to College and Career Success* more closely fit your course and goals by integrating your own materials, including only the parts of the text you intend to use in your course, or both. Contact your local Bedford/St. Martin's sales representative for more information.

Student Resources and Packaging Options

For more information about the items listed below, visit **bedfordstmartins.com/stepbystep/catalog** or go directly to the Web addresses listed.

Your College Experience companion Web site offers a variety of rich learning resources designed to enhance the student experience—all for **free**: videos illustrating important concepts and skills, with accompanying discussion questions; podcasts with quick advice on note-taking, money management, and other topics; links to sites offering more information and support; and more. Go to **bedfordstmartins.com/Gardner**.

CourseSmart e-Book for Step by Step to College and Career Success is a downloadable version of *Step by Step*, Fourth Edition, at about half the price of the print book. To learn more about this low-cost alternative, produced through partnership with CourseSmart, go to **www.coursesmart.com**.

VideoCentral: College Success is a growing collection of online videos for the college success classroom. The exciting new documentary *French Fries Are Not Vegetables and Other College Lessons* (see above) is available here, as are brief clips illustrating important concepts and skills. *VideoCentral* can be packaged with a print book or purchased separately.

Bedford/St. Martin's Insider's Guides are concise and student-friendly booklets on topics critical to college success and are a perfect complement to your textbook and course. Bundle one with any Bedford/St. Martin's textbook at no additional cost. Topics include:

- **NEW** Insider's Guide to Global Citizenship
- **NEW** Insider's Guide to Personal Responsibility
- **NEW** Insider's Guide to College Etiquette
- Insider's Guide to Credit Cards
- Insider's Guide to Beating Test Anxiety

- Insider's Guide to Time Management
- Insider's Guide to Getting Involved on Campus
- Insider's Guide to Community College

The Bedford/St. Martin's Planner includes everything that students need to plan and use their time effectively, with advice on preparing schedules and to-do lists and blank schedules and calendars (monthly and weekly) for planning. Integrated into the planner are quick tips on fixing common grammar errors, taking notes, and succeeding on tests; an address book; and an annotated list of useful Web sites. The planner fits easily into a backpack or purse.

The **Writing Journal**, designed to give students an opportunity to use writing as a way to explore their thoughts and feelings, includes a generous supply of inspirational quotes placed throughout the pages, tips for journaling, and suggested journal topics.

TradeUp allows you to bring more value and choice to your students' first-year experience by packaging *Step by Step to College and Career Success* with one of a thousand titles from Macmillan publishers at a 50 percent discount off the regular price. See the inside front cover or contact your local Bedford/St. Martin's sales representative for more information.

About the Authors

John N. Gardner brings unparalleled experience to this authoritative text for first-year seminar courses. John is the recipient of his institution's highest award for teaching excellence. He has twenty-five years of experience directing and teaching in the most respected and most widely emulated first-year seminar in the country, the University 101 course at the University of South Carolina. John is universally recognized as one of the country's leading educators for his role in initiating and orchestrating an international reform movement to improve the beginning college experience, a concept he coined as "the first-year experience." He is the founding executive director/president of two influential higher education centers that support campuses in their efforts to improve the learning and retention of beginning college students: the National Resource Center for The First-Year Experience and Students in Transition at the University of South Carolina (www.sc.edu/fye), and the John N. Gardner Institute for Excellence in Undergraduate Education (www.jngi.org), based in Brevard, North

Carolina. The experiential basis for all of his work is his own miserable first year of college on academic probation, an experience he hopes to prevent for this book's readers. Today, as a much happier adult, John is married to fellow author of this book, Betsy Barefoot.

Betsy O. Barefoot is a writer, researcher, and teacher whose special area of scholarship is the first year of college. During her tenure at the University of South Carolina from 1988 to 1999, she served as codirector for research and publications at the National Resource Center for The First-Year Experience and Students in Transition. She taught University 101, in addition to special-topics graduate courses on the first-year experience and the principles of college teaching. She conducts first-year seminar faculty training workshops around the United States and in other countries and is frequently called on to evaluate first-year seminar outcomes. Betsy currently serves as vice president and senior scholar of the John N. Gardner Institute for Excellence in Undergraduate Education, in Brevard, North Carolina. In this role she led a major national research project to identify institutions of excellence in the first college year. She currently works with both two- and four-year campuses in evaluating all components of the first year.

Acknowledgments

Although this text speaks with the voices of its two authors, it represents contributions from many others. We gratefully acknowledge these contributions and thank these individuals, whose special expertise has made it possible to introduce new college students to their college experience through the holistic approach we deeply believe in.

Chris Gurrie has been active in the first-year experience and first-year issues for several years. Recently he was the chair of the first-year committee and is currently an academic adviser at the University of Tampa. Chris's research areas include technology, generational characteristics, and the use and misuse of PowerPoint in higher education. He teaches the first-year seminar, Gateways; public speaking; business communication; and education abroad. Chris holds a B.A. from Purdue University, an M.S. from Florida State University, and an Ed.D. from Nova Southeastern University. Chris coauthored the new Chapter 9, Technology in College.

Catherine Andersen is Associate Provost for Enrollment at Gallaudet University. Prior to this appointment, she was Gallaudet's Interim Dean of Enrollment Management and General Studies as well Director of the First-Year Experience for ten years. She is a Teagle Assessment Scholar (a national group that assists liberal arts colleges and universities in assessing student outcomes), an affiliate of the John N. Gardner Institute for Excellence in Undergraduate Education, and a certified master trainer in Emotional Intelligence assessment. Catherine received her B.S. from Ohio University, her M.S. from Hofstra University, and her Ph.D. from Indiana University. Catherine contributed her valuable and considerable expertise to the writing of the Emotional Intelligence section of Chapter 3, How You Learn.

Throughout her career of more than thirty years, **Natala Kleather (Tally) Hart** has served students with limited opportunities for higher education. Her work includes service in financial aid offices at several four-year public institutions: University of California, San Diego, Purdue University, Indiana University, and Ohio State University; public service as the head of the Indiana State Scholarship and Loan Commission; and service to institutions of higher education at the College Board. She has contributed widely to college student financial literacy initiatives to improve student retention and completion. Her current role is as the founding head of the Economic Access Initiative at Ohio State, which works to develop and evaluate mechanisms to encourage college attendance among low-income fourth- through tenth-grade Ohio students and enrollment in graduate and professional programs for first-generation college students. Tally contributed her valuable and considerable expertise to the writing of the new Chapter 10, Managing Money.

Kate Trombitas is the Assistant Director of Ohio State University's Student Wellness Center, where she serves as a financial specialist for undergraduate, graduate, and professional students. She holds a bachelor's degree in business administration from the Fisher College of Business, Ohio State, and a master's degree in communications, also from Ohio State. Kate contributed her valuable and considerable expertise to the writing of the new Chapter 10, Managing Money.

Julie Alexander-Hamilton is the Associate Vice President for Assessment Administration at the John N. Gardner Institute for Excellence in Undergraduate Education. She actively engages with colleges and universities as they prepare for and conduct an intensive self-study of the first year of college. Julie holds an M.A. in college student development and a B.S. in psychology from Appalachian State University. While at Appalachian, Julie taught the three-credit-hour first-year seminar and was involved in faculty development and support, peer leader recruitment and training, and planning and implementing of Appalachian's residential summer bridge program. Julie developed and wrote the end-of-chapter review exercises and activities in this book.

We would also like to acknowledge and thank the numerous colleagues who have contributed to this book in its previous editions: Michelle Murphy Burcin, University of South Carolina at Columbia; Tom Carskadon, Mississippi State University; Juan Flores, Folsom Lake College; Philip Gardner, Michigan State University; Jeanne L. Higbee, University of Minnesota, Twin Cities; Mary Ellen O'Leary, University of South Carolina at Columbia; Constance Staley, University of Colorado at Colorado Springs; R. Stephen Staley, Colorado Technical University; and Edward Zlotkowski, Bentley College.

We are also indebted to the following reviewers who offered us thoughtful and constructive feedback on the book:

Andy Alt, *Bowling Green State University*

Heather Castro, *Wright State University*

Julie Chi, *Minneapolis Community and Technical College*

Audra Cooke, *Rock Valley College*

Patricia Santoianni, *Sinclair Community College*

Bruce Skolnick, *Edinboro University of Pennsylvania*

Mike Wood, *Missouri State University*

Jennifer Rockwood, *University of Toledo*

Jodi Webb, *Bowling Green State University*

Robert Buford, *University of New Mexico*

Lynn Burgess, *Tallahassee Community College*

Jennifer Crissman Ishler, *Penn State University*

Evelyn Dufner, *International Academy of Design and Technology*

Patsy Krech, *The University of Memphis*

Judy Lynch, *Kansas State University*

Carrie McLean, *North Carolina State University*

Donna Richardson-Hall, *Mercer County Community College*

Sara Smith, *Highland Community College*

Dorothy Ward, *University of Texas at El Paso*

As we look to the future, we are excited about the numerous improvements to this text that our creative Bedford/St. Martin's team has made and will continue to make.

Special thanks to Joan Feinberg, President of Bedford/St. Martin's; Denise Wydra, Editorial Director; Karen Henry, Editor in Chief; Carrie Brandon, Executive Editor; Julie Kelly, Development Editor; Martha Bustin, Senior Development Editor; Christina Shea, Marketing Manager; Nicholas Murphy, Editorial Assistant; Elise Kaiser, Associate Director, Editorial Production; and Christina Horn, Senior Production Editor.

Most of all, we thank you, the users of our book, for you are the true inspiration for this work.

Step by Step
to College
and Career
Success

01 Beginning College

No matter what your age and background, the fact that you are going to college means that you have the opportunity to change your life for the better. Success in college will depend on your commitment and your willingness to take advantage of all that your institution has to offer. Some entering students find college far more challenging than they thought it would be. This book is a step-by-step guide to college success; reading and remembering the information in each chapter will help you avoid the kinds of problems that sometimes trip up even the best students in the first year.

Don't forget that college life is more than academic work. It is also about making the most of new and continuing relationships and finding your niche on campus. You'll have many opportunities to meet other students and instructors in and out of class. And whether you live at home or on campus, you'll want to communicate regularly with members of your family. During your first term, investigate opportunities for becoming involved in a campus group or organization. Meeting others who share your talents or interests will help you feel at home in this new environment.

You're on an exciting journey and this book can be your roadmap. If you follow these strategies, you will achieve more than you might have dreamed possible in college and your career.

How Do You Measure Up?

1. I know how to set short-term goals for my academic success.
   - ○ Agree
   - ○ Don't Know
   - ○ Disagree

2. I plan to get to know my instructors.
   - ○ Agree
   - ○ Don't Know
   - ○ Disagree

3. I intend to join at least one campus group or organization in my first year.
   - ○ Agree
   - ○ Don't Know
   - ○ Disagree

4. I want to help my family members feel a part of my college experience.
   - ○ Agree
   - ○ Don't Know
   - ○ Disagree

Review the items you marked "don't know" or "disagree." Paying attention to all these aspects of your college experience can be very important to your success. After reading this chapter, come back to this list and think about ways you can work on these areas.

02

03

04

05

06

07

08

09

10

11

12

13

Making a Commitment and Staying Focused

Jane Tabuchi

18-year-old student in her first semester

My brother is ruining my life.

Okay, so that's not exactly true. But it feels true. I mean, here I am at college—making new friends, enjoying my seminar course, and wanting to join a campus group, as my instructor, Ms. Burns, suggests. But my older brother Rudy was such a crazy joiner that he flunked out his second semester. He was never great at time management and always left his homework till the last minute, but as soon as he got to campus, he joined an intramural soccer team, a political association, and a hiking club. He got overextended, big time, and our parents were upset, to say the least, when his college career came to a crashing halt. Now there is a club that I would like to join, one involved with volunteer community service, and the deadline to join is a week away. I've actually thought about joining the group behind my parents' backs. But they're pretty cool, at least if I promise them that I will keep things in a better balance than Rudy did and that I will not let my class work or my grades slip. I wonder, though, if I will really be able to make good on that promise.

What would you do if you were Jane?

Why do so many students have problems in the first year? For those fresh out of high school, a major challenge is newfound freedom. Your college instructors are not going to tell you what, how, or when to study. If you live on campus, your parents aren't there to wake you in the morning, see that you eat well and get enough sleep, monitor whether or how carefully you do your homework, and remind you to allow enough time to get to class. Getting it done now depends on you.

For returning students, the opposite is true: Most experience an overwhelming lack of freedom. Working, caring for a family, and meeting other commitments and responsibilities compete for the time and attention it takes to do their best or even simply to persist in college.

Whichever challenges you are facing, what will motivate you to stay focused? And what about the enormous investment of time and money that getting a college degree requires? Are you convinced that the investment will pay off? Have you selected a major, or is this on your list of things to do after you arrive? Do you know where to go when you need help with a personal or financial problem? If you are a minority student on your campus, are you concerned about how you will be treated?

Thoughts like these are very common. Although your classmates might not say it out loud, many of them share your concerns, doubts, and fears. This course will be a safe place for you to talk about all of these issues with people who care about you and your success in college.

Making the Transition

The differences between high school and college can also make starting college difficult. You may be attending a college far from home, one in which you are part of a more diverse or a larger student body. Your classes also may be larger and may meet for longer periods of time. Because college classes meet on various days, managing your time and juggling other commitments will be a challenge. In most colleges there are literally hundreds of courses to choose from, and you will be expected to do academic work out of class, including your own original research.

Your experience in your classes will also be different. College tests are given less frequently than you might be used to, but you will probably do more writing than you did in high school. In high school, courses tend to be textbook-focused, but you may find that your college instructors rarely focus on the textbook and instead use a variety of sources to prepare their lectures.

Advantages of a College Education

According to the Carnegie Commission on Higher Education, these are some of the benefits enjoyed by college graduates:

- You will have a more stable job history.
- You will earn more promotions.
- You will likely be happier with your work.
- You will be less likely than a nongraduate to become unemployed.
- Not only will you earn more with a college degree, but you also will find it easier to get a job and hold on to it.

Of course, college will affect you in other ways. A well-rounded college education will expand life's possibilities for you. As a result:

- You will learn how to work independently and discover new knowledge.
- You will encounter and learn more about how to appreciate the cultural, artistic, and spiritual dimensions of life.
- You will learn more about how to seek appropriate information before making a decision.
- You will grow intellectually through learning about and interacting with cultures, languages, ethnic groups, religions, nationalities, and socioeconomic groups other than your own.

One of the best aspects of college is that you will have the opportunity to meet people who are different from you and to make many new friends, some of whom may be friends for life.

Returning Students versus Traditional Students

Similarly, returning students must deal with major life changes when they begin college. Sometimes going to college while working can be stressful, but reexploring higher education can also be exciting and invigorating. Those whose grown children have moved away may find college to be a new beginning, a stimulating challenge, or a path to a new career. Generally speaking, returning students tend to take their studies more seriously and work harder than some younger students. Therefore they earn higher grades. Age brings with it a wealth of wisdom and experience that can help returning students achieve, and even exceed, their goals.

Setting Goals for Success

What can you do to achieve success? One method is to set specific goals as you start your courses that will help you reach your potential.

College is an ideal time to begin setting and fulfilling short- and long-term goals. A short-term goal might be to read twenty pages from your history text twice a week, anticipating an exam that will cover the first hundred pages of the book. A long-term goal might be to begin predicting which college courses will help you attain your career goals. (It's okay if you don't know which career to pursue; more than 60 percent of college students change majors at least once.)

Follow these guidelines to set some short-term goals:

1. State your goal in measurable terms. Be specific about what you want to achieve and when.

2. Be sure that the goal is achievable. Allow enough time to pursue it. If you don't have the necessary skills, strengths, and resources to achieve your goal, modify it appropriately.

3. Be sure you genuinely want to achieve the goal. Don't set out to work toward something only because you want to please others.

4. Know why the goal matters. Be sure your goal fits into a larger plan and has the potential to give you a sense of accomplishment.

5. Identify difficulties you might encounter. Plan for ways you might overcome obstacles.

6. Decide which goal comes next. How will you begin? Create steps and a time line for reaching your next goal.

try it!

How College Is Different from High School

Think back to your high school. What did you enjoy most about it? How does your experience so far in college compare to your high school experience? Is it better or worse? Why?

Connecting with Your Instructors

One of the most important types of relationships you can develop in college is with your course instructors. The basis of such relationships is mutual respect. Instructors who respect students treat them fairly and are willing to help them both in and out of class. Students who respect instructors come to class regularly and take their work seriously.

What Your Instructors Expect from You

While instructors' expectations might vary depending on a particular course, most instructors expect their students to exhibit attitudes and behaviors that are basic to student success. They expect you to come to class, do the assigned work to the best of your ability, listen and participate, think critically about course material, and persist—that is, not give up when a concept is difficult to master. Instructors also expect honesty and candor. Many instructors will invite you to express your feelings about the course anonymously in writing through one-minute papers or other forms of class assessment. Generally college instructors expect that you're going to be self-motivated to do your best. Your grade school and high school teachers might have spent a great deal of time thinking about how to motivate you, but college faculty will usually consider this need for motivation to be your personal responsibility.

What You Can Expect from Your Instructors

The expectations you have for college instructors may be based on what you have heard, both positive and negative, from friends, fellow students, and family members. In your actual classes, you will find that instructors vary in basic personality and in experience. You might have instructors who are in their first year of teaching, either as graduate students or as new professors. Other instructors might be seasoned professors who have taught generations of new students. Some will be introverted and difficult to approach; others will be open, friendly, and willing to talk to you and your classmates. No matter what their level of experience, basic personality, or skill as a lecturer, you should expect your instructors to grade you fairly and provide meaningful feedback on your papers and

exams. Your instructors should be organized, prepared, and enthusiastic about their academic field. And they should be accessible. You should always be able to approach your instructors if you need assistance or if you have a personal problem that affects your academic work.

try it!

Getting to Know Your Instructors

Which of your instructors would you most like to get to know? Sometime in the next two weeks, make an appointment to see that instructor. Find out what that instructor expects of students in his or her classes.

Making the Most of the Learning Relationship

Contrary to what you might have heard, most college instructors appreciate your willingness to ask for appointments. Though it might seem a little scary, the best way to establish an appropriate relationship with an instructor is to schedule an appointment early in the term. At this meeting, introduce yourself, tell why you are taking the course (besides the fact that it's required), and what you hope to learn from it. Ask about the instructor's academic background and why he or she chose college teaching as a career. You can learn a great deal about your instructor from simply looking around the office. There will often be pictures of family members or animals or travel locations.

The relationships you develop with instructors will be valuable to you both now and in the future. People who become college faculty members do so because they have a real passion for learning about a particular subject and working with students. If you and your professor share an interest in a particular field of study, you will have the opportunity to develop a true friendship based on mutual interests. Instructors who know you well can also write that all-important letter of reference when you are applying to graduate or professional school or seeking your first job after college.

Understanding Academic Freedom

Colleges and universities have promoted the advancement of knowledge by granting professors academic freedom—virtually unlimited freedom of speech and inquiry as long as human lives, rights, and privacy are not violated. Such freedom is not usually possible in other professions. Most college instructors believe in the freedom to speak out, whether in a classroom discussion about economic policy or at a political rally. Think of where education would be if instructors were required to keep their own ideas to themselves. You won't always agree with your instructors, but you will benefit by listening to what they have to say and respecting their ideas and opinions. Academic freedom also extends to students. Within the limits of civility and respect for others you will be free to express your opinions in a way that might be different from your experience in high school or work settings.

When Things Go Wrong between You and an Instructor

Although there is a potential in any environment for things to go wrong, problems between students and instructors that cannot be resolved are rare. First, ask for a meeting to discuss your problem. See whether the two of you can work things out. If the instructor refuses, go up the administrative ladder, starting at the bottom: department head to dean, and so on. If the problem is a grade, keep in mind that academic freedom includes the right of an instructor to grade you as he or she sees fit and that no one can force the instructor to change that grade. Most important, don't let a bad experience sour you on college. Even the most trying instructor will be out of your life by the end of the term. When all else fails, resolve to stick with the class until the final exam is behind you. Then shop carefully for instructors for next term by asking fellow students, your academic adviser, and others whose advice you can trust.

Making the Most of Relationships with Your Instructors

Attend class regularly and be on time. Learning what your instructors have to offer is much easier when you're there every day.

Participate in class. Seek instructors who favor active student engagement in learning; you'll find learning is more fun this way, you'll learn more, and you'll earn higher grades.

Learn from your instructors' criticism. Criticism can be healthy and helpful. It's how we all learn. If you get a low grade, ask to meet with your instructor to discuss what you should do to improve your work.

Meet with your instructors. You should make it a point to meet with instructors if you have something to discuss. Students who do so tend to do better academically. Your instructors are required to have office hours; they expect you to visit.

How Relationships Change in College

As a college student, are classes and studies the first things on your mind? Your instructors may think so. Your family may hope so. But student journals suggest that what often takes center stage are relationships—with boyfriends, girlfriends, or spouses; with friends and enemies; with parents and family; with roommates, classmates, and coworkers; and with new people and new groups.

Parents

Whether you live on campus or at home, becoming a college student right after you leave high school will change your relationship with your parents. Home will never be quite the same, and you will not be who you were before. You may find that your parents try to make decisions on your behalf, such as what major you should choose, where and how much you should work, and what you should do on weekends. You also may find that it's hard for you to make any decisions without talking to your parents first. While communication with your parents is important, your college or university advisers or counselors can help you draw the line between what decisions should be yours alone and what decisions your parents should help you make.

Many college students are living in blended families, so that more than one set of parents is involved in their college experience. If your father or mother has remarried or has a new partner, you may have to negotiate with both family units.

So how can you have a good relationship with your parents during this period of transition? A first step in establishing a good relationship with them is to be aware of their concerns. Parents are often worried that you'll harm yourself in some way. They might still see you as young and innocent, and they don't want you to make the same mistakes they might have made or experience situations that have been publicized in the media. They might be concerned that your family values or cultural values will change or that you'll never really come home again. For some students, this is exactly what happens.

Parents often have genuine concerns. To help them feel comfortable with your life in college, try setting aside regular times to update them on how college and your life in general are going. Ask for and consider their advice—even if you end up not taking it.

Spouses, Partners, and Families

If you live with a spouse, partner, or children of your own, your college transition will affect them as well. They may have concerns and fears about whether and how you will change, and your responsibilities to them will certainly add to your time management challenges. But families can also be a special source of support as you pursue your academic goals. Help them feel a part of the college experience by including them in campus activities designed for family members. Spend time sharing your hopes and dreams, and let them know how your college success will make a positive difference for everyone in the family.

Roommates

If you live on campus, adjusting to a roommate is a significant transition experience. You may make a friend for life—or an acquaintance you wish you'd never known. A roommate doesn't have to be a best friend, just someone with whom you can comfortably share your living space. Your best friend may not make the best roommate.

With roommates, it's important to establish your mutual rights and responsibilities. If you have problems, talk them out promptly. Speak directly—politely but plainly. If your problems persist, or if you don't know how to address them, seek professional counseling, which usually is available free of charge at your campus's counseling center. Normally, you can tolerate (and learn from) a less than ideal situation. But if things get really bad and do not improve, insist on a change.

Friends

One of the best parts of going to college is meeting new people. Studies of college students have found that they learn more from other students than they learn from professors. Although not everyone you hang out with will be a close friend, you will likely form some special relationships that may even last a lifetime.

Choose your friends carefully. You are who you associate with—or you soon will be. If you want a friend, be a friend. Here's how:

- Be an attentive listener.
- Give your opinion when asked.
- Keep your comments polite and positive.
- Never violate a confidence.
- Offer an encouraging word and a helping hand when you can.

Your friends usually have attitudes, goals, and experiences similar to your own. But in your personal life, just as in class, you have the most to learn from people who are different from you. You'll find it an enriching experience to diversify—to make friends with students who come from another state or country, are from a different racial or ethnic group, or are of a different sexual orientation or age.

Social Networking and Electronic Relationships

Social networking Web sites such as Facebook and MySpace are very popular with college students. There are both positives and negatives associated with using social networking sites. Entering college students should definitely examine the words and images they post online, the effects their online statements have on others, and the benefits and pitfalls of using social networking.

Social networking Web sites are wonderful tools to help you keep connected to your friends from high school and to your new friends in college. What you might not know is that you can also use social networking sites for more than just staying in touch with friends. Facebook can help you become more engaged in life on your campus. If you are a returning adult student, you might feel that learning how to use something like Facebook will be a daunting task. However, returning adult students, like traditional-age students, can learn a great deal about academic life and the campus community from being involved on Facebook.

You might also use Facebook to help you learn more about your instructors. When students read an instructor's Facebook profile, they might be surprised to learn that instructors are people too and engage in everyday activities such as exercising and watching movies. Learning a bit more about your professors can help you feel more comfortable participating in class discussion and asking for help.

Now for the downside: It is easy to get lost in reading profiles, status updates, and notes and in checking out your friends' photos. Students often describe social networking Web sites as "addicting," and the time you spend on such sites can interfere with your academic success and your well-being. You might find that you spend much more time on Facebook than you expected and don't have enough time to finish your work. Some students use technology to the exclusion of other activities in their lives. If you find yourself struggling to keep up with your real-world commitments and relationships because you are spending so much time on Facebook, it might be a good idea to talk to someone at your campus counseling center.

Being Active in Campus and Community Life

01

Colleges and universities can seem huge and unfriendly, especially if you went to a small high school or grew up in a small town. Whether you are attending a school close to home or farther away, and whether you are living at home or on your own for the first time, the adjustment may be overwhelming. To feel comfortable in your new environment, you need to find your comfort zone or niche. Many students discover that becoming involved in campus organizations eases the transition. They also find that it helps them make connections with other students, faculty, and staff members and prepares them for the world of work.

It's not hard to find a place where you belong, but it will take some initiative. Consider your interests and the activities that you enjoy most, and explore opportunities related to them. You might be interested in joining an intramural team, performing community service, running for a student government office, or getting involved in the residence hall. Or you might prefer joining a more structured club or organization that has chapters on many campuses. Campus organizations can be recreational; your school may have a rock-climbing club, billiards league, or glee club, for example. You'll find others that are more academically and career oriented, such as the Spanish Club, the Electrical Engineering Society, and the Student Nurses' Association. And many campuses have groups that provide resources and social outlets for students in similar situations (for example, Students with Children, and the International Students' Association).

To find the organization that's right for you, check out campus newspapers, activity fairs, printed guides, open houses, and Web pages. Many campuses also have a student activities office located in a central facility, often called the student union, for student clubs and programs. And your first-year seminar instructor may spend time in class describing different clubs and organizations and talking about the overall benefits of campus involvement. If you become interested in a certain group or activity, consider attending a meeting before you make the decision to join. See what the organization is like, what the expectations of time and money are, and whether you feel comfortable with the members. As you explore your options, consider that new students who become involved with at least one organization are more likely to be successful in their first year and remain in college.

Your campus is part of a larger community. If you live on campus, find a way to learn more about the community around you. Even if this community is your hometown, you will learn much about it that is new when you experience the community with a fresh eye. Some campuses offer students the opportunity to interact with a community mentor—an older individual who may or may not be an alumnus of the institution and who can help you find things to do, places to go, and people to meet in the local area. Consider participating in a community service project. Your college may offer service opportunities as part of first-year courses (service learning), or your campus's division of student affairs may have a volunteer or community service office.

Joining On-Campus Groups

On any college campus, there are many ways to become involved and find your niche. It doesn't really matter which type of involvement you choose, but participating in one or more out-of-class clubs or organizations will enrich your college experience.

Is Greek life right for you? Some, but not all, colleges and universities are the home for Greek organizations, commonly called fraternities or sororities—social groups for men and women known by their Greek letter names. Fraternities and sororities can be a rich source of friends and support, and some students love them. But other students may not think a Greek organization is the right fit for them and may choose not to participate in one.

Fraternities and sororities provide a quick connection to a large number of individuals on your campus and beyond—a link to a social network, camaraderie, and support. Some campuses have several fraternities and sororities to choose from, each differing in philosophy and image. There are even fraternities and sororities created by and for specific racial or ethnic groups. These have existed for a number of years and were established by students of color who felt the need for campus groups that allowed them to connect to their community and culture while in school. Nu Alpha Kappa Fraternity, Alpha Rho Lambda Sorority, Omega Psi Phi Fraternity, Alpha Kappa Alpha Sorority, Lamba Phi Epsilon Fraternity, and Sigma Omicron Pi Sorority are just a few of the many ethnically based Greek organizations that exist across the country. Such organizations have provided many students with a means to become familiar with their campus and to gain friendship and support, while promoting their culture and ethnicity.

Fraternities and sororities are powerful social influences, so you'll definitely want to take a good look at the sophomores, juniors, and seniors in them. If what you see is what you want to be and if you are willing to pay the fees and recurring membership dues, consider joining. But if you decide that Greek life is not for you, there are many other great ways to make close friends.

Career/major organizations   You might find your niche on campus by taking part in activities that reflect your major and career interests. Belonging to an organization that focuses on a specific field of study can help you to have a well-rounded college experience and also can further your future or current career. Join a club that is affiliated with your major or that reflects your career interest. Becoming a member will help you find out more about your field of interest and allow you to make contacts that can enhance your career options. Many campus clubs participate in challenges and contests with similar groups from other colleges and contribute to campus activities through exhibitions and events. The Psychology Club; the Math, Engineering, and Science Association; and the Association of Student Filmmakers are examples of groups dedicated to specific academic fields.

Political/activist organizations   You may want to get involved on campus by joining a politically active group. Campuses are home to many organizations that are dedicated to specific political affiliations and causes. Campus Republicans, Young Democrats, Amnesty International, Native Students in Social Action, and other groups provide students with a platform to express their political views and share their causes with others. These organizations typically host debating events and forums to address current issues and events.

Special-interest groups   Perhaps the largest subgroup of student clubs is the special-interest category, which comprises everything from recreational interests to hobbies. On your campus you may find special-interest organizations as varied as the Brazilian Jujitsu Club, the Kite Flyers' Club, the Flamenco Club, and the Video Gamers' Society. Students can cultivate an interest in bird watching or indulge their curiosity about ballroom dance without ever leaving campus. Many of these clubs sponsor campus events highlighting their specific interests and talents; these occasions provide an ideal way to learn about the organizations. Check out the ones you're most curious about. If a club is not available, create it yourself and contribute to the social opportunities on your campus!

Becoming involved—on or off campus, or both—helps you gain valuable knowledge, broaden your exposure to new ideas, make useful contacts, and develop a support network. You'll find that time spent in these outside-of-class endeavors can be just as important as the time inside your classes. Remember: Not all learning occurs in the classroom. Participating enriches your time in college and connects you to the wider campus and the external community.

try it!

Finding Your Niche on Campus

Search your school's Web page for information on campus organizations and groups. Which ones dovetail with some of your present interests and talents? Which ones focus on activities and programs that are new to you but that you are interested in exploring? List the groups and organizations that catch your attention, along with the contact information for each, and take steps to learn more about them.

01 Chapter Review

One-minute paper . . .

Chapter 1 explores how deciding to go to college, experiencing college life, and finding your own path can be a unique journey. Sometimes things that seem simple have more depth if they are given some thought. Take a minute (or several) to think about and note what you found most useful or meaningful during this class. Did anything that was covered in this chapter leave you with more questions than answers? If so, what are your questions?

Applying what you've learned . . .

Now that you have read and discussed this chapter, consider how you can apply what you have learned to your academic and personal life. The following prompts will help you reflect on chapter material and its relevance to you both now and in the future.

1. Review the "Advantages of a College Education" box on page 5. While landing a lucrative career is probably high on your list of goals after college, take a look at the other possible advantages of obtaining a college degree. List five advantages from this section that you can relate to the most. If you think of an advantage that is not noted in the chapter, add it to your top five. Why are these advantages important to you?

2. College students often feel the stress of trying to balance their personal and academic lives. The ups and downs of life are inevitable, but we can control our choices and attitudes. As a first-year student, you will want to begin developing a personal strategy for bouncing back after a particularly difficult time. Your strategy should include at least three steps you can take to get back on track and move forward.

Building your portfolio . . .

What's in it for me? Skills matrix

How might the courses in which you are enrolled right now affect your future? Although it might be hard to imagine that there is a direct connection to your career or lifestyle after college, the classes and experiences you are now engaged in can play an important role in your future.

Developing a skills matrix will help you reflect on your college experiences and track the skills that will eventually help you land a great summer job, the hard-to-get internship, a scholarship, and, one day, a career.

1. Using Microsoft Excel, develop a skills matrix like the one on page 13 to identify courses and out-of-class experiences that enhance the following skills: communication, critical thinking, leadership, and teamwork.

2. Add any additional skills categories or courses you would like to track.

3. Indicate what you did in your courses or activities that helped you learn one of these skills. Be specific about the assignment, project, or activity that helped you learn.

4. Save your skills matrix on your computer, flash drive, or external hard drive.

5. Update your matrix often. Add new skills categories, courses, and activities. Change the title to indicate the appropriate time period (e.g., Skills Learned in My First Two Years of College).

6. Start an electronic collection of your college work. Save papers, projects, and other relevant material in one location on your computer or on an external storage device. Be sure to back up your work to avoid digital disasters!

My First-Term Courses and Activities

Skills Learned	English	Math	History	French	First-Year Seminar	Activities
Communication	Improved my writing skills			E-mailed French students	Gave 3 presentations	Joined Toastmasters
Critical Thinking	Wrote original poetry		Debated war in Afghanistan			
Leadership					Led a group project	Participated in Emerging Leaders
Teamwork		Joined a study group				Participated in intramural soccer

Where to go for help . . .

On Campus

To find the college support services you need, ask your academic adviser or counselor; consult your college catalog, phone book, and home page on the Internet; or call or visit student services (or student affairs).

Academic advisement center: This center offers help in choosing courses and also has information on degree requirements.

Academic skills center: The academic skills center offers tutoring, help in study and memory skills, and help in studying for exams.

Adult reentry center: This center offers programs for returning students, supportive contacts with other adult students, and information about services such as child care.

Career center: Career centers usually have a career library and offer interest assessments, counseling, help in finding a major, and job and internship listings.

Commuter services: These centers display a list of options for off-campus housing, transportation information, and roommate lists, as well as to orient students to the community.

Computer center: Your campus computer center offers minicourses and also has handouts on campus computer resources.

Counseling center: The counseling center offers confidential counseling on personal concerns and stress-management programs.

Disabled student services: This center offers assistance in overcoming physical barriers and learning disabilities.

Housing/residential life office: This office can help you locate on- or off-campus housing.

Student activities office: This center can help you identify opportunities for campus involvement.

My Institution's Resources

_____

_____

_____

_____

_____

_____

_____

_____

_____

_____

_____

_____

02 Managing Your Time

How do you approach time? Because people have different personalities and come from different cultures, you and others may view time in different ways.

The way you look at time may also have to do with your preferred style of learning. For example, if you're a natural organizer, you probably enter on your calendar all due dates for assignments, exams, and quizzes as soon as you receive each course syllabus, and you may be good at adhering to a strict schedule. On the other hand, if you take a laid-back approach to life, you may prefer to be more flexible, or "go with the flow," rather than follow a daily or weekly schedule. You may excel at dealing with the unexpected. You may also be a procrastinator.

Time management involves six components: knowing your goals, setting priorities to meet them, anticipating the unexpected, placing yourself in control of your time, making a commitment to being punctual, and carrying out your plans. This chapter addresses essential strategies to help you manage your time. Being a good time manager is one of the key skills of successful college students and a quality that every employer values and seeks in new employees.

How Do You Measure Up?

1. I set academic and personal goals every term to guide how I prioritize my time.
   - ○ Always
   - ○ Occasionally
   - ○ Never

2. I am able to focus on the task at hand instead of getting distracted or procrastinating.
   - ○ Always
   - ○ Occasionally
   - ○ Never

3. I use a daily or weekly planner, to-do lists, or other planning devices to keep track of my commitments.
   - ○ Always
   - ○ Occasionally
   - ○ Never

4. I am able to balance my social life and my need for personal time with my academic requirements.
   - ○ Always
   - ○ Occasionally
   - ○ Never

Review the items you marked "occasionally" or "never." Paying attention to all these aspects of your college experience can be important to your success. After reading this chapter, come back to this list and think about ways you can work on these areas.

Taking Control of Your Time

Nick Larsen

20-year-old student in his first semester

On the first day of class, my English instructor spent more time talking about deadlines than books. "Review the syllabus and enter all your upcoming tests and papers in your datebook," Professor Hughes said. So, okay, I typed everything into my iPod calendar. But I was also thinking about my job, my next class, and my band's gig on Saturday, and it's sort of hard to think about the future when your here-and-now is packed.

"Your final research paper should run at least 20 pages and will count for 25 percent of your final grade," Professor Hughes added. "Find a topic and start gathering resource materials *now*." I jotted down a couple of ideas and figured I'd go to the library later in the week to get help.

Cut to a week before the deadline: I still hadn't made it to the library.

I now felt so panicked that I could barely get out of bed. I knew that I'd never make the deadline unless. . . . Okay, I'd never make the deadline.

What would you do if you were in Nick's position, both to get out of the current jam and to stay out of similar situations in the future?

The first step to effective time management is recognizing that you can be in control. Being in control means that you make your own decisions. Two of the most often-cited differences between high school and college are increased autonomy, or independence, and greater responsibility. If you are a returning student rather than a recent high school graduate, it's likely that you already have considerable independence. But returning to college creates responsibilities above and beyond those you already have, such as those related to employment, family, community service, or other activities.

Whether you are beginning college immediately after high school or continuing your education after a break, now is the time to establish new priorities for managing your time. To take control of your life and your time and to guide your decisions, it is wise to begin by setting some goals for the future.

Setting Goals

Where do you see yourself five or ten years from now? What are some of your goals for the coming decade? One goal is probably to earn a two-year or four-year degree or technical certificate. You already may have decided on the career that you want to pursue. Or perhaps you plan to go on to graduate or professional school. As you look to the future, you may see yourself buying a new car, owning a home, starting a family, owning a business, or retiring early. Time management is one of the most effective tools to assist you in meeting such goals.

Take a few minutes to complete the "Try It!" exercise. List your top three personal goals for the coming decade. Your goals can be challenging, but they should also be attainable. Then determine at least two methods for achieving each goal. The difference between a goal and an objective is that a goal is what you want to achieve, while an objective is a tangible, measurable method for getting there.

More than likely, one goal you will set is to find a good job upon completion of your degree, or a job that is significantly better than your current job. Your objectives may include defining a "good job," making yourself a competitive candidate in a job search, and completing an internship in a related field, among others.

In a job search, a college degree and good grades may not be enough. So when setting goals and objectives for allocating your time, consider the importance of having a well-rounded résumé when you graduate. Such a résumé might show that you made a commitment to participating in extracurricular activities, gaining leadership experience, engaging in community service or in an internship or co-op opportunities, developing job-related skills, keeping up-to-date on technological advances, or pursuing relevant part- or full-time employment while attending classes.

When it is time to look for a permanent job, you want to demonstrate that you have used your college years wisely. Doing so will require planning and effective time-management skills, which are highly valued by employers. Your college or university's career center can help you arrange for an internship, a co-op program, or community service that will give you valuable experience and strengthen your résumé.

Establishing Priorities

Once you have established goals and objectives, prioritize your time. Which goals and objectives are the most important to you? For example, is it more important to study for a test tomorrow or to attend a job fair today? That decision will be up to you. Keep in mind that it isn't always a good idea to ignore long-term goals in order to meet short-term goals. Using good time management, you can study during the week before the test so that you can attend the job fair the day before the

test. One way that skilled time managers establish priorities is to maintain a to-do list (discussed in more detail later in this chapter), rank the items on the list, and then determine schedules and deadlines for each task.

Another aspect of setting priorities in college is finding an appropriate way to balance an academic schedule, social life, family life, and time for yourself. All work and no play can make you dull or uninteresting and can undermine your academic motivation. That is, social activities are an important part of the college experience. Being involved in campus life can enhance your satisfaction with college and thus your achievement and your determination to continue in college. However, never having time alone or time to study and think can leave you feeling overwhelmed. And employment, family, and community obligations are also important, time-consuming, and not "optional." For many students the greatest challenge of prioritizing is to balance college with these other valuable dimensions of life.

Staying Focused

Many of the decisions you make today are reversible. You may change your major, and your career and life goals may shift as well. But the decision to take control of your life—to establish your own goals for the future, to set your priorities, and to manage your time accordingly—is an important one for the present and the future.

If you are an adult reentering college, you may question your decision to go back to school, and you may feel temporarily overwhelmed by the academic responsibilities that are suddenly heaped on top of your other commitments. Prioritizing, rethinking some commitments, letting some things go, and weighing the advantages and disadvantages of attending college part-time versus full-time can help you work through this adjustment period. Again, keep your long-term goals in mind.

Successful people frequently say that staying focused is a key to their success. To help you stay focused, make a plan. Begin with your priorities, and then think about the necessities of life.

Finish what needs to be done before you move from work to pleasure.

try it!

Goal Setting

A. Name your top three goals for the coming decade.

1. _____
2. _____
3. _____

B. List two measurable objectives for achieving each of the goals set above.

1. a. _____
   b. _____
2. a. _____
   b. _____
3. a. _____
   b. _____

Creating a Workable Class Schedule

If you are a first-year student, you may not have had much flexibility in determining your course schedule; by the time you could register for classes, some sections of your required courses already may have been closed. You also may not have known whether you would prefer taking classes back-to-back or having a break between classes.

Over time, have you found that you prefer spreading your classes over five or six days of the week? Or have you discovered that you like to go to class just two or three days a week, or only once a week for a longer class period? Your attention span as well as your other commitments may influence your decisions about your class schedule. Before you register for the next term, think about how to make your class schedule work for you—how you can create a schedule that allows you to use your time most efficiently and effectively.

Using a Daily or Weekly Planner

In college, as in life, you will quickly learn that managing time is a key to not only survival but also success. A good way to start is to look at the big picture. Consider buying a week-at-a-glance organizer for the current year. Your campus bookstore may sell one designed just for your college or university, with important dates and deadlines already provided. If you prefer to use an electronic planner, that's fine—your PC, laptop, or PDA comes equipped with a calendar.

Regardless of the format you prefer (electronic or paper), carry your planner with you at all times and continue to enter all due dates as soon as you know them. Write in meeting times and locations, scheduled social events, study time for each class, and so forth. Add phone numbers and e-mail addresses, too, in case something comes up and you need to cancel. Get into the habit of using a planner to help you keep track of commitments and maintain control of your schedule. This practice will become invaluable to you in the world of work. Choose a specific time of day to check your notes daily for the current week and the coming week. It takes just a moment to be certain that you aren't forgetting something important, and it helps relieve stress!

Maintaining a To-Do List

Keeping a to-do list can also help you avoid feeling stressed or out of control. Some people start a new list every day or once a week. Others keep a running list and only throw a page away when everything on the list is done. Use your to-do list to keep track of all the tasks you need to remember, not just academics. You might include errands you need to run, appointments you must make, e-mail messages you need to send, and so on.

Develop a system for prioritizing the items on your list: highlight; use colored ink; or mark with one, two, or three stars or A, B, C. You can use your to-do list in conjunction with your planner. As you complete each task, cross it off. You will feel good about how much you have accomplished, and this positive feeling will help you to stay motivated.

Scheduling Your Time Week by Week

Use the following steps to schedule your time for a whole week at a time:

- Begin by entering all of your commitments for the week—classes, work hours, family commitments, and so on—on your schedule.

- Try to reserve at least 2 hours of study time for each hour spent in class. This 2-for-1 rule reflects many faculty members' expectations for how much work you should do to master the material in their classes. This rule says that if you are taking a typical full-time class load of fifteen credits, for example, you should plan to study an additional 30 hours per week. Think of this 45-hour-per-week commitment as comparable to a full-time job. Then if you are also working, reconsider how many hours per week it will be reasonable for you to be employed above and beyond this commitment, or consider reducing your credit load. At many institutions you need to carry a minimum of twelve or thirteen credits to be considered a full-time student, and this status can be important for financial aid and various forms of insurance.

Figure 2.1

Daily and Weekly To-Do Lists

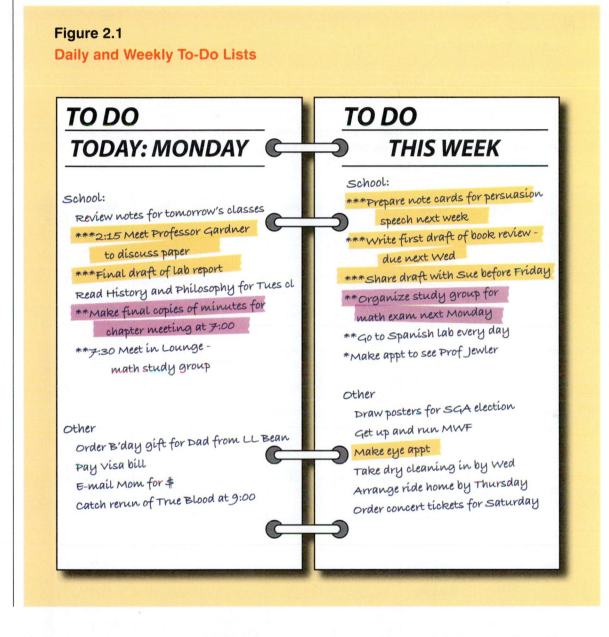

TO DO
TODAY: MONDAY

School:
Review notes for tomorrow's classes
***2:15 Meet Professor Gardner
to discuss paper
***Final draft of lab report
Read History and Philosophy for Tues cl
**Make final copies of minutes for
chapter meeting at 7:00
**7:30 Meet in Lounge –
math study group

Other
Order B'day gift for Dad from LL Bean
Pay Visa bill
E-mail Mom for $
Catch rerun of True Blood at 9:00

TO DO
THIS WEEK

School:
***Prepare note cards for persuasion
speech next week
***Write first draft of book review –
due next Wed
***Share draft with Sue before Friday
**Organize study group for
math exam next Monday
**Go to Spanish lab every day
*Make appt to see Prof Jewler

Other
Draw posters for SGA election
Get up and run MWF
Make eye appt
Take dry cleaning in by Wed
Arrange ride home by Thursday
Order concert tickets for Saturday

- Depending on your body clock, obligations, and potential distractions, decide whether you will study more effectively in the day or in the evening or by using a combination of both. Determine whether you are capable of getting up very early in the morning to study, or how late you can stay up at night and still wake up for morning classes.

- Estimate how much time you will need for each assignment, and plan to begin your work early. A good time manager frequently finishes assignments before actual due dates to allow for emergencies.

- Set aside time for research and other preparatory tasks. For example, instructors may expect you to be computer literate, but they usually

Figure 2.2

Weekly Timetable

Create your own weekly timetable. You can find blank templates on the book's Web site at **bedfordstmartins.com/gardner**. As you complete your timetable, keep in mind the suggestions in this chapter. Do you want your classes back-to-back or with breaks in between? How early in the morning are you willing to start classes? Do you prefer—or do work or family commitments require you—to take evening classes? Are there times of day when you are more alert? Less alert? Plan how you will spend your time for the coming week.

	Sunday	Monday	Tuesday	Wednesday	Thursday	Friday	Saturday
6:00							
7:00							
8:00			BREAKFAST	———————→			
9:00	SLEEP IN!	Review English	PSYCH 101	Review English	PSYCH 101	Review English	
10:00		English 101	Review PSYCH	English 101	Review PSYCH	English 101	ENJOY!
11:00		LUNCH		LUNCH			
12:00	PICNIC	HISTORY 101	LUNCH	HISTORY 101	LUNCH	HISTORY 101	
1:00	W/JANE,						
2:00	ALEX,	BIO 101		BIO 101	BIO 101 LAB	WORK	BE LAZY!
3:00	MICHELLE, etc.				↓		
4:00		WORK		WORK		↓	
5:00							GO
6:00	STUDY ENGLISH	DINNER	DINNER	DINNER	DINNER	DINNER	OUT
7:00	HISTORY		STUDY ENGLISH		STUDY ENGLISH		WITH
8:00			HISTORY		HISTORY		FRIENDS
9:00		STUDY PSYCH	BIO	STUDY PSYCH			
11:00							
11:00							

don't have time to explain how to use a word processor, spreadsheet, or statistical computer program. Most campuses have learning centers or computer centers that offer tutoring, walk-in assistance, or workshops to assist you with computer programs, e-mail, and Internet searches. Your library may offer sessions on searching for information using various computer databases. Such services will save you time and usually are free.

- Schedule at least three aerobic workouts per week. (Walking to and from classes doesn't count.) Taking a break for physical activity relaxes your body, clears your mind, and is a powerful motivator. Allow enough time to maintain an elevated heart rate for 30 minutes, plus time for warming up, stretching, and cooling down.

try it!

Working Together: Comparing Class Schedules

In a small group, share your current class schedules with the other students. Exchange ideas on how to handle time-management problems and the challenges you see in others' schedules. Discuss how you would arrange your schedule differently for the next term.

Organizing Your Day

Being a good student does not necessarily mean studying day and night and doing little else.

Keep the following points in mind as you organize your day:

- Set realistic goals for your study time. Assess how long it takes to read a chapter in different types of textbooks and how long it takes to review your notes from different instructors, and then schedule your time accordingly. Allow adequate time to review and then test your knowledge when preparing for exams.

- Use waiting time (on the bus, before class, waiting for appointments) to review.

- Schedule time to review immediately or as soon as possible after class; you will remember more of what you learned in class.

- Take advantage of your best times of day to study. Schedule other activities, such as doing laundry, responding to e-mail, and spending time with friends, for times when it will be difficult to concentrate.

- Schedule time right before and after meals for leisure activities; it's hard to study on an empty or a full stomach.

- Use the same study area regularly. Have everything handy that you may need, such as a dictionary, writing implements, a highlighter, and note cards. Make sure that you have adequate lighting, a chair with sufficient back support, and enough desk space to spread out everything you need. When working at a computer, position the keyboard at an appropriate height and adjust monitor settings to avoid eyestrain.

- Assess your attention level. Make sure that you are studying actively and that you can meaningfully put what you have learned into words.

- Study difficult or boring subjects first, when you are fresh. (Exception: If you are having trouble getting started, it might be easier to begin with your favorite subject.)

- Divide study time into 50-minute blocks. Study for 50 minutes; then take a 10- or 15-minute break; then study for another 50-minute block. Try not to study for more than three 50-minute blocks in a row, or you will find that you are not accomplishing 50 minutes' worth of work. (In economics, this drop-off in productivity is known as the "law of diminishing returns.")

- Break extended study sessions into a variety of activities, each with a specific objective. For example, begin by reading, then develop flash cards by writing key terms and their definitions or key formulas on note cards, and finally test yourself on what you have read. You cannot maintain maximum concentration when reading the same text for 3 consecutive hours.

- Restrict repetitive, distracting, and time-consuming tasks such as checking your e-mail to a certain time, not every hour.

- Avoid multitasking. Even though you may be good at juggling many tasks at once, or at least think that you are, the reality is that you will study more effectively and retain more if you concentrate on one task at a time.

- Be flexible! You cannot anticipate every disruption to your plans. Build extra time into your study schedule so that unexpected interruptions do not prevent you from meeting your goals.

- Reward yourself! Develop a system of short- and long-term study goals and rewards for meeting those goals. Doing so will keep your motivation high.

Make Your Daily Time-Management Plan Work

Consider what kind of schedule will work best for you. If you live on campus, you may want to create a schedule that situates you near a dining hall at mealtimes or allows you to spend breaks between classes at the library. Or you may need breaks in your schedule for relaxation, like spending time in a student lounge or at the campus center. You may want to avoid returning to your residence hall room to take a nap between classes if a nap will make you feel lethargic or make you oversleep and miss later classes. Be realistic about your personal habits when choosing class times and locations. Also, if you attend a large college or university, be sure that you allow adequate time to get from building to building.

If you are a commuting student, or if you must work off campus to afford going to school, you may prefer scheduling your classes together in blocks without breaks. *Block scheduling,* which means enrolling in back-to-back classes, allows you to cut travel time by attending classes one or two days a week, and it may provide more flexibil-

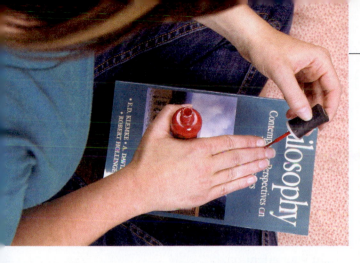

02

ity for scheduling employment or family commitments. But it also can have significant drawbacks.

When all your classes are scheduled in a block of time, you run several risks. If you become ill on a class day, you could fall behind in all your classes. You might also become fatigued from sitting in class after class. When one class immediately follows another, it will be difficult for you to have a last-minute study period immediately before a test because you will be attending another class and are likely to have no more than a 15-minute break. Finally, remember that for back-to-back classes, several exams might be held on the same day. Scheduling classes in blocks might work better if you have the option of attending lectures at alternative times in case you are absent, if you alternate classes with free periods, and if you seek out instructors who are flexible with due dates for assignments.

Don't Overextend Yourself

Being overextended is a primary source of stress for college students. Determine what is a realistic workload for you. Do not take on more than you can handle. Learn to say "no." Do not feel obligated to provide a reason; you have the right to decline requests that will prevent you from getting your own work done.

With the best intentions, even students who use a time-management plan can become overextended. If there is not enough time to carry your course load and to meet your commitments, drop a course before the drop date so you won't have a low grade on your permanent record.

If dropping a course is not feasible and if other activities are lower on your list of priorities, assess your other time commitments and let go of one or more. Doing so can be difficult, especially if you think that you are letting other people down. However, it is far preferable to excuse yourself from an activity in a way that is respectful to others than to fail to come through at the last minute because you are overcommitted.

Reduce Distractions and Follow a Routine

Where is the best place to study? Some students find that it's best not to study in places associated with leisure, such as at the kitchen table or the living room in front of the TV, because such locations lend themselves to interruptions by other people and to a number of distractions. Similarly, it might be unwise to study on your bed. You may find yourself drifting off to sleep when you need to study, or you may learn to associate your bed with studying and not be able to go to sleep when you need to. Instead, find quiet places, both on campus and at home, where you can concentrate and develop a study mind-set each time you sit down to do your work.

Stick to a study routine. The more firmly you have established a specific time and a quiet place to study, the more effective you will be in keeping up with your schedule. If you have larger blocks of time available on the weekend, for example, take advantage of them to review or to catch up on major projects, such as term papers, that you can't complete in 50-minute blocks. By breaking down large tasks and taking one thing at a time, you will make steady progress toward your academic goals and thereby stay motivated.

Here are additional tips to help you deal with distraction while studying:		
1. Leave the TV, CD player, DVD player, MP3 player, and radio off unless the background noise or music truly helps you concentrate on your studies or drowns out more distracting noises.	**2.** Don't let personal concerns interfere with studying. If necessary, call a friend or write in a journal before you start to study, and then put your worries away.	**3.** Develop an agreement with the people who live with you about quiet hours.

Overcoming Procrastination and Respecting Others' Time

The way people manage time can tell you a great deal about their level of self-discipline and their attitude toward others. Individuals who routinely procrastinate often have difficulty controlling not only their time, but also other aspects of their life. Like procrastination, being habitually late for appointments or for class might be an indication that your life is out of control, but such behavior might also cause others to assume that you don't care enough about the activity or about them to be on time.

Overcoming Procrastination

Procrastination can trip up many otherwise capable people. Students may procrastinate for a number of reasons. Some procrastinate because they are perfectionists; not doing a task may be easier than having to live up to their own or others' expectations. Or they procrastinate because they are afraid of the task, feeling it is too hard, unfamiliar, or confusing for them to tackle. Others procrastinate because they find an assigned task boring or irrelevant.

Simply not enjoying an assignment is not a good excuse to put it off. Throughout life you'll be faced with tasks that you don't find interesting, and in many cases you won't have the option not to do them. For instance, when you work in an entry-level job, you might find that you are assigned tedious tasks that are generally reserved for new employees. On a more personal level, you might put off cleaning your house or your room until the day comes when you can't find an important file or document or a visitor is coming.

Regardless of its source, procrastination may be your single greatest enemy. Here are some ways to beat procrastination and to stay motivated:

- Remind yourself of the possible consequences if you do not get down to work; then get started.
- Create a to-do list. Check off things as you finish them. Use the list to focus on tasks that aren't getting done. Move them to the top of your next day's list, and make up your mind to do them. Working from a list will give you a feeling of accomplishment.

- Break down big jobs into smaller steps. Tackle short, easy-to-accomplish tasks first.
- Before you begin to work, promise yourself a reward for finishing the task.
- Control your study environment. Eliminate distractions. Say "no" to friends and family who want your attention.
- Don't talk on the phone, send e-mails or text messages, or surf the Web during planned study sessions. Close your door.

If these ideas fail to motivate you, reexamine your values and priorities. Keep coming back to some basic questions: Why am I in college here and now? Why am I in this course? What is really important to me? If you are not willing to stop procrastinating and tackle the tasks at hand, you may want to reconsider whether you should be in college at this time.

Researchers at Carleton University in Canada have found that college students who procrastinate in their studies also avoid confronting other tasks and problems and are more likely to develop unhealthy habits, such as drinking too much alcohol, smoking, not sleeping or eating well, and not exercising.[1] If you cannot get procrastination under control, it is in your best interest to seek help at your campus counseling service before you begin to feel that you are also losing control over other aspects of your life.

Respecting Others' Time

How does time management relate to respect? Think of the last time you made an appointment with someone who either forgot the appointment entirely or was very late. Were you upset or disappointed by the person for wasting your time? Most of us have experienced the frustration of having someone else disrespect our time. In college, if you repeatedly arrive late for class or leave before class periods have officially ended, you are breaking the basic rules of politeness. You are intentionally or unintentionally showing a lack of respect for your instructors and your classmates.

---

[1] Timothy A. Pychyl and Fuschia M. Sirois, *Procrastination: Costs to Health and Well-being.* Presentation at the APA Convention, August 22, 2002, Chicago.

02

Here are a few basic guidelines for respectful behavior in class and in other interactions with instructors.

- Be in class on time. Arrive early enough to remove outerwear, shuttle through your backpack, and have your assignments, notebooks, and writing tools ready to go.

- Avoid behavior in class that shows a lack of respect for the instructor and other students. Such inconsiderate behavior includes walking out in the middle of class to plug a parking meter; answering your cell phone, text-messaging, or surfing the Web; doing homework for another class; yawning; falling asleep; and whispering or talking.

- Make adequate transportation plans in advance, get enough sleep at night, wake up early enough to be on time for class, and complete assignments prior to class.

- Manage your time when participating in class discussions and activities. Don't "hog the floor"; give others the opportunity to express their ideas. Take the time to listen respectfully, to suspend judgment, and to weigh the merits of different arguments before forming and expressing your own opinions and answers.

- Be on time for scheduled appointments with your instructor or adviser. If you fail to show up on time, you cause inconvenience not only to the faculty or staff member but also potentially to other students, who, like you, face constant challenges in managing their time.

Time management is a lifelong skill. Securing a good job after college will likely mean managing your own time and possibly that of other people you supervise. If you decide to go to graduate or professional school, time management will continue to be essential to your success. Time management is important not only for you but also is a way in which you show respect for others: your friends, family, and your college instructors.

At times what instructors perceive as inappropriate or disrespectful behavior may be the result of a cultural misunderstanding. All cultures view time differently. In American academic culture, punctuality is a virtue. Being strictly on time may be a difficult adjustment for you if you grew up in a culture that is more flexible in its approach to time, but it is important to recognize the values of the new culture you are encountering. Although you should not have to alter your cultural identity to succeed in college, you must be aware of the expectations that faculty members typically have for students.

02 Chapter Review

One-minute paper . . .

Chapter 2 gives you a lot of tips for managing your time. It can be frustrating to realize that you have to spend time organizing yourself to manage your time effectively. Did any of the time-management tips in this chapter appeal to you? If so, which ones and why? Did anything in this chapter leave you with more questions than answers? If so, what are your questions?

Applying what you've learned . . .

Now that you have read and discussed this chapter, consider how you can apply what you have learned to your academic and personal life. The following prompts will help you to reflect on chapter material and its relevance to you both now and in the future.

1. Review the "Overcoming Procrastination" section of this chapter. Think of one upcoming assignment in any of your current classes and describe how you can avoid waiting until the last minute to get it done. Break down the assignment, and list each step that you will take to complete the assignment. Give yourself a due date for each step and one for completing the assignment.

2. After reading about effective time-management strategies, consider the way in which you manage your own time. If you were grading your current set of time-management skills, what grade (A, B, C, or lower) would you give yourself? Why? What is your biggest challenge to becoming a more effective time manager?

Building your portfolio . . .

Time is of the essence

This chapter includes many great tips for effectively managing your time. Those skills are necessary for reducing the stress of everyday life, but have you thought about managing your time over the long term? What are your long-term goals? Preparing yourself for a particular career is probably high on your list, and it's not too early to begin thinking about what kind of preparation is necessary for the career (or careers) you are considering.

First, to help you determine the careers you are most interested in pursuing, schedule an appointment with a counselor in the career center on your campus and ask for information on career assessments to help you identify your preferences and interests. This portfolio assignment will help you realize that it is important to plan ahead and consider what implications your long-term goals have for managing your time right now.

1. In a Word document or Excel spreadsheet, create a chart like the example opposite.

2. Choose a career or careers in which you're most interested. In this example, a student needs to plan ahead for activities that will help to prepare for a future as a certified public accountant. It is okay if you have not decided on just one major or career; you can repeat this process as your interests change. An "action step" is something you need to do within a certain time frame.

3. Talk with someone in the career center, a professor, an upperclass student in your desired major, or a professional in your chosen career to get an idea of what you need to be considering, even now.

4. Fill in the action steps, to-dos, time line, and notes sections of your own chart, and update the chart as you learn more about the career you are exploring.

5. Save your work in your portfolio on your personal computer or flash drive.

Example Career: Certified Public Accountant (CPA)

Action Step	To-Do	Time Line	Notes
Make sure I'm taking the courses necessary to pursue this career.	Set up an appointment to talk with my academic adviser.	I should do this as soon as possible.	What prerequisites do I need for these courses?
Consider job shadowing.	Check with the career center to learn whether they can help me job shadow with college alumni in this career.	I should do this as soon as possible.	This action step will help me to determine whether this is really a career that I wish to pursue.
Check out campus clubs, organizations, and volunteer work.	Join a club or organization and consider becoming an officer, such as treasurer.	I should do this as soon as possible.	Joining a campus organization will give me practical experience that relates to my field.
Determine whether I need a master's degree, certificate, or license.	Explore these options and the benefits of each.	I should begin thinking about these options in my junior and senior years.	I need to know how long a degree will take and consider how to finance it.
Consider internships.	Find out whether this is a requirement.	I should begin thinking about an internship in my junior and senior years.	Where would I do an internship?

Where to go for help . . .

On Campus

Academic skills center: Along with assistance in studying for exams, reading textbooks, and taking notes, your campus academic skills center has specialists in time management who can offer advice for your specific problems.

Counseling center: If your problems with time management involve emotional issues you are unable to resolve, consider visiting your school's counseling office.

Your academic adviser/counselor: If you have a good relationship with this person, he or she might be able to offer advice or to refer you to another person on campus, including those in the offices mentioned above.

A fellow student: A friend who is a good student and willing to help you with time management can be one of your most valuable resources.

My Institution's Resources

_____

_____

_____

_____

_____

_____

_____

_____

_____

_____

_____

_____

_____

03 How You Learn

Research reveals that students who become genuinely engaged in their college experience have a greater chance of success than those who do not. "Engagement" means participating actively in your academic life and approaching every challenge with determination. One way to begin is to get to know your instructors, especially those who offer you the chance to learn actively. Whenever your instructor asks you a question, assigns groups to solve a problem, or requires you to make an oral presentation to the class, you become actively engaged in learning. Learning should be not only easier but also more rewarding and successful as a result.

To do well in college, it is also important to understand and use your preferred learning style. Experts agree that there is no one best way to learn. You may have trouble listening to a long lecture, or listening may be the way you learn best. You may love classroom discussion, or you may consider hearing other students' opinions a waste of time.

Another component of college success is "emotional intelligence." People who have a high level of emotional intelligence are able to control their own emotions and manage their reactions to difficult or frustrating situations. If you are not satisfied with your current level of emotional intelligence, the good news is that it can be improved. The first step is becoming more aware of how you react in various life situations and the effects of your reactions on others.

This chapter will help you engage actively with your coursework, classmates, and instructors and will ask you to complete a learning inventory to shed light on how you learn best. It will examine emotional intelligence and offer advice and resources for recognizing and treating common learning disabilities. The knowledge and insights you gain should help you get the most out of your learning and maximize your "return" on your college investment.

How Do You Measure Up?

1. I know the benefits of studying in groups.
   - ○ Agree
   - ○ Don't Know
   - ○ Disagree

2. I understand which of my courses ask me to learn in different ways.
   - ○ Agree
   - ○ Don't Know
   - ○ Disagree

3. I understand why emotional intelligence is important to success in college and in life.
   - ○ Agree
   - ○ Don't Know
   - ○ Disagree

4. I can recognize the signs of common learning disabilities, and I know where to get help with a learning problem I might have.
   - ○ Agree
   - ○ Don't Know
   - ○ Disagree

Review the items you marked "don't know" or "disagree." Paying attention to all these aspects of your college experience can be important to your success. After reading this chapter, come back to this list and think about ways you can work on these areas.

Being an Engaged Learner

Ben Kulish

25-year-old returning student

Just as calculus class was ending, Professor Berman dropped the news on us. "And I want every student here to participate in a study group," he said. A chorus of groans went up, but after that little moment, everyone started looking at the available times on the sign-up sheet he had made and started committing to a group. I sat at my desk and packed up my books. I aced every math course I took in high school, including pre-cal. So what if that was years ago? I'm good at math. Why would anyone need to show me how to study? A study group would be a waste of my time.

In the days before the first test, I studied like a crazy man—on my own. I figured I'd get the highest grade in the class. Yeah, so I'd skipped a couple of classes, and if I'd known any of the other students, I would have asked them for the notes. But I felt sure I hadn't missed anything major.

Fast-forward a week: When I scanned the grades posted on Dr. Berman's door, mine was one of the lowest. And after Dr. Berman returned the test, I saw that I had gotten the first two problems right but screwed up the last three. I couldn't believe it. What else had I missed in class?

This was only the first test, so Ben has the rest of the term to boost his grade in the course. What steps should he take? Does Professor Berman have any further responsibility to help him? Why or why not?

Engaging with learning requires you to prepare before and after every class, not just before exams. You might need to do library research, make appointments to talk with faculty members, prepare outlines from your class notes, ask someone to read your written assignment to see if it's clear, or have a serious discussion with students whose personal values are different from yours. This active approach to learning has the potential to make you well rounded in all aspects of your life. With good active learning skills, you will feel more comfortable socially, gain a greater appreciation for diversity and education, and be better able to clarify your academic major and future career.

Benefits of Collaborative Learning Teams

More than likely, you will be working with others after college, so now is a good time to learn how to collaborate. Students who engage in learning through a team approach not only learn better but often enjoy their learning experiences more. Whether on teams or by themselves, engaged learners are willing to try new ideas and discover new knowledge by exploring the world around them instead of just memorizing facts.

Experts on collaborative learning point to these benefits of learning teams:

- Learners learn from one another as well as from the instructor.

- Collaborative learning is by its nature active learning, and so it tends to increase learning through engagement.

- "Two heads are better than one." Collaboration can lead to more ideas, alternative approaches, new perspectives, and better solutions.

- If you're uneasy about speaking out in large classes, you will tend to be more comfortable participating in small groups, and better communication and better ideas will result.

- You will develop stronger bonds with other students in the class, which may increase everyone's interest in attending.

• "Positive competition" among groups happens when several groups are asked to solve the same problem—with the instructor clarifying that the purpose is for the good of all.

• Working in teams may help you develop leadership skills.[1]

Making learning teams productive Not all learning teams are equally effective. Sometimes teamwork fails to reach its potential because no thought was given to how the group was formed or how it should function. Use the following strategies to develop high-quality learning teams that maximize the power of peer collaboration:

1. Use learning teams for more than just preparing for exams. Effective student learning teams collaborate regularly for other academic tasks besides test review sessions.

2. Seek out team members who will contribute quality and diversity to the group. Resist the urge to limit the group to people who are just like you. Look for students who are motivated, attend class regularly, are attentive and participate actively while in class, and complete assignments.

3. Keep the team small (four to six teammates). Small groups allow for more face-to-face interaction and eye contact and less opportunity for any one individual to shirk responsibility to the team.

4. Hold individual team members personally accountable for contributing to the learning of their teammates. One way to ensure accountability is to have each member come to group meetings with specific information or answers to share with teammates, as well as with questions to ask the group.

---

[1] Joseph Cuseo, *Igniting Student Involvement, Peer Interaction, and Teamwork: A Taxonomy of Specific Cooperative Learning Structures and Collaborative Learning Strategies* (Stillwater, OK: New Forums Press, 2002).

How to make the most of learning teams Learning teams can serve a number of valuable purposes:

- **Note-taking.** Team up with other students immediately after class to share and compare notes. Look at the level of detail in one another's notes, and adopt the best of one another's styles. Discuss places where you got lost. Talk about technical terms and symbols you didn't understand or couldn't decipher on the board, and ask about questions raised in class that you didn't completely understand. If there are points that the whole group doesn't understand, consult with the instructor about the confusing information. If you absolutely have to miss a class, consult with members of your study group for notes and the assignment. Catch up before the next class. Otherwise you will get further and further behind.

- **Reading.** After completing reading assignments, team with other students to compare your highlighting and margin notes. See if all agree.

- **Library research.** Develop a support group for reducing "library anxiety" and for locating and sharing sources of information (which does not constitute cheating or plagiarizing as long as the final product you turn in represents your own work).

- **Team/instructor conferences.** Schedule a time for your learning team to visit the instructor during office hours to seek additional assistance as needed.

- **Preparing for tests.** Divide the job of making a study outline. Each person should bring his or her section. Team members can discuss and modify the outlines before a final version is created for all. Group members can quiz one another, focusing on facts and specific pieces of information for an objective test and on the relationship of those pieces to one another for an essay exam. Members then can write practice questions for each other, or the group might create an entire sample exam and take it together under timed conditions.

- **Reviewing test results.** After receiving test results, join with your team to review your individual tests together. Help one another identify the sources of mistakes, and share any answers that received high scores.

- **Teaching each other.** Split up difficult questions or problems and assign them to various members to prepare and present to the group. Remember that the best way to learn something is to explain it to someone else.

- **Asking questions.** Never criticize a question in your study group; respond positively and express appreciation for all contributions. If you notice someone is lost, give that person an opportunity to ask a question by reviewing the work: "Let's see if we all understand what we've done so far. . . ." If you are explaining your solution to a problem, try leading the others through it by asking a series of simple questions. Above all, come to the group meeting prepared—not with all the answers, but knowing what specific questions you have.

Using Learning Teams in Mathematics and Science

Although working with students in a learning team is important for all courses, a learning team that serves as a study group is especially effective in science and math. In his groundbreaking research on the factors that predict success in calculus, Professor Uri Treisman of the University of Texas at Austin determined that the most effective strategy for success in calculus turned out to be active participation in a study group! It is now widely accepted that, by working together, a group of students can significantly enhance one another's performance, particularly in problem-solving courses and especially when one member of the group is an advanced math student.

It seems that the larger the class and the more complex the material, the more valuable the study group. Although Treisman-style workshops in calculus, chemistry, physics, and other subjects have been established by schools across the country, most study groups are informal and organized by students themselves. Study groups work best when members take their commitment to one another seriously, make faithful attendance a priority, and set specific goals for each session.

03

Learning How You Learn Best: The VARK Learning Styles Inventory

You will be more likely to succeed in college if you know and use your most effective learning style. There are many models for thinking about and describing learning styles, such as the Kolb Learning Styles Inventory and the Myers-Briggs Type Indicator. We focus here on one popular model—the VARK—and present its learning styles inventory to help you determine your best mode of learning.

The VARK (Visual, Aural, Read/Write, and Kinesthetic) Learning Styles Inventory

Unlike learning styles theories that rely on personality or intelligence, the VARK focuses on how learners prefer to use their senses to learn. The acronym VARK stands for "Visual," "Aural," "Read/Write," and "Kinesthetic." Visual learners prefer to learn information through charts, graphs, symbols, and other visual means. Aural learners favor hearing information. Read/Write learners prefer to learn information that is displayed as words. Kinesthetic learners are most comfortable learning through experience and practice, whether simulated or real. To determine your learning style according to the VARK Inventory, respond to the questionnaire that follows.

The VARK Questionnaire

(Version 7.0, 2006)

Choose the answers that best explain your preference and circle the letter next to it. Please circle more than one if a single answer does not match your perception. Leave blank any question that does not apply.

1. You are helping someone who wants to go to your airport, town center, or railway station. You would:
   a. go with her.
   b. tell her the directions.
   c. write down the directions as a list (without a map).
   d. draw or give her a map.

2. You are not sure whether a word should be spelled "dependent" or "dependant." You would:
   a. see the words in your mind and choose by the way they look.
   b. think about how each word sounds and choose one.
   c. find it in a dictionary.
   d. write both words on paper and choose one.

3. You are planning a holiday for a group. You want some feedback from the group about your plan. You would:
   a. describe some of the highlights.
   b. use a map or Web site to show them the places.
   c. give them a copy of the printed itinerary.
   d. phone, text, or e-mail them.

4. You are going to cook something as a special treat for your family. You would:
   a. cook something you know without the need for instructions.
   b. ask friends for suggestions.
   c. look through the cookbook for ideas from the pictures.
   d. use a cookbook where you know there is a good recipe.

5. A group of tourists wants to learn about the parks or wildlife reserves in your area. You would:
   a. talk about, or arrange a talk for them about, parks or wildlife reserves.
   b. show them Internet pictures, photographs, or picture books.
   c. take them to a park or wildlife reserve and walk with them.
   d. give them a book or pamphlets about the parks or wildlife reserves.

6. You are about to purchase a digital camera or mobile phone. Other than price, what would most influence your decision?
   a. Trying or testing it.
   b. Reading the details about its features.
   c. It is a modern design and looks good.
   d. The salesperson telling you about its features.

7. Remember a time when you learned how to do something new. Try to avoid choosing a physical skill (e.g., riding a bike). You learned best by:
   a. watching a demonstration.
   b. listening to somebody explaining it and asking questions.

03

c. diagrams and charts—visual clues.

d. written instructions (e.g., a manual or text-book).

8. You have a problem with your knee. You would prefer that the doctor:

a. gave you a web address or something to read about it.

b. used a plastic model of a knee to show what was wrong.

c. described what was wrong.

d. showed you a diagram of what was wrong.

9. You want to learn a new program, skill, or game on a computer. You would:

a. read the written instructions that came with the program.

b. talk with people who know about the program.

c. use the controls or keyboard.

d. follow the diagrams in the book that came with it.

10. You like Web sites that have:

a. things you can click on, shift, or try.

b. interesting design and visual features.

c. interesting written descriptions, lists, and explanations.

d. audio channels where you can hear music, radio programs, or interviews.

11. Other than price, what would most influence your decision to buy a new nonfiction book?

a. The way it looks is appealing.

b. Quickly reading parts of it.

c. A friend talks about it and recommends it.

d. It has real-life stories, experiences, and examples.

12. You are using a book, CD, or Web site to learn how to take photos with your new digital camera. You would like to have:

a. a chance to ask questions and talk about the camera and its features.

b. clear written instructions with lists and bullet points about what to do.

c. diagrams showing the camera and what each part does.

d. many examples of good and poor photos and how to improve them.

13. Do you prefer a teacher or a presenter who uses:

a. demonstrations, models, or practical sessions?

b. question-and-answer sessions, group discussion, or guest speakers?

c. handouts, books, or readings?

d. diagrams, charts, or graphs?

14. You have finished a competition or test and would like some feedback. You would like to have feedback:

a. using examples from what you have done.

b. using a written description of your results.

c. from somebody who talks it through with you.

d. using graphs showing what you had achieved.

15. You are going to choose food at a restaurant or cafe. You would:

a. choose something that you have had there before.

b. listen to the waiter or ask friends to recommend choices.

c. choose from the descriptions in the menu.

d. look at what others are eating or look at pictures of each dish.

16. You have to make an important speech at a conference or special occasion. You would:

a. make diagrams or get graphs to help explain things.

b. write a few key words and practice saying your speech over and over.

c. write out your speech and learn from reading it over several times.

d. gather many examples and stories to make the talk real and practical.

Scoring the VARK

Use the following scoring chart to find the VARK category that each of your answers corresponds to. Circle the letters that correspond to your answers. For example, if you answered b and c for question 3, circle V and R in the question 3 row.

VARK Scoring Guide

Question	A category	B category	C category	D category
3	K	(V)	(R)	A

Scoring Chart

Question	A category	B category	C category	D category
1	K	(A)	R	V
2	V	A	(R)	K
3	K	V	R	(A)
4	(K)	A	V	R
5	(A)	V	K	R
6	K	R	(V)	A
7	(K)	A	V	R
8	R	K	(A)	V
9	R	(A)	K	V
10	K	V	R	A
11	(V)	R	A	K
12	(A)	R	V	K
13	(K)	A	R	V
14	K	R	(A)	V
15	(K)	A	R	(V)
16	V	A	(R)	K

Count the number of each of the VARK letters you have circled to get your score for each VARK category.

||| Total number of **V**s circled = ___3___

|| ||| Total number of **A**s circled = ___7___

|| Total number of **R**s circled = ___2___

|||| Total number of **K**s circled = ___4___

Because you could choose more than one answer for each question, the scoring is not just a simple matter of counting. It is like four stepping stones across some water. Enter your scores **from highest to lowest** on the stones below, with their V, A, R, and K labels.

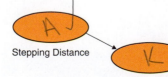

Stepping Distance

Scoring VARK - Stepping Stones

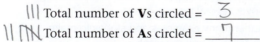

Your **stepping distance** comes from this table:

Total of my four VARK scores is	My stepping distance is
16–21	1
22–27	2
28–32	3
More than 32	4

03

Follow these steps to establish your preferences.

1. Your first preference is always your highest score. Check that first stone as one of your preferences.

2. Now subtract your second highest score from your first. If that figure is larger than your stepping distance (see above table), you have a single preference. Otherwise check this stone as another preference and continue with step 3 below.

3. Subtract your third score from your second one. If that figure is larger than your stepping distance, you have a bimodal preference. If not, check your third stone as a preference and continue with step 4 below.

4. Lastly, subtract your fourth score from your third one. If that figure is larger than your stepping distance, you have a trimodal preference. Otherwise, check your fourth stone as a preference, and you have all four modes as your preferences.

Note: If you are bimodal, trimodal, or have checked all four modes as your preferences, you can be described as *multimodal* in your VARK preferences.

Using VARK Results to Study More Effectively

How can knowing your VARK score help you do better in your college classes? Here are ways of using learning styles to develop your own study strategies:

- If you have a visual learning preference, underline or highlight your notes; use symbols, charts, or graphs to display your notes; use different arrangements of words on the page; and redraw your pages from memory.

- If you are an aural learner, talk with others to verify the accuracy of your lecture notes. Put your notes on tape and listen, or tape class lectures. Read your notes out loud; ask yourself questions and speak your answers.

- If you have a read/write learning preference, write and rewrite your notes, and read your notes silently. Organize diagrams or flow charts into statements, and write imaginary exam questions and respond in writing.

- If you are a kinesthetic learner, you will need to use all your senses in learning—sight, touch, taste, smell, and hearing. Supplement your notes with real-world examples; move and gesture while you are reading or speaking your notes.

Understanding Emotional Intelligence

Particularly in the first year of college, many students who are intellectually capable of succeeding have difficulty establishing positive relationships with others, dealing with pressure, or making wise decisions. Other students exude optimism and happiness and seem to adapt to their new environment without any trouble. The difference lies not in academic talent but in emotional intelligence (EI), or the ability to recognize and manage moods, feelings, and attitudes. A growing body of evidence shows a clear connection between students' EI and whether or not they stay in college.

What Is Emotional Intelligence?

Emotional intelligence is the ability to identify, use, understand, and manage emotions. Emotions are a big part of who you are; you should not ignore them. The better the emotional read you have on a situation, the more appropriately you can respond to it. Being aware of your own and others' feelings helps you to gather accurate information about the world around you and allows you to respond in appropriate ways.

There are many competing theories about EI, some of them complex. While experts vary in their definitions and models, all agree that emotions are real, can be changed for the better, and have a profound impact on whether or not a person is successful.

In the simplest terms, emotional intelligence consists of two general abilities:

- **Understanding emotions** involves the capacity to monitor and label feelings accurately (nervous, happy, angry, relieved, and so forth) and to determine why you feel the way you do. It also involves predicting how others might feel in a given situation. Emotions contain information, and the ability to understand and think about that information plays an important role in behavior.

- **Managing emotions** builds on the belief that feelings can be modified, even improved. At times, you need to stay open to your feelings, learn from them, and use them to take appropriate action. Other times, it is better to disengage from an emotion and return to it later. Anger, for example, can blind you and lead you to act in negative or antisocial ways; used positively, however, the same emotion can help you overcome adversity, bias, and injustice.

Identifying and using emotions can help you know which moods are best for different situations and learn how to put yourself in the "right" mood. Developing an awareness of emotions allows you to use your feelings to enhance your thinking. If you are feeling sad, for instance, you might view the world in a certain way, while if you feel happy, you are likely to interpret the same events differently. Once you start paying attention to emotions, you can learn not only how to cope with life's pressures and demands, but also how to harness your knowledge of the way you feel for more effective problem solving, reasoning, decision making, and creative endeavors.[2]

A number of sophisticated tools can be used to assess emotional intelligence. But even without a formal test, you can take a number of steps to get in touch with your own EI. You'll have to dig deep inside yourself and be willing to be honest about how you really think and how you really behave. This process can take time, and that's fine. Think of your EI as a work in progress.

How Emotions Affect Success

Emotions are strongly tied to physical and psychological well-being. For example, some studies have suggested that cancer patients who have strong EI live longer. A large study done at the

---

[2] Adapted with permission from EI Skills Group, "Ability Model of Emotional Intelligence," http://www.emotionaliq.com/. © 2005–2009.

Emotional Intelligence Questionnaire

Your daily life gives you many opportunities to take a hard look at how you handle emotions. Here are some questions that can help you begin thinking about your own EI.

1. What do you do when you are under stress?

a) I tend to deal with it calmly and rationally.

b) I get upset, but it usually blows over quickly.

c) I get upset but keep it to myself.

2. My friends would say that:

a) I will play, but only after I get my work done.

b) I am ready for fun anytime.

c) I hardly ever go out.

3. When something changes at the last minute:

a) I easily adapt.

b) I get frustrated.

c) It doesn't matter, since I don't really expect things to happen as I plan.

4. My friends would say that:

a) I am sensitive to their concerns.

b) I spend too much time worrying about other people's needs.

c) I don't like to deal with other people's petty problems.

5. When I have a problem to solve, such as too many things due at the end of the week:

a) I write down a list of the tasks I must complete, come up with a plan indicating specifically what I can accomplish and what I cannot, and follow my plan.

b) I am very optimistic about getting things done and just dig right in and get to work.

c) I get a little frazzled. Usually I get a number of things done and then push aside the things that I can't do.

Review your responses. **A** responses indicate that you probably have a good basis for strong emotional intelligence. **B** responses indicate you may have some strengths and some challenges in your EI. **C** responses indicate that your success in life and school could be negatively affected by your EI.

03

University of Pennsylvania found that the best athletes do well in part because they are extremely optimistic. Even with tremendous obstacles and the odds stacked against them, emotionally intelligent people nonetheless go on to succeed.

A number of studies link strong EI skills to college success in particular. Here are a few highlights:

- **Emotionally intelligent students get higher grades.** Researchers looked at students' grade point averages at the end of the first year of college. Students who had tested high for intrapersonal skills, stress tolerance, and adaptability when they entered in the fall did better academically than those who had lower overall EI test scores.

- **Students who can't manage their emotions struggle academically.** Some students have experienced full-blown panic attacks before tests. Others who are depressed can't concentrate on coursework. And far too many turn to risky behaviors (drug and alcohol abuse, eating disorders, and worse) in an effort to cope. Dr. Richard Kadison, Chief of Mental Health Services at Harvard University, notes that "the emotional well-being of students goes hand-in-hand with their academic development. If they're not doing well emotionally, they are not going to reach their academic potential."[3]

---

[3] Richard Kadison and Theresa Foy DiGeronimo, *College of the Overwhelmed: The Campus Mental Health Crisis and What to Do About It* (San Francisco: Jossey-Bass, 2004), p. 156.

- **Students who can delay gratification tend to do better overall.** Impulse control leads to achievement. In the famous "Marshmallow Study" performed at Stanford University, researchers examined the long-term behaviors of individuals who, as four-year-olds, did or did not practice delayed gratification. The children were given one marshmallow and told that if they didn't eat it right away, they could have another. Fourteen years later, the children who ate their marshmallow immediately were more likely to experience significant stress, irritability, and inability to focus on goals. The children who waited scored an average of 210 points higher on the SAT; had better confidence, concentration, and reliability; held better-paying jobs; and reported being more satisfied with life.

- **EI skills can be enhanced in a first-year seminar.** In two separate studies, one conducted in Australia and another conducted in the United States, researchers found that college students enrolled in a first-year seminar who demonstrated good EI skills were more likely to do better in college than students who did not exhibit those behaviors.

Without strong EI in college, it is possible to do well enough to get by, but you might miss out on the full range and depth of competencies and skills that can help you to succeed in your chosen field and have a fulfilling and meaningful life.

How to Improve Your Emotional Intelligence

Developing your EI is an important step toward getting the full benefit of a college education. Think about it. Do you often give up because something is just too hard or you can't figure it out? Do you take responsibility for what you do, or do you blame others if you fail? How can you communicate effectively if you are not assertive or if you are overly aggressive? If you're inflexible, how can you solve problems, get along with coworkers and family members, or learn from other people's points of view?

The good news is that you can improve your EI. It might not be easy—old habits are hard to change—but it can definitely be done. Here are some suggestions:

1. **Identify your strengths and weaknesses.** Take a hard look at yourself, and consider how you respond to situations. Most people have trouble assessing their own behaviors realistically, so ask someone you trust and respect for insight.

2. **Set realistic goals.** As you identify areas of emotional intelligence that you would like to improve, be as specific as possible. Instead of deciding to be more assertive, for example, focus on a particular issue that is giving you trouble.

3. **Formulate a plan.** With a particular goal in mind, identify a series of steps you could take to achieve the goal, and define the results that would indicate success.

4. **Check your progress on a regular basis.** Continually reassess whether or not you have met your goals, and adjust your strategy as needed.

It's important not to try to improve everything at once. Instead, identify specific EI competencies that you can define, describe, and identify, and then set measurable goals for change. Don't expect success overnight. Remember that it took you a while to develop your specific approach to life, and it will take commitment and practice to change it.

Learning with a Learning Disability

While everyone has a learning style, a portion of the population has what is characterized as a "learning disability." Learning disabilities are usually recognized and diagnosed in grade school. But occasionally students successfully compensate for a learning problem and reach college never having been properly diagnosed or assisted.

Learning disabilities affect people's ability to interpret what they see and hear or to link information across different parts of the brain. These limitations can show up as specific difficulties with spoken and written language, coordination, self-control, or attention. Such difficulties can impede learning to read, write, or do math. Because the term *learning disability* covers a broad range of possible causes, symptoms, treatments, and outcomes, it is difficult to diagnose a learning disability or pinpoint the causes. The types of learning disabilities that most commonly affect college students are attention disorders and disorders that affect the development of academic skills, including reading, writing, and mathematics.

Attention Disorders

Attention disorders are common in children, adolescents, and adults. Some students who have attention disorders appear to daydream excessively, and once you get their attention, they can be easily distracted. Individuals with attention deficit disorder (ADD) or attention deficit hyperactivity disorder (ADHD) often have trouble organizing tasks or completing their work. They don't seem to listen to or follow directions, and their work might be messy or appear careless. Although they are not strictly classified as learning disabilities, ADD and ADHD can seriously interfere with academic performance, leading some educators to classify them along with other learning disabilities.

If you have trouble paying attention or getting organized, you won't really know whether you have ADD or ADHD until you are evaluated. Check out resources on campus or in the community. After you have been evaluated, follow the advice you get, which might or might not mean taking medication. If you do receive a prescription for medication, be sure to take it according to the physician's directions. In the meantime, if you're having trouble getting and staying organized, whether or not you have an attention disorder, you can improve your focus through your own behavioral choices. The National Institutes of Mental Health offer the following suggestions (found on its Web site) for adults with attention disorders:

> Adults with ADD or ADHD can learn how to organize their lives by using "props," such as a large calendar posted where it will be seen in the morning, date books, lists, and reminder notes. They can have a special place for keys, bills, and the paperwork of everyday life. Tasks can be organized into sections so that completion of each part can give a sense of accomplishment. Above all, adults who have ADD or ADHD should learn as much as they can about their disorder (**http://www.nimh.nih.gov/health/publications/attentiondeficit-hyperactivity-disorder/can-adults-have-adhd.shtml**).

Cognitive Learning Disabilities

Other learning disabilities are related to cognitive skills. Dyslexia, for example, is a common developmental reading disorder. A person can have problems with any of the tasks involved in reading. However, scientists have found that a significant number of people with dyslexia share an inability to distinguish or separate the sounds in spoken words. For instance, dyslexic individuals sometimes have difficulty assigning the appropriate sounds to letters, either individually or when letters combine to form words. However, there is more to reading than recognizing words. If the brain is unable to form images or relate new ideas to those stored in memory, the reader can't understand or remember the new concepts. So other types of reading disabilities can appear when the focus of reading shifts from word identification to comprehension.

03

Writing, too, involves several brain areas and functions. The brain networks for vocabulary, grammar, hand movement, and memory must all be in good working order. So a developmental writing disorder might result from problems in any of these areas. Someone who can't distinguish the sequence of sounds in a word will often have problems with spelling. People with writing disabilities, particularly expressive language disorders (the inability to express oneself using accurate language or sentence structure), are often unable to compose complete, grammatical sentences.

A student with a developmental arithmetic disorder will have difficulty recognizing numbers and symbols, memorizing facts such as the multiplication table, aligning numbers, and understanding abstract concepts such as place value and fractions.

The following questions may help you determine whether you or someone you know should seek further screening for a possible learning disability:

- Do you perform poorly on tests even when you feel you have studied and are capable of performing better?
- Do you have trouble spelling words?
- Do you work harder than your classmates at basic reading and writing?
- Do your instructors tell you that your performance in class is inconsistent, such as answering questions correctly in class but incorrectly on a written test?
- Do you have a really short attention span, or do your family members or instructors say that you do things without thinking?

Although responding "yes" to any of these questions does not mean that you have a disability, the resources of your campus learning center or the office for student disability services can help you address any potential problems and devise ways to learn more effectively.

A final important message: A learning disability is a learning difference but is in no way related to intelligence. Having a learning disability is not a sign that you are stupid. In fact, some of the most intelligent individuals in human history have had a learning disability.

03

try it!

Find out whether your college or university has a special office that is able to diagnose and help treat learning disabilities. Visit this office or your campus library to learn how individuals with learning disabilities can still succeed in college and in life.

03 Chapter Review

One-minute paper . . .

Recognizing that people have different ways of learning can be a relief. After reading this chapter, do you have a better understanding of your own learning style? What did you find to be the most interesting point in this chapter? What would you like to learn more about?

Applying what you've learned . . .

Now that you have read and discussed this chapter, consider how you can apply what you have learned to your academic and personal life. The following prompts will help you reflect on the chapter material and its relevance to you both now and in the future.

1. Managing stress is an important skill in college. Take a look through your course syllabi, and make a list of assignments, exams, and due dates. Do any of your assignments or exams seem to cluster around the same time in the term? Can you anticipate times when you might be especially likely to get stressed? What can you do in advance to avoid becoming overwhelmed and overstressed?

2. It is important to understand various learning styles and how your own style(s) of learning affect(s) your experience in the classroom. Considering your own learning styles, what kinds of teaching and learning methods do you think will work best for you? What teaching and learning methods will be especially challenging?

Building your portfolio . . .

Know thyself

Understanding your own behavior can sometimes be more difficult than understanding someone else's. Review the questionnaire on page 39 of this chapter. Were you honest in your assessment of yourself?

1. In a Word document, list the questions from page 39 that you answered with a B or a C. For example, did you rate yourself with a B or a C on a statement such as "something changes at the last minute"?

2. For each question that you have listed, describe your strategy for improving your response to certain situations. For example, when things change suddenly, you might say, "I am going to take a few minutes to think about what I need to do next. I will remind myself that I am still in control of my actions."

3. Save your responses in your portfolio on your personal computer or flash drive. Revisit your responses to the questions listed above as you experience similar situations.

Pay special attention to how your emotional intelligence affects your daily life. As you become more aware of your emotions and actions, you will begin to see how you can improve in the areas that are most difficult for you.

Where to go for help . . .

On Campus

Learning (assistance/support) center: Almost every campus has one or more of these. Sometimes they provide help for students in all subjects at all levels; sometimes they are specific to one discipline. The staff will know many, if not all, of your instructors and can provide good advice for using active learning strategies.

These centers typically retain outstanding undergraduate students who serve as tutors. From their experiences, they can teach you how to make active learning easier and more enjoyable. Above all, remember: Learning centers are not just for students who are having academic trouble—they are for all students who want to improve their learning skills.

Counseling center: Maybe your first term in college is putting you under excessive stress—a fairly common issue among new college students. There's help right on campus at the counseling center, which provides free and confidential support for students. You can get feedback on the sources of your stress and learn new coping mechanisms. You already have paid for such services in your basic tuition and fees. Seeking a counselor simply means that, as a new student with concerns, you are taking steps to get the assistance you need.

Faculty members: Probably some of your professors strike you as approachable and sympathetic. Make an appointment to see one of them and share your concerns.

Academic adviser/counselor: Make a special effort to meet your adviser/counselor, especially if you're having problems in any of your courses or if circumstances are keeping you from earning higher grades. If you don't feel comfortable with your adviser, you have the right to ask for a new one.

Your first-year seminar instructor: To learn more about learning styles and learning disabilities, talk to your first-year seminar instructor about campus resources. You also may have professors in the areas of education and psychology who have a strong interest in the processes of learning. Finally, don't forget your library or the Internet. A great deal of published information is available to describe how we learn.

Books

Edward M. Hallowell (Foreword), Jonathan Mooney, and David Cole, *Learning outside the Lines: Two Ivy League Students with Learning Disabilities and ADHD Give You the Tools for Academic Success and Educational Revolution* (New York: Fireside, 2000).

Kathleen G. Nadeau, *Survival Guide for College Students with ADD or LD* (Washington, DC: Magination Press, 1994).

Patricia O. Quinn, MD, ed., *ADD and the College Student: A Guide for High School and College Students with Attention Deficit Disorder* (Washington, DC: Magination Press, 2001).

Online

Active Learning: Creating Excitement in the Classroom: **http://www.ntlf.com/html/lib/bib/91-9dig.htm**. Check out the authors' interpretation of the active learning process.

Tools for Teaching: http://teaching.berkeley.edu/bgd/collaborative.html. Read the information designed for instructors on collaborative learning.

LD Pride: http://www.ldpride.net/learningstyles.MI.htm. This site was developed in 1998 by Liz Bogod, an adult with learning disabilities. It provides general information about learning styles and learning disabilities and offers an interactive diagnostic tool to determine your learning style.

Support 4 Learning: http://www.support4learning.org.uk/education/learning_styles.cfm. This site is supported by HERO, Higher Education and Research Opportunities, which is the official online gateway to UK universities, colleges, and research organizations. The site provides learning styles inventories and helpful hints about how to use your learning style to do well in college courses.

National Center for Learning Disabilities: http://www.ncld.org. This is the official Web site for the National Center for Learning Disabilities. The site provides a variety of resources for diagnosing and understanding learning disabilities.

04 Thinking Critically

One of the main purposes of a college education is to empower you to become a good critical thinker. Becoming a critical thinker does not mean that you will become more argumentative and "critical" but that you will be able to evaluate information by using logical and rational processes. In our nation and world, there are many authorities, including politicians, religious leaders, media pundits, and marketers, who want others to accept what they say as "the truth." But before you accept any viewpoint, it is important that you consider it through the lens of critical thinking. You will often find that there is no "one right answer" to a particular question; the best answer may depend on the particular context or situation. Thinking critically may cause you to challenge some of your own viewpoints. As you develop your own critical thinking skills, you will be more cautious about accepting the opinions of others before you weigh the evidence and make your own decision.

Some of your courses will require more critical thinking than others. For instance, learning in the social and behavioral sciences requires you to evaluate different theories and opinions. But even mathematicians and accountants disagree about the best way to work a problem or find the right answer. So be on the lookout for critical thinking opportunities, even in courses that seem less open to debate.

This chapter will provide you valuable strategies for critical thinking. It will also help you understand why critical thinking is one of the most important and desirable skills for success in college and the workplace and for living in a democracy.

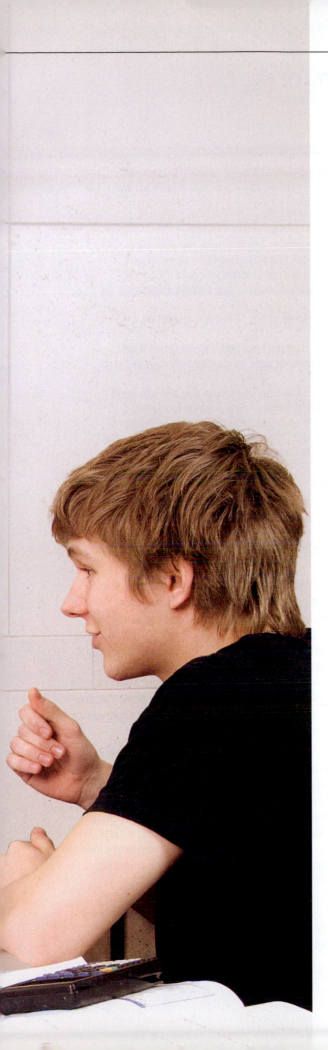

How Do You Measure Up?

1. Even when I find some people irritating, I try to listen to what they have to say.
   - ○ Always
   - ○ Occasionally
   - ○ Never

2. I can recognize when facts just don't add up, even though they appear to be logical.
   - ○ Always
   - ○ Occasionally
   - ○ Never

3. I try to not allow my emotions to get in the way of making the right decision.
   - ○ Always
   - ○ Occasionally
   - ○ Never

4. I am careful to double-check information I find on the Internet to make sure it's legitimate.
   - ○ Always
   - ○ Occasionally
   - ○ Never

Review the items you marked "occasionally" or "never." Paying attention to all these aspects of your college experience can be important to your success. After reading this chapter, come back to this list and think about ways you can work on these areas.

Becoming a Critical Thinker

Tom Nyugen

20-year-old second-year student

In the beginning, I didn't know anything about choosing a professor. My first term, my academic adviser set my schedule, so my instructors were totally random. But this semester, I knew what classes I wanted and needed to take. I also knew that getting the right professor could mean the difference between learning how to nap with my eyes open and having my mind totally expanded. So I decided to check out all the candidates.

"Oh, I've already done the research on that," said a classmate, Greg. "For the real deal on a teacher, just go to RateMyProfessors.com."

I logged on and looked up the professors who teach the courses I needed. I wrote down their names along with their scores (excellent, good, fair, poor). An hour later, I presented my ratings list to my academic adviser, who promptly freaked out.

"What makes you think these are accurate?" she asked. "Some professors on that site are rated by only one student—maybe even someone who didn't take that class." She pointed to my list. "Look at Professor Schwartz: He's highly regarded in his field and gets glowing student evaluations. Yet RateMyProfessors listed him as 'poor'! She shook her head. "Come on, Tom. You *really* think this Web site is the best way to learn about professors? College is about being a good critical thinker— not just taking one opinion as fact."

Tom felt torn: He knew his adviser was trying to help him, but he also wanted to believe his fellow students. What should he do? How can he be sure he's making the right choices?

In essence, critical thinking is a search for truth. In college and in life, you'll be confronted by a mass of information and ideas. Much of what you read and hear will seem suspect, and a lot of it will be contradictory. (If you have ever talked back to a television commercial or doubted a politician's campaign promises, you know this already.) How do you decide what to believe?

On the Web site for the Foundation for Critical Thinking, Richard Paul and Linda Elder offer this definition: "Critical thinking is that mode of thinking about any subject, content, or problem in which the thinker improves the quality of his or her thinking by skillfully . . . imposing intellectual standards upon [his or her thoughts]."[1] They believe that much of our thinking, left to itself, is biased, distorted, partial, uninformed, or downright prejudiced.

Paul and Elder also caution that shoddy thinking is costly. How so? You probably know people who simply follow authority. They do not question, are not curious, and do not challenge people or groups who claim special knowledge or insight. These people do not usually think for themselves but rely on others to think for them. They might indulge in wishful, hopeful, and emotional thinking. As you might have noticed, such people tend not to have much control over their circumstances or to possess any real power in business or society.

Paul and Elder remind us that there may be more than one right answer to any given question. The task is to determine which of the "truths" you read or hear are the most plausible and then draw on them to develop ideas of your own. Difficult problems practically demand that you weigh options and think through consequences before you can reach an informed decision. Critical thinking also involves improving the way you think about a subject, statement, or idea. To do that, you'll need to ask questions, consider several different points of view, and draw your own conclusions.

[1] http://www.criticalthinking.org/print-page .cfm?pageID=766.

Ask Questions

The first step to thinking critically is to engage your curiosity. When you come across an idea or a "fact" that strikes you as interesting, confusing, or suspicious, ask yourself first what it means. Do you fully understand what is being said, or do you need to pause and think to make sense of the idea? Do you agree with the statement? Why or why not? Can the material be interpreted in more than one way?

Don't stop there. Ask whether you can trust the person or institution making a particular claim, and ask whether they have provided enough evidence to back up an assertion (more on this later). Finally, ask yourself about the implications and consequences of accepting something as truth. Will you have to change your perspective or give up a long-held belief? Will it require you to do something differently? Will it be necessary to investigate the issue further? Do you anticipate having to try to bring other people around to a new way of thinking?

Consider Multiple Points of View

Once you start asking questions, you will typically discover a slew of different possible answers competing for your attention. Don't be too quick to latch on to one and move on. To be a critical thinker, you need to be fair and open-minded, even if you don't agree with certain ideas at first. Give them all a fair hearing, because your goal is to find the truth or the best action, not to confirm what you already believe.

Often, you will recognize the existence of competing points of view on your own, perhaps because they're held by people you know personally. You might discover them in what you read, watch, or listen to for pleasure. Reading assignments might deliberately expose you to conflicting arguments and theories about a subject, or you might encounter differences of opinion as you do research for a project.

The more ideas you entertain, the more sophisticated your own thinking will become. Ultimately, you will discover not only that it is okay to change your mind, but also that a willingness to do so is the mark of a reasonable, educated person.

Draw Conclusions

Once you have considered different points of view, it's up to you to reach your own conclusions, to craft a new idea based on what you've learned, or to make a decision about what you'll do with the information you have.

This process isn't necessarily a matter of figuring out the best idea. Depending on the goals of the activity, it might be simply the one that you think is the most fun or the most practical, or it might be a new idea of your own creation.

Drawing conclusions involves looking at the outcome of your inquiry in a more demanding, critical way. If you are looking for solutions to a problem, which ones really seem most promising after you have conducted an exhaustive search for materials? If you have found new evidence, what does that new evidence show? Do your original beliefs hold up? Do they need to be modified? Which notions should be abandoned? Most important, consider what you would need to do or say to persuade someone else that your ideas are valid. Thoughtful conclusions are not very useful if you can't share them with others.

04

try it!

Being Alert for False Promises

Looking at the Internet, television, or magazines, pay attention to commercials that make outrageous or false promises. Pick two or three to share with your classmates. Discuss why such commercials can be effective with some people.

Being Aware of Logical Fallacies

A critical thinker has an attitude—an attitude of wanting to avoid nonsense, to find the truth, and to discover the best action. It's an attitude that rejects intuiting what is right in favor of requiring reasons. Instead of being defensive or emotional, critical thinkers aim to be logical.

Although logical reasoning is essential to solving any problem, whether simple or complex, you need to go one step further to make sure that an argument hasn't been compromised by faulty reasoning. Here are some of the most common missteps people make in their use of logic:

- **Attacking the person.** It's perfectly acceptable to argue against other people's positions or to attack their arguments. It is not okay, however, to go after their personalities. Any argument that resorts to personal attack ("Why should we believe a cheater?") is unworthy of consideration.

- **Begging.** "Please, officer, don't give me a ticket because if you do, I'll lose my license, and I have five little children to feed and won't be able to feed them if I can't drive my truck." None of the driver's statements offer any evidence, in any legal sense, as to why she shouldn't be given a ticket. Pleading *might* work, if the officer is feeling generous, but an appeal to facts and reason would be more effective: "I fed the meter, but it didn't register the coins. Since the machine is broken, I'm sure you'll agree that I don't deserve a ticket."

- **Appealing to false authority.** Citing authorities, such as experts in a field or the opinions of qualified researchers, can offer valuable support for an argument. But a claim based on the authority of someone whose expertise is questionable relies on the appearance of authority rather than real evidence. We see this all the time in advertising: Sports stars who are not doctors, dieticians, or nutritionists urge us to eat a certain brand of food, or famous actors and singers who are not dermatologists extol the medical benefits of a pricey remedy for acne.

LUSTRE-CREME is the favorite beauty shampoo of 4 out of 5 top Hollywood stars... and you'll love it in its new Lotion Form, too!

Marilyn Monroe
starring in
"GENTLEMEN PREFER BLONDES"
A 20th Century-Fox Production
Color by Technicolor

- **Jumping on a bandwagon.** Sometimes we are more likely to believe something if a lot of other people believe it. Even the most widely accepted truths, however, can turn out to be wrong. There was a time when nearly everyone believed that the world was flat — until someone came up with evidence to the contrary.

- **Assuming that something is true because it hasn't been proven false.** Go to a bookstore, and you'll find dozens of books detailing close encounters with flying saucers and extraterrestrial beings. These books describe the person who had the close encounter as beyond reproach in integrity and sanity. Because critics could not disprove the claims of the witnesses, the events are said to have really occurred. Even in science, few things are ever proved completely false, but evidence can be discredited.

- **Falling victim to false cause.** Frequently, we make the assumption that just because one event followed another, the first event must have caused the second. This reasoning is the basis for many superstitions. The ancient Chinese once believed that they could make the sun reappear after an eclipse by striking a large gong, because they knew that the sun reappeared after a large gong had been struck on one such occasion. Most effects, however, are usually the result of a complex web of causes. Don't be satisfied with easy before-and-after claims; they are rarely correct.

- **Making hasty generalizations.** If someone selected one green marble from a barrel containing a hundred marbles, you wouldn't assume that the next marble would be green. After all, there are still ninety-nine marbles in the barrel, and you know nothing about the colors of those marbles. However, given fifty draws from the barrel, each of which produced a green marble after the barrel had been shaken thoroughly, you would be more willing to conclude that the next marble drawn would be green, too. Reaching a conclusion based on the opinion of one source is like figuring that all the marbles in the barrel are green after pulling out only one.

04

try it!
Discovering Logical Fallacies in Your Own Thinking

Have you ever used any of these fallacies to justify a decision? Why was it wrong to do so? Can you think of other errors of logic that might push you farther from the truth?

Fallacies like these can slip into even the most careful reasoning. One false claim can derail an entire argument, so be on the lookout for weak logic in what you read and write. Never forget that accurate reasoning is a key factor for success in college and in life.

Thinking Critically about Arguments

What does the word *argument* mean to you? If you're like most people, the first image it conjures up might be an ugly fight you had with a friend, a yelling match you witnessed on the street, or a heated disagreement between family members. True, such unpleasant confrontations are arguments. But the word also refers to a calm, reasoned effort to persuade someone of the value of an idea.

When you think of it this way, you'll quickly recognize that arguments are central to academic study, work, and life in general. Scholarly articles, business memos, and requests for spending money all have something in common: The effective ones make a general claim, provide reasons to support it, and back up those reasons with evidence. That's what argument is.

As we have already seen, it's important to consider multiple points of view, or arguments, in tackling new ideas and complex questions. Arguments are not, however, all equally valid. Good critical thinking involves thinking creatively about the assumptions that might have been left out and scrutinizing the quality of the evidence that is used to support a claim. Whether examining an argument or communicating one, a good critical thinker is careful to ensure that ideas are presented in an understandable, logical way.

Challenge Assumptions

All too often, our beliefs are based on gut feelings or on blind acceptance of something we've heard or read. To some extent, those patterns of acceptance are unavoidable. If we made a habit of questioning absolutely everything, we would have trouble making it through the day. Yet some assumptions should be examined more thoughtfully, especially if they will influence an important decision or serve as the foundation for an argument.

For an example, imagine that the mayor of the city where your school is located has announced that he wants to make a bid to host the Olympic Games. Many people on campus are excited at the prospect, but your friend Richard is less than thrilled.

"The Olympic Games just about ruined my hometown," Richard tells you. "Road signs all over Atlanta had to be changed so that visitors could find the game sites easily. Because the city couldn't supply enough workers to complete the task on time, the organizers brought thousands of immigrants to town to help with the task, and some of them were illegal aliens. The Games are intended to foster national and international pride, but these immigrants could care less about that. They were there to earn money for their families. The Hispanic population nearly doubled once the Games were over. And if people understood how much political corruption went on behind the scenes, they would understand why the Olympic Games are not healthy for a host city."

Another friend, Sally, overhears your conversation, and she's not buying Richard's conclusions. "How do you know all of that is accurate?" she asks. "I just know it," says Richard.

Eager to get at the truth of the matter, Sally decides to look into other points of view. She does a quick Web search and finds an article about the Atlanta Olympics in the *American Historical Review*, the journal of record for the history profession in the United States. Its author notes that "the Games provided an enormous engine for growth" and comments that the city's "surging population is the most obvious marker of Atlanta's post-Olympic transformation." The article continues: "By the 1996 Games the metro population had reached three million, and today [is] 4,458,253. Winning the Olympic bid marked a turning point that put Atlanta on the world's radar screen."[2]

Although Sally has found good information from a reputable source, you should be uncomfortable with the totally upbeat tone of the article. If you and Sally dig a little further, you might land on the Web site of the Utah Office of Tourism, which includes a report that was prepared when that state was investigating the potential impacts of hosting the 2002 Winter Games in Salt Lake City. According to the report, "Among the key legacies of the Atlanta Olympics was the regeneration of certain downtown districts that had fallen into urban decay." The authors also note that "the Olympic-spurred development in

---

[2] Mary G. Rolinson, visiting lecturer in the Georgia State University History Department, "Atlanta before and after the Olympics." Copyright © American Historical Association. Available at http://www.historians.org/perspectives/issues/2006/0611/0611ann6.cfm.

[Atlanta] has provided a much-needed stimulus for revitalization."[3]

Finding a second positive analysis would give you a compelling reason to believe that the Olympic Games are good for a city, but Richard might easily discover a report from the European Tour Operators Association, which concludes that visitors are likely to stay away from host countries during and following the Games, causing a significant long-term decline in revenue for hotels and other businesses that depend on tourism.[4]

Unfortunately, simply learning more about the benefits and costs of hosting the Olympics doesn't yield any concrete answers. Even so, you, Richard, and Sally have uncovered assumptions and have developed a better understanding of the issue. That's an important first step.

Examine the Evidence

The evidence that is offered as support for an argument can vary in quality. While Richard started with no proof other than his convictions ("I just know it"), Sally looked to expert opinion and research studies for answers to her question. Even so, one of her sources sounded overly positive, prompting a need to confirm the author's claims with additional evidence from other sources.

Like Sally, critical thinkers are careful to check that the evidence supporting an argument—whether someone else's or their own—is of the highest possible quality. To do that, simply ask a few questions about the arguments as you consider them:

- What general idea am I being asked to accept?
- Are good and sufficient reasons given to support the overall claim?
- Are those reasons backed up with evidence in the form of facts, statistics, and quotations?
- Does the evidence support the conclusions?
- Is the argument based on logical reasoning, or does it appeal mainly to the emotions?

- Do I recognize any questionable assumptions?
- Can I think of any counterarguments? What facts can I muster as proof?
- What do I know about the person or organization making the argument?

If, after you have evaluated the evidence used in support of a claim, you're still not certain of its quality, it's best to keep looking. Drawing on questionable evidence for an argument has a tendency to backfire. In most cases, a little persistence will help you find something better.

try it!

Observing How Instructors Challenge Your Thinking

Think about your experiences in your classes so far this term, and answer these questions:

- Have your instructors pointed out any conflicts or contradictions in the ideas they have presented? Or have you noted any contradictions that they have not acknowledged?

- Have they asked questions for which they sometimes don't seem to have the answers? Give concrete examples.

- Have they challenged you or other members of the class to explain yourselves more fully? In what ways?

---

[3] Utah Office of Tourism, *Observations from Past Olympic Host Communities: Executive Summary.* Available at http://travel.utah.gov/research_and_planning/2002_olympics.

[4] "Olympics Have Negative Effect on Tourism," July 10, 2008. Available at http://www.travelbite.co.uk.

Critically Evaluating Sources

It is easy to assume that huge amounts of available information automatically provide knowledge. Some students might at first be excited about receiving 20,800,000 hits from a Google search on political ethics, but shock takes hold when they realize their discovery is utterly unsorted. They might respond by using only the first several hits, irrespective of quality. A more productive approach is to think critically about the usefulness of potential sources by measuring them against three important criteria: relevance, authority, and bias.

Relevance

The first thing to consider in looking at a possible source is how well it fits your needs. That, in turn, will be affected by the nature of your research project and the kind of information you are seeking.

- **Is it introductory?** Introductory information is very basic and elementary. It neither assumes nor requires prior knowledge about the topic. Introductory sources can be useful when you're first learning about a subject. They are less useful when you're drawing conclusions about a particular aspect of the subject.

- **Is it definitional?** Definitional information provides some descriptive details about a subject. It might help you introduce a topic to others or clarify the focus of your investigation.

- **Is it analytical?** Analytical information supplies and interprets data about origins, behaviors, differences, and uses. In most cases it's the kind of information you want.

- **Is it comprehensive?** The more detail, the better. Avoid unsubstantiated opinions, and look instead for sources that consider the topic in depth and offer plenty of evidence to support their conclusions.

- **Is it current?** You should usually give preference to recent sources, although older ones can sometimes be useful (for instance, if your subject is historical or the source is still cited by others in a field).

- **Can you conclude anything from it?** Use the "so what?" test: How important is this information? Why does it matter to my project?

Authority

Once you have determined that a source is relevant to your project, check that it was created by somebody who has the qualifications to write or speak on the subject. Whether or not the author is qualified will depend on your subject and the nature of your inquiry (a fifth grader's opinion might be exactly what you're looking for), but in most cases you'll want expert conclusions based on rigorous evidence.

Make sure you can identify the author and be ready to explain why that author is a reliable source. Good qualifications might include academic degrees, institutional affiliations, an established record of researching and publishing on a topic, or personal experience with a subject. Be wary, on the other hand, of anonymous or commercial sources or those written by someone whose credibility is questionable.

Understand, as well, whether your project calls for scholarly publications, popular magazines, or both. Do you know the difference?

try it!

Discovering Valid Sources

How do you find sources for an important paper? Do you go to the first several hits on Google, or do you use a more deliberate process? What strategies can you use to make sure your Internet or library research results in valid information?

Scholarly Journals	**Popular Magazines**
Long articles	Shorter articles
In-depth information on topic	Broad overview of topic
Written by academic experts	Written by journalists or reporters
Graphs, tables, and charts	Photos of people and events
Articles "refereed" or reviewed	Articles not rigidly evaluated
Formally documented	Sources credited informally

You don't necessarily have to dismiss popular magazines. Many journalists and columnists are extremely well qualified, and their work might well be appropriate for your needs. But as a rule scholarly sources will be more credible.

Bias

When you are searching for sources, you should realize that there can be a heavy dose of bias or point of view in some of them. Although nothing is inherently wrong with someone's having a particular point of view, it is dangerous for a reader not to know that the bias is there. A great source for keeping you informed about potential bias is *Magazines for Libraries,*[5] which will tell you about a periodical's editorial and political leanings. *The Nation,* for instance, is generally considered liberal, while *National Review* is conservative. Some signs of bias indicate that you should avoid using a source. If you detect overly positive or overly harsh language, hints of an agenda, or a stubborn refusal to consider other points of view,

think carefully about how well you can trust the information in a document.

A Note on Internet Sources

Be especially cautious of material you find online. It is often difficult to tell where something on the Internet came from or who wrote it. The lack of this information can make it very difficult to judge the credibility of the source. And while an editorial board reviews most conventional print matter (books, articles, and so forth) for accuracy and overall quality, it's frequently difficult to confirm that the same is true for information on a Web site—with some exceptions. If you are searching through an online database such as the Human Genome Database or Eldis: The Gateway to Development Information (a poverty database), it is highly likely that documents in these collections have been reviewed. Online versions of print magazines and journals, likewise, have usually been checked out by editors. And information from academic and government Web sites (those whose URLs end in .edu or .gov, respectively) is generally—but not always—trustworthy.

---

[5] Cheryl LaGuardia, Bill Katz, and Linda S. Katz, *Magazines for Libraries,* 13th ed. (New Providence, NJ: RR Bowker LC, 2004).

04 Chapter Review

One-minute paper . . .

One major shift from being a high school student to being a college student involves the level of critical thinking your college instructors expect of you. After reading this chapter, how would you describe critical thinking to a high school student?

Applying what you've learned . . .

Now that you have read and discussed this chapter, consider how you can apply what you have learned to your academic and personal life. The following prompts will help you reflect on chapter material and its relevance to you both now and in the future.

1. After reading this chapter, think of professions (for example, physicians, engineers, marketing professionals) for whom problem solving and thinking "outside of the box" is necessary. Choose one career, and describe why you think critical thinking is a necessary and valuable skill.

2. In your opinion, is it harder to think critically than to base your arguments on how you feel about a topic? Why or why not? What are the advantages of finding answers based on your feelings? Based on critical thinking? How might you use both approaches in seeking answers?

Building your portfolio . . .

My influences

Our past experiences have shaped the way in which we think and perceive the world around us. Sometimes it is easy to interpret things without stopping to think about why we feel the way we do. How have other people shaped the way you see the world today?

1. In your personal portfolio, create a Word document and

- Describe at least three people (such as family, friends, celebrities, national leaders) who you feel have most influenced the way you think.

- Describe how these individuals' values, actions, expectations, and words have shaped the way you think about yourself and the world.

2. Describe a situation that you have dealt with since coming to college that has challenged you to think about an issue in a new and different way.

3. Save your work on your personal computer or flash drive.

Where to go for help . . .

On Campus

Logic courses: Check out your philosophy department's course in introduction to logic. This course may be the single best one to take for learning critical thinking skills.

Argument courses and critical thinking courses: Argument courses are usually offered in the English department. They will help you develop the ability to formulate logical arguments and to avoid such pitfalls as logical fallacies.

Debating skills: Some of the best critical thinkers have participated in debating during college. Go to either your student activities office or your department of speech/drama and find out if your campus has a debate club/society or a debate team.

Literature

12 Angry Men by Reginald Rose (New York: Penguin Classics, 2006). This work is a reprint of the original teleplay, which was written in 1954 and made into a film in 1958. It is also available on DVD. The stirring courtroom drama pits twelve jurors against one another as they argue the outcome of a murder trial in which the defendant is a teenage boy. Where critical thinking is needed to arrive at the truth, all but one juror employ every noncritical argument in the book to arrive at a guilty verdict until the analysis of the one holdout produces remarkable changes in their attitudes.

Online

Check the following Web site for a critical review of the *Encyclopedia of Stupidity:* **http://arts.independent.co.uk/books/reviews/article112328.ece.**

A Guide to Critical Thinking about What You See on the Web: **http://www.ithaca.edu/library/training/think.html.**

My Institution's Resources

_____

_____

_____

_____

_____

_____

_____

_____

_____

_____

_____

_____

05 Listening & Taking Notes

In every college class you take, you will need to master two skills to earn high grades: listening and note-taking. By taking an active role in your classes—genuinely participating by asking questions, contributing to discussions, and providing answers—you will listen better and take more meaningful notes. The reward for your efforts will be an enhanced ability to understand abstract ideas, find new possibilities, organize those ideas, and recall the material once the class is over. This increased capacity to analyze and understand complex material will result in better academic performance while you are in college and also will be valued by a wide range of employers.

This chapter provides valuable suggestions for becoming a skilled listener, note-taker, and class participant. Decide which techniques work best for you. Practice them regularly until they become part of your study routine.

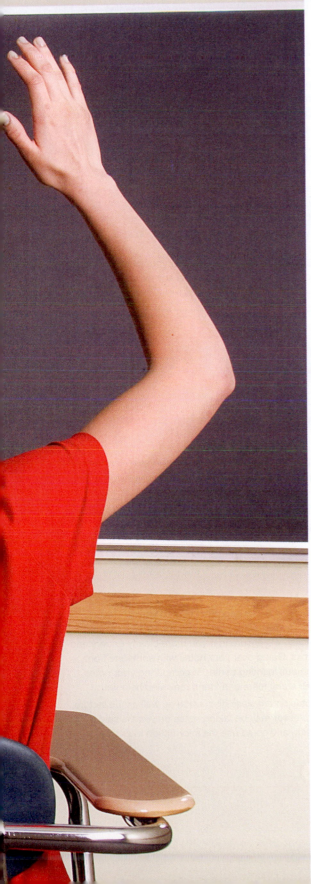

How Do You Measure Up?

1. During class I write down all key points in my notes.
   - ○ Always
   - ○ Occasionally
   - ○ Never

2. If I do not understand something, I do not hesitate to ask questions in class, even in large lecture sections.
   - ○ Always
   - ○ Occasionally
   - ○ Never

3. In math or science courses, I write down everything the instructor puts on the board or screen.
   - ○ Always
   - ○ Occasionally
   - ○ Never

4. I look for opportunities to join study groups for each of my classes.
   - ○ Always
   - ○ Occasionally
   - ○ Never

Review the items you marked "occasionally" or "never." Paying attention to all these aspects of your college experience can be important to your success. After reading this chapter, come back to this list and think about ways you can work on these areas.

Knowing the Basics of Listening and Note-Taking

Amy Gailliard

35-year-old returning student

"So, Amy, why do you think Harper Lee chose to give *To Kill a Mockingbird* a child narrator?" my professor asked me at our second literature class. Minutes earlier I'd been tapping my pencil on my notebook, feeling happy as we discussed my favorite book; suddenly I was grasping for something to say.

"Er," I managed. Thirty-two 20-something-year-old faces were looking at me. I felt my face go beet-red. They don't want to hear from the "old lady" in the class.

"Anyone else?" he asked, looking around. "Speak up."

"Scout has an innocent perspective," said the girl sitting next to me.

"Exactly," said Professor Kelso. "And why is that such an effective device here?"

Because the difference between what the reader sees happening in the book and what Scout perceives generates a lot of irony, I thought to myself. Because we see her learn something important. Because her childlike tone disguises the serious purpose of the plot.

"Because we see her start to understand how her world works—in good and bad ways," said a boy across the room.

The professor crossed his arms and nodded. "Good job, Aziz. That's a point toward your class participation grade." Then he caught a glance at my stricken face. "Amy, did you have something to add?"

"Uh, well . . . I, um," I said. Yep, I was doomed.

How does Amy's reticence about speaking in front of her younger classmates affect her performance in college? Experts say that learning how to speak in front of a crowd is like learning to ride a bike: It just takes practice. If so, how could she begin to overcome her shyness?

Listening and note-taking are critical to your academic success because your professors are likely to introduce material in class that your texts don't cover. Chances are good that much of this material will resurface on quizzes and exams.

While you are taking notes, also be sure to participate in class discussion. Whether you are in class or in another situation, you will tend to remember what you have said more than what others are saying to you.

Remembering What Happens in Class

Here are tips for ensuring that you will retain what is important from class:

- Before class, review your study notes from the previous class.
- Consider recording the lecture, but be sure to request the instructor's permission first. Even if you are recording, take notes, too.
- Be aware that an instructor often thinks that what is discussed in class is more important than what the text says. Therefore, you are more likely to see class material on a test.

- Ask questions in class (or after class if your professor prefers). The instructor is always the best source, and this practice will ensure that you more clearly understand your notes. Going over your notes with someone from your campus learning center or comparing your notes with your study team or a friend may also help you.
- Take notes on the class discussion as well as the lecture. Your professor may be taking notes on what is said in discussion and could use the information in exams.

Note-Taking Systems

You can make the best use of your class time by using your listening skills to take effective notes. But first, you have to decide on a system.

Cornell format   In the Cornell format, you create a "recall" column on each page of your notebook by drawing a vertical line a few inches from the left border (see Figure 5.1). As you take notes during the lecture—whether writing down ideas, making lists, or using an outline or paragraph format—write only in the wider column on the right; leave the recall column blank. The recall column is the place where you write down the main ideas and important details as you sift through your notes as soon after class as feasible. Many students have found the recall column to be an important study device for tests and exams.

Outline format   You probably already know what a formal outline looks like, with key ideas represented by Roman numerals and other ideas relating to each key idea represented in order by uppercase letters, numbers, and lowercase letters. If you use this approach, try to determine how the instructor is outlining the lecture or presentation and recreate that outline in your notes (see Figure 5.2).

Figure 5.1

Note-Taking in the Cornell Format

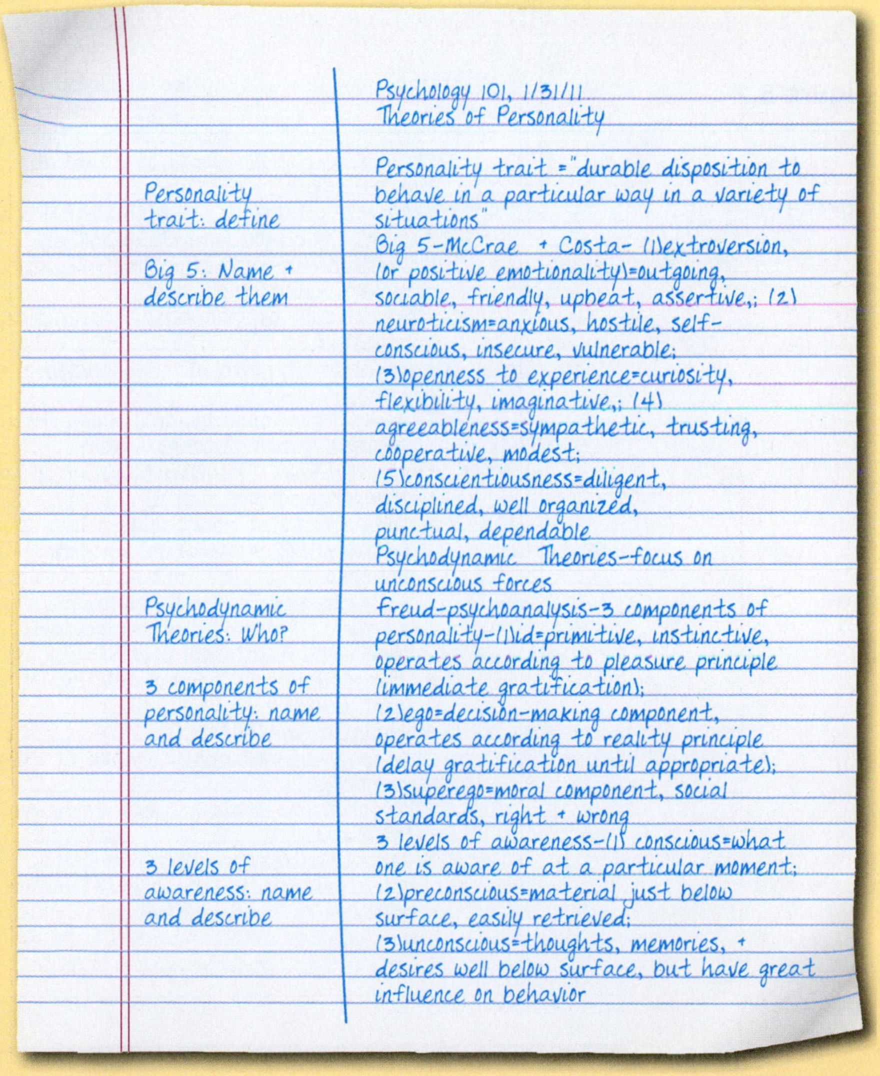

Psychology 101, 1/31/11
Theories of Personality

Personality trait: define — Personality trait = "durable disposition to behave in a particular way in a variety of situations"

Big 5: Name + describe them — Big 5—McCrae + Costa— (1)extroversion, (or positive emotionality)=outgoing, sociable, friendly, upbeat, assertive,; (2) neuroticism=anxious, hostile, self-conscious, insecure, vulnerable; (3)openness to experience=curiosity, flexibility, imaginative,; (4) agreeableness=sympathetic, trusting, cooperative, modest; (5)conscientiousness=diligent, disciplined, well organized, punctual, dependable

Psychodynamic Theories: Who? — Psychodynamic Theories—focus on unconscious forces
freud-psychoanalysis—3 components of personality

3 components of personality: name and describe — (1)id=primitive, instinctive, operates according to pleasure principle (immediate gratification); (2)ego=decision-making component, operates according to reality principle (delay gratification until appropriate); (3)superego=moral component, social standards, right + wrong

3 levels of awareness: name and describe — 3 levels of awareness—(1) conscious=what one is aware of at a particular moment; (2)preconscious=material just below surface, easily retrieved; (3)unconscious=thoughts, memories, + desires well below surface, but have great influence on behavior

Paragraph format The paragraph format involves writing detailed paragraphs, with each containing a summary of a topic. You might decide to write summary paragraphs when you are taking notes on what you are reading. This method might not work as well for class notes because it's difficult to summarize a topic until your instructor has covered it completely.

List format The list format can be effective when taking notes on terms and definitions, sequences, or facts. It is easy to use lists in combination with the Cornell format, with key terms on the left and their definitions and explanations on the right.

Note-Taking Techniques

Once you've decided on a note-taking system, use these techniques to put that system to work.

1. **Identify the main ideas.** Well-organized lectures always contain key points. The first principle of effective note-taking is to write down the main ideas around which the lecture is built.

Some instructors announce the purpose of a lecture or offer an outline, thus providing the class with the skeleton of main ideas, followed by the details. Others develop overhead trans-

Figure 5.2

Note-Taking in the Outline Format

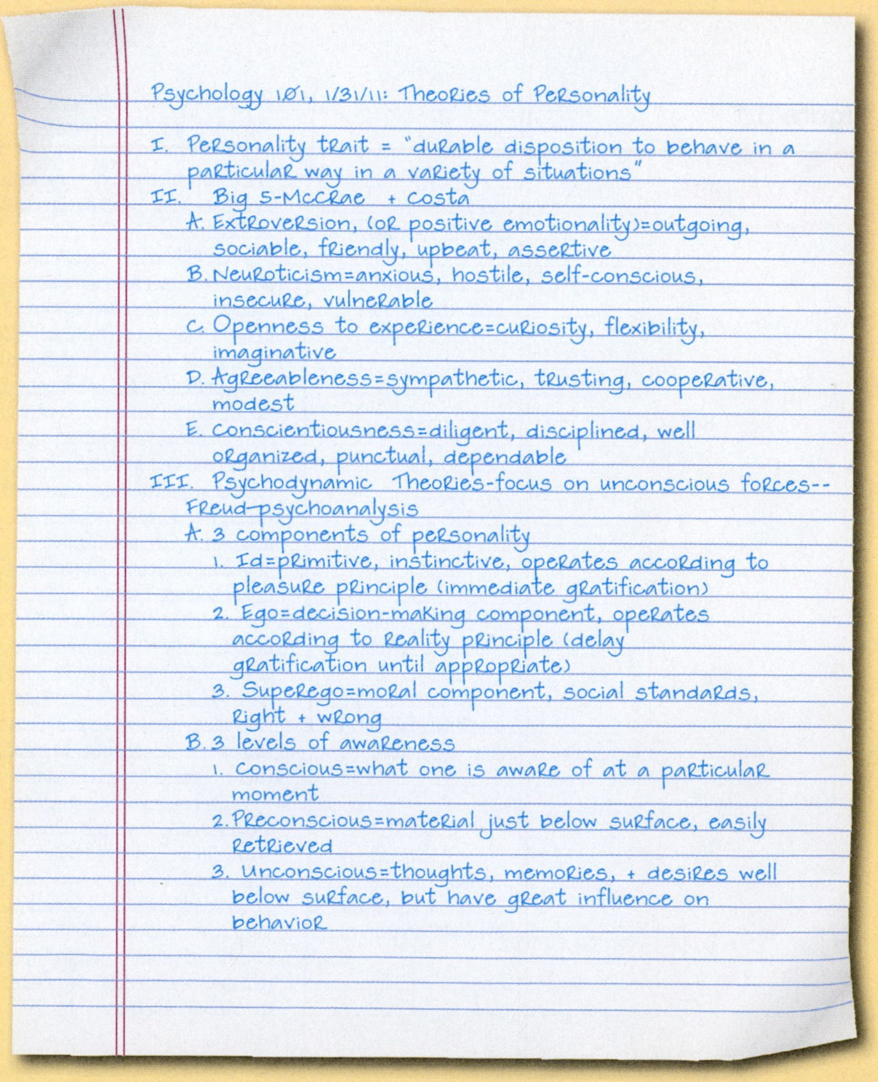

Psychology 101, 1/31/11: Theories of Personality

I. Personality trait = "durable disposition to behave in a particular way in a variety of situations"

II. Big 5 - McCrae + Costa
  A. Extroversion, (or positive emotionality) = outgoing, sociable, friendly, upbeat, assertive
  B. Neuroticism = anxious, hostile, self-conscious, insecure, vulnerable
  C. Openness to experience = curiosity, flexibility, imaginative
  D. Agreeableness = sympathetic, trusting, cooperative, modest
  E. Conscientiousness = diligent, disciplined, well organized, punctual, dependable

III. Psychodynamic Theories - focus on unconscious forces -- Freud - psychoanalysis
  A. 3 components of personality
    1. Id = primitive, instinctive, operates according to pleasure principle (immediate gratification)
    2. Ego = decision-making component, operates according to reality principle (delay gratification until appropriate)
    3. Superego = moral component, social standards, right + wrong
  B. 3 levels of awareness
    1. Conscious = what one is aware of at a particular moment
    2. Preconscious = material just below surface, easily retrieved
    3. Unconscious = thoughts, memories, + desires well below surface, but have great influence on behavior

parencies or PowerPoint presentations and may make these materials available on a class Web site before the lecture.

2. **Don't try to write down everything.** Attempting to record every word from a class lecture or discussion will distract you from an essential activity: thinking. If you're an active listener, you will ultimately have shorter but more useful notes.

3. **Don't be thrown by a disorganized lecturer.** When a lecturer is disorganized, it's your job to try to organize what she says into general and specific frameworks. When the order is not apparent, indicate in your notes where the gaps lie. After the lecture, consult your reading material, study team, or a classmate to fill in these gaps, or visit the instructor during office hours with your questions.

4. **Prepare to use your notes as a study tool.** As soon after class as feasible, preferably within an hour or two, sift through your notes and create a recall column to identify the main ideas and important details for tests and examinations. In anticipation of using your notes later, treat each page of your notes as part of an exam preparation system.

Q5

Figure 5.3

Note-Taking in the List Format

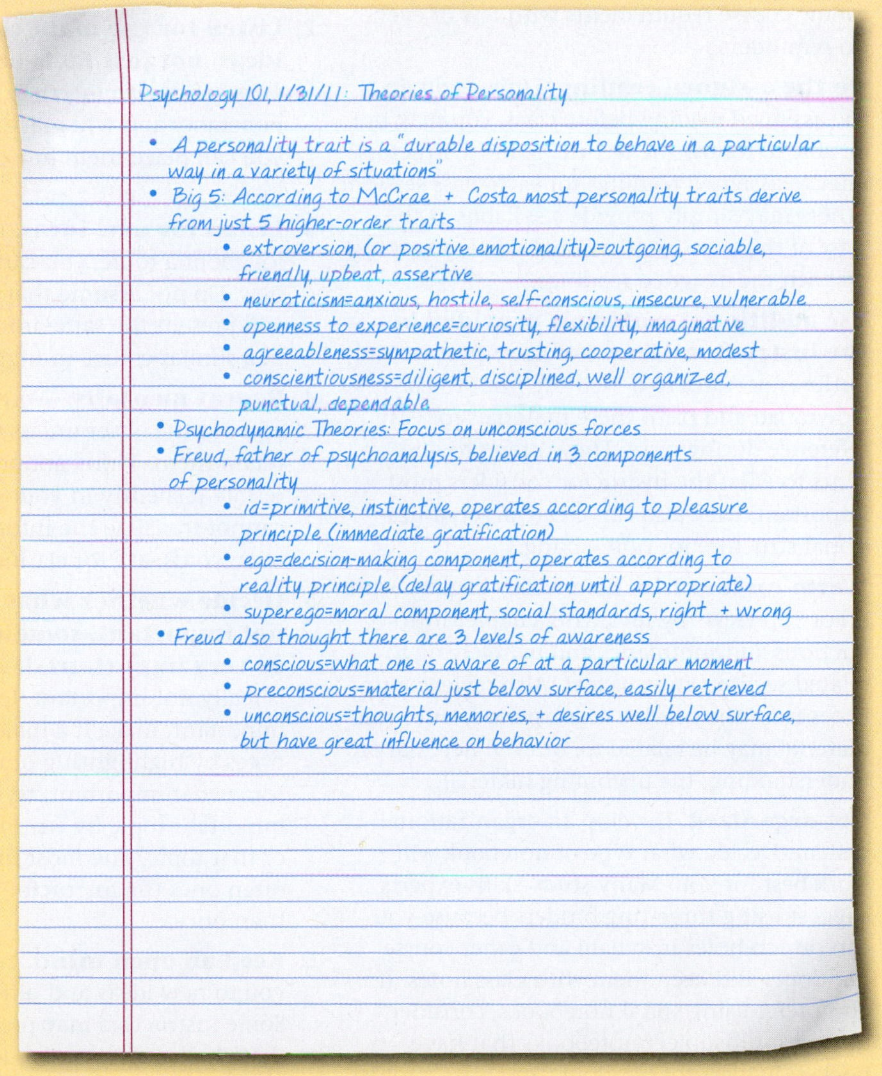

Psychology 101, 1/31/11: Theories of Personality

- A personality trait is a "durable disposition to behave in a particular way in a variety of situations"
- Big 5: According to McCrae + Costa most personality traits derive from just 5 higher-order traits
  - extroversion, (or positive emotionality)=outgoing, sociable, friendly, upbeat, assertive
  - neuroticism=anxious, hostile, self-conscious, insecure, vulnerable
  - openness to experience=curiosity, flexibility, imaginative
  - agreeableness=sympathetic, trusting, cooperative, modest
  - conscientiousness=diligent, disciplined, well organized, punctual, dependable
- Psychodynamic Theories: Focus on unconscious forces
- Freud, father of psychoanalysis, believed in 3 components of personality
  - id=primitive, instinctive, operates according to pleasure principle (immediate gratification)
  - ego=decision-making component, operates according to reality principle (delay gratification until appropriate)
  - superego=moral component, social standards, right + wrong
- Freud also thought there are 3 levels of awareness
  - conscious=what one is aware of at a particular moment
  - preconscious=material just below surface, easily retrieved
  - unconscious=thoughts, memories, + desires well below surface, but have great influence on behavior

Preparing for and Participating in Class

Believe it or not, doing well in class is not just a matter of showing up and taking notes. Getting the most out of lectures and discussions requires preparing before class as well as listening and participating during each class session.

Prepare to Remember

Even if lectures don't allow for active participation, you can take a number of active learning steps before your classes to make your listening and note-taking efficient.

1. **Pay attention to your course syllabus.** Syllabi are formal statements of course expectations, requirements, and procedures. Many instructors assume that once students have received the syllabus, they will understand and follow course requirements with few or even no reminders.

2. **Do the assigned reading.** Unless you do the assigned reading before class, you may not be able to follow the lecture. Some instructors refer to assigned readings for each class session; others may simply provide a syllabus at the start of the course and assume you are keeping up with the assigned readings.

3. **Use additional materials provided by the instructor.** Many professors post lecture outlines or notes to a Web site prior to class. Download and print these materials for easy reference during class. They often provide hints to what the instructor considers most important; they also can create an organizational structure for note-taking.

4. **Warm up for class.** Before class begins, warm up or "preview" by reviewing chapter introductions and summaries and by referring to related sections in your text. Also review your notes from the previous class period, since that material may be related to, or even necessary to understanding, the upcoming material.

5. **Get organized.** Develop an organizational system. Decide what type of notebook will work best for you. Many study skills experts suggest using three-ring binders because you can punch holes in syllabi and other course handouts and keep them with class notes. If you prefer using spiral notebooks, consider buying multisubject notebooks that have pocket dividers for handouts, or create a folder for each course.

Listen Critically

Listening in class is not like listening to a TV program, a friend, or even a speaker at a meeting. Knowing how to listen in class can help you recall and understand what you have heard and can save you time. Here are some suggestions.

1. **Be ready for the message.** Prepare yourself to hear, to listen, and to receive the message. If you have done the assigned reading, you will know what details are already in the text so that you can focus your notes on key concepts during the lecture. You will also know what information is not covered in the text, and you will be prepared to pay especially close attention when the instructor is presenting unfamiliar material.

2. **Listen for the main concepts and central ideas, not just facts and figures.** Although facts are important, they will be easier to remember and will make more sense when you can place them in a context of themes and ideas.

3. **Listen for new ideas.** Even if you know a lot about a topic, you can still learn something new. Do not assume that college instructors will present the same information you learned in a similar course in high school.

4. **Repeat mentally.** Words can go in one ear and out the other unless you make an effort to retain them. Think about what you hear and restate it silently in your own words. If you cannot translate the information into your own words, ask for clarification.

5. **Decide whether what you have heard is not important, somewhat important, or very important.** If a point in the lecture is really not important, let it go. If it's very important, make it a major point in your notes by highlighting or underscoring it. If it's somewhat important, try to relate it to a very important topic by writing it down as a subset of that topic. The most important points are often ones the instructor has repeated more than once.

6. **Keep an open mind.** Your classes will expose you to new ideas and different perspectives. Some instructors may present information that challenges your value system. One of the purposes of college is to teach you to think

in new and different ways and to learn to feel confident about your own beliefs. Instructors want you to think for yourself, and they do not necessarily expect you to agree with everything they or your classmates say.

7. **Listen to the entire message.** Concentrate on the big picture, but also pay attention to specific details and examples that can assist you in understanding and retaining the information.

8. **Sort, organize, and categorize.** When you listen, try to match what you are hearing with what you already know. Take an active role in deciding how best to recall what you are learning.

Speak Up

Naturally, you will be more likely to participate in a class where the instructor emphasizes interactive discussion, calls on students by name, shows students signs of approval and interest, and avoids criticizing anyone for an incorrect answer. Often, answers that you and others offer that are not quite correct can lead to new perspectives on a topic.

In large classes instructors often use the lecture method, and large classes can be intimidating. If you ask a question in a class of one hundred and think you've made a fool of yourself, it's usually because you fear that ninety-nine other people know the answer. That conclusion is unrealistic. Since you've probably asked a question that others were too timid to ask, they'll silently thank you for doing so. If you're lucky, you might even find that the instructor in a large class takes time out to ask or answer questions. To take full advantage of these opportunities, try using the following techniques:

1. **Sit as close to the front as possible.** If you're seated by name and your name begins with Z, visit your professor during office hours and request to be moved up front.

2. **Keep your eyes on the teacher.** Sitting close to the front of the classroom will make this easier for you to do.

3. **Focus on the lecture.** Do not let yourself be distracted. It might be wise not to sit near friends, who can be distracting without meaning to be.

4. **Raise your hand when you don't understand something.** The instructor might answer you immediately, ask you to wait until later in the class, or throw your question to the rest of the class. In each case, you benefit in several ways. The instructor gets to know you, other students get to know you, and you learn from both the instructor and your classmates. But don't overdo it. The instructor and your peers will tire of too many questions that disrupt the flow of the class.

5. **Speak up in class.** Ask a question or volunteer to answer a question or make a comment. It becomes easier every time you do so.

6. **Never feel that you're asking a "stupid" question.** If you don't understand something, you have a right to ask for an explanation.

7. **When the instructor calls on you to answer a question, don't bluff.** If you know the answer, give it. If you're not certain, begin with "I think . . . , but I'm not sure I have it all correct." If you don't know, just say so.

8. **If you've recently read a book or an article that is relevant to the class topic, bring it in.** Use related outside reading either to ask questions about the material or to provide additional information that was not covered in class.

Taking Notes in Nonlecture and Quantitative Courses

Nonlecture and quantitative courses—like mathematics, chemistry, or physics—pose special challenges when it comes to note-taking. The following advice and tips will help you improve the skills you've learned in this chapter and apply them to these kinds of courses.

Nonlecture Courses

Be ready to adapt your note-taking methods to match the situation. Group discussion has become a popular way to teach in college because it involves active learning. On your campus you may also have Supplemental Instruction (SI) classes that provide further opportunity to discuss the information presented in lectures. If you do have this option, take advantage of it, and keep a record of what's happening in such classes.

Assume you are taking notes in a problem-solving group assignment. You would begin your notes by asking yourself, "What is the problem?" and writing the problem down. As the discussion progresses, you would list the solutions offered. These solutions would be your main ideas. The important details might include the positive and negative aspects of each view or solution. The important thing to remember when taking notes in nonlecture courses is that you need to record the information presented by your classmates as well as by the instructor and to consider all reasonable ideas, even though they may differ from your own.

How to organize the notes you take in a class discussion depends on the purpose or form of the discussion. It usually makes good sense to begin with the list of issues or topics that the discussion leader announces. Another approach is to list the questions that the participants raise for discussion. If the discussion is exploring reasons for and against a particular argument, it is reasonable to divide your notes into columns or sections for pros and cons. When conflicting views arise in the discussion, it is important to record the different perspectives and the rationales behind them.

Quantitative Courses

Many quantitative courses such as mathematics, chemistry, and physics often build on each other from term to term and from year to year. When you take notes in these courses, you are likely to need to refer back to them in future terms. For example, when taking organic chemistry, you may need to go back to notes taken in earlier chemistry courses. This review process can be particularly important when time has passed since your last course, such as after a summer break. Here are some ideas for getting organized:

1. Keep your notes and supplementary materials (such as instructors' handouts) for each course in a separate three-ring binder labeled with the course number and name.

2. Before class, download any notes, outlines, or diagrams, charts, graphs, and other visual representations of the material provided on the instructor's Web site, and bring them to class. You can save yourself considerable time and distraction during the lecture if you do not have to copy complicated graphs and diagrams while the instructor is talking.

3. Take notes only on the front of each piece of loose-leaf paper. Later, you can use the back of each sheet to add further details, annotations, corrections, comments, questions, and a summary of each lecture. Alternatively, once you've placed what have now become the left-hand pages in the binder, you can use them the same way that you would use the recall column in the Cornell format, noting key ideas to be used for testing yourself when preparing for exams.

4. Consider taking your notes in pencil or erasable pen. When copying long equations while also trying to pay attention to what the instructor is saying, or when copying problems that students are solving at the board, it is not unusual to need to erase or make changes. You want to keep your notes as neat as possible.

Tips for Note-Taking in Math and Science Courses

- Write down any equations, formulas, diagrams, charts, graphs, and definitions that the instructor puts on the board or screen.
- Quote the instructor's words as precisely as possible. Technical terms often have exact meanings and cannot be paraphrased.
- Use standard symbols, abbreviations, and scientific notation.
- Write down all worked problems and examples, step by step. They often provide the format for exam questions. Actively try to solve the problem yourself as it is solved

at the front of the class. Be sure that you can follow the logic and understand the sequence of steps.

- Listen carefully to other students' questions and the instructor's answers. Take notes on the discussion and during question-and-answer periods.
- Use asterisks, exclamation points, question marks, or symbols of your own to highlight important points or questions in your notes.
- Refer back to the textbook after class; it may contain more accurate diagrams and other visual representations than you are able to draw while taking notes in class.

5. Organize your notes in your binder chronologically. Then create separate tabbed sections for homework, lab assignments, returned tests, and other materials.

6. If the instructor distributes handouts in class, label them and place them in your binder either immediately before or immediately after the notes for that day.

7. Keep your binders for math and science courses until you graduate (or even longer if there is any chance that you will attend graduate school in the future). They will serve as beneficial review materials for later classes in math and science sequences and for preparing for standardized tests such as the Graduate Record Exam (GRE) or the Medical College Admission Test (MCAT).

Taking notes in math and science courses can be different from taking notes for other types of classes, where it may not be a good idea to try to write down every word the instructor says. At the top of the page are some tips geared specifically to taking notes in math and science classes.

05

try it!

Developing a System for Keeping Your Notes

If you are not currently keeping your notes and handouts for your science or math courses, now is the time to begin. Working from the suggestions in this chapter, create your own unique filing system. For instance, you might want to scan these materials and maintain them in electronic, rather than paper, files.

Reviewing Your Notes

Most forgetting takes place within the first twenty-four hours of encountering the information, a phenomenon known as "the forgetting curve." If you do not review your notes almost immediately after class, it can be difficult to retrieve the material later. In two weeks, you will have forgotten up to 70 percent of the material or information! Don't let the forgetting curve take its toll on you. As soon after class as possible, review your notes and fill in the details you still remember but missed writing down. If you are an aural learner, you might want to repeat your notes out loud.

For interactive learners, the best way to learn something might be to teach it to someone else. You will understand something better and remember it longer if you try to explain it. Explaining material to someone else helps you discover your own reactions and uncover gaps in your comprehension. (Asking and answering questions in class can also provide you with the feedback you need to make certain your understanding is accurate.) Now you're ready to embed the major points from your notes in your memory. Use the following three important steps for remembering the key points from the lecture.

1. **Write down the main ideas.** For 5 or 10 minutes, quickly review your notes and select key words or phrases that will act as labels or tags for main ideas and key information in your notes.

2. **Recite your ideas out loud.** Recite a brief version of what you understand from the class. If you don't have a few minutes after class when you can concentrate on reviewing your notes, find some other time during that same day to review what you have written. You might also want to ask your instructor to glance at your notes to determine whether you have identified the major ideas.

3. **Review your notes from the previous class just before the next class session.** As you sit in class the next time it meets, waiting for the lecture to begin, use the time to quickly review your notes from the previous class session. This review will put you in tune with the lecture that is about to begin and prompt you to ask questions about material from the previous lecture that might not have been clear to you.

What if you have three classes in a row and no time for studying between them? Recall and recite as soon after class as possible. Review the most recent class first. Never delay recall and recitation longer than one day; if you do, it will take you longer to review, select main ideas, and recite. With practice, you can complete the review of your main ideas from your notes quickly, perhaps between classes, during lunch, or while riding the bus.

Comparing Notes

You might be able to improve your notes by comparing notes with another student or in a study group, Supplemental Instruction session, or a learning community, if one is available to you. Knowing that your notes will be seen by someone else will prompt you to make your notes well organized, clear, and accurate. Compare your notes: Are they as clear and concise as those of other students? Do you agree on the most important points? Share with one another how you take and organize your notes. Take turns testing one another on what you have learned. This practice will help you predict exam questions and determine whether you can answer them. Comparing notes is not the same as copying somebody else's notes. You simply cannot learn as well from someone else's notes, no matter how good they are, if you have not attended class.

If your campus has a note-taking service, check with your instructor about making use of this for-pay service, but keep in mind that such notes are intended to supplement the ones you take, not to substitute for them. Some students choose to copy their own notes as a means of review or because they think their notes are messy and that they will not be able to understand them later. Unless you are a tactile learner, copying or typing your notes might not help you learn the material. A more profitable approach might be to summarize your notes in your own words.

Finally, have a backup plan in case you need to be absent because of illness or a family emergency. Exchange phone numbers and e-mail addresses with other students so that you can contact one of them to learn what you missed and get a copy of his or her notes. Also contact your instructor to explain your absence and set up an appointment during office hours to make sure you understand the work you missed.

try it!
Working Together by Comparing Notes

Pair up with another student and compare your class notes for this course. Are your notes clear? Do you agree on what is important? Take a few minutes to explain your note-taking systems to each other. Agree to use a recall column during the next class meeting. Afterward, share your notes again and check on how each of you used the recall column. Again, compare your notes and what each of you deemed important.

Class Notes and Homework

Good class notes can help you complete homework assignments, too. Follow these steps.

1. Take 10 minutes to review your class notes. Skim the notes and put a question mark next to anything you do not understand at first reading. Draw stars next to topics that are especially important.

2. Do a warm-up for your homework. Before starting the assignment, look through your notes again. Use a separate sheet of paper to rework examples, problems, or exercises. If there is related assigned material in the textbook, review it. Go back to the text examples. Cover the solutions and attempt to answer each question or complete each problem.

3. Do assigned problems and answer assigned questions. When you start your homework, read each question or problem and ask: What am I supposed to find or find out? What is essential and what is extraneous? Read each problem several times and state it in your own words. Work the problem without referring to your notes or the text.

4. Don't give up. When you encounter a problem or question that you cannot readily handle, move on only after a reasonable effort. After you have completed the entire assignment, return to the items that stumped you. Try once more, and then take a break. You may need to mull over a particularly difficult problem for several days.

5. Complete your work. When you finish an assignment, consider what you learned from the exercise. Think about how the problems and questions were different from one another, which strategies you used to solve them, and what form the answers took. Review any material you have not mastered. Ask the professor, a classmate, your study group, someone in the campus learning center, or a tutor to help you with difficult problems and questions.

05

05 Chapter Review

One-minute paper . . .

This chapter explores multiple strategies for being an effective listener and student, engaged in class. What new strategies did you learn that you had never thought about or used before? What questions about effective note-taking do you still have?

Applying what you've learned . . .

Now that you have read and discussed this chapter, consider how you can apply what you have learned to your academic and personal life. The following prompts will help you to reflect on the material and its relevance to you both now and in the future.

1. Review the content in this chapter on note-taking systems. How would you describe your current method of taking notes? Are you organized or disorganized? How is your current method of taking notes similar to or different from any of the methods suggested? Do your notes help you study for exams? If not, what suggestions from this chapter might help you become a better note-taker?

2. How would you rate your current level of participation in the classes you are taking this term? Do you speak up, contribute to discussion, and ask questions? Or do you sit silently? Do your instructors encourage you to participate, or do they seem to discourage your involvement? Research finds that students learn more when they contribute to class discussions and feel comfortable asking and responding to questions. Think about how your own level of participation relates to learning and enjoyment in the classes you're currently taking.

Building your portfolio . . .

Making meaning

This chapter includes several examples of note-taking strategies, but did you catch the emphasis on what you should do with your notes after class? Sometimes it is helpful to associate a concept with an interest you have. And preparing to teach someone else how to do something or explaining a complex idea to others can help you to understand the information more fully.

Test this idea for yourself.

1. Choose a set of current class notes (it doesn't matter which class they are from), and specifically look for connections between the subject matter and your personal interests and goals (future career, social issue, sports, hobbies, etc.).

2. Next, develop a 5-minute presentation using PowerPoint that both outlines your class notes and shows the connection to your interests. Develop the presentation as though you were going to teach a group of students about the concept. Use a combination of graphics, photos, music, and video clips to help your imaginary audience connect with the material in a new and interesting way.

3. Save the PowerPoint in your portfolio on your personal computer or flash drive. Use your PowerPoint presentation as one way to study for your next exam in that course.

You probably won't be creating PowerPoint presentations for all of your class notes, but making a habit of connecting class content to your life is an easy way to help yourself remember information. When it is time to prepare for a test, try pulling your notes into a presentation that you would feel comfortable presenting to your classmates.

Where to go for help . . .

On Campus

Learning assistance center: Present on almost every campus, the mission or purpose of these helpful centers is to support students in their learning and development of good study skills. The skills in this chapter are among the specialties of these learning assistance centers. More and more, the best students—and good students who want to be the best students—use the campus learning center as often as students who are having academic difficulties. These services are offered by both full-time professionals and highly skilled student tutors who are available at times convenient for you.

Fellow college students: Often the best help you can get is from your fellow students—but of course, not just any students. Keep an eye out in your classes, residence hall, co-curricular groups, and other places for the most serious, purposeful, and directed students. They are the ones to seek out. Find a student tutor. Join a study group. Students who use these readily available peer resources are much more likely to stay in college and succeed. It does not diminish you in any way to seek assistance from your peers.

Online

Toastmasters International offers public speaking tips at http://www.toastmasters.org.

See guidelines for speaking in class at http://www .school-for-champions.com/grades/speaking.htm.

My Institution's Resources

_____

_____

_____

_____

_____

_____

_____

_____

_____

_____

_____

_____

_____

_____

06 Reading for Success

Why is reading college textbooks more challenging than reading high school texts or reading for pleasure? The answer is that college textbooks are loaded with terms, concepts, and complex information that you are expected to learn on your own in a short time. To succeed, you will need to learn, and use, a reading method such as the one described in this chapter.

A textbook reading plan can pay off. It can increase your focus and concentration, promote greater understanding of what you read, and prepare you to study for tests and exams. This system is based on four main steps: previewing, reading, marking, and reviewing.

How Do You Measure Up?

1. I skim or "preview" a chapter before I begin to read.
   - ○ Always
   - ○ Occasionally
   - ○ Never

2. I wait to underline, highlight, or annotate the text until after I have read a page or section.
   - ○ Always
   - ○ Occasionally
   - ○ Never

3. As I read textbooks, I look for key ideas and record them in my notes.
   - ○ Always
   - ○ Occasionally
   - ○ Never

4. When reading a textbook, I use a dictionary to check the meaning of unfamiliar words.
   - ○ Always
   - ○ Occasionally
   - ○ Never

Review the items you marked "occasionally" or "never." Paying attention to all these aspects of your college experience can be important to your success. After reading this chapter, come back to this list and think about ways you can work on these areas.

Preparing to Read and Getting Started

Titus Indra

First-year student returning to school after a four-year break

The day after I registered for classes, and after I got my list of assigned reading material, I walked over to the bookstore. My biology textbook alone had a price tag of $100. The way I figured it, borrowing the textbook from a classmate or from the library wouldn't be that bad. I could even photocopy a few sections if necessary, or I could pick up an old edition somewhere at a discount. We'd probably cover most of the chapters in class anyway.

That was the plan. But the professor assigned reading constantly, and nobody else in my class wanted to share a book for *one minute*. They were all pre-med and studied nonstop. My lab partner finally said that I could borrow his book on *Saturday nights,* as long as I had it back to him the next morning at 8. And since the thing ran about 400 pages and was as thick as a toaster, photocopying didn't work out well.

In the meantime, I realized three things: (1) that the lone and hugely popular library copy of the book would *never* be available; (2) that old editions were hard to find and didn't have the updates that the professor wanted us to know; and (3) that a huge part of learning in college involves teaching yourself. That $100 came to seem like a bargain, in giving me a lot of information I could study on my own.

Why is it so important to keep up with your outside reading assignments in college?

Previewing before You Read

The purpose of previewing is to get the big picture, to understand how what you are about to read is connected to what you already know and to the material the instructor is covering in class. Begin by reading the title of the chapter. Next, quickly read the introductory paragraphs, and then read the summary at the beginning or end of the chapter (if there is a summary). Skim through the chapter headings and subheadings. Finally, note any study exercises at the end of the chapter.

As part of your preview, check the number of pages the chapter contains. Estimate how many pages you can reasonably expect to cover in your first 50-minute study period. Different types of textbooks may require more or less time to read. For example, depending on your interests and previous knowledge, you may be able to read a psychology text more quickly than a logic text that presents a whole new system of symbols.

As you preview the text material, look for connections between the text and the related lecture material. Call to mind the related terms and

try it!

Preparing to Read, Think, and Mark

Choose a reading assignment for one of your classes. After previewing the material, begin reading until you reach a major heading or until you have read at least a page or two. Now stop and write down what you remember from the material. Next go back to the same material and mark what you believe are the main ideas. Don't fall into the trap of marking too much. Now list four of the main ideas from the reading:

1. _____
2. _____
3. _____
4. _____

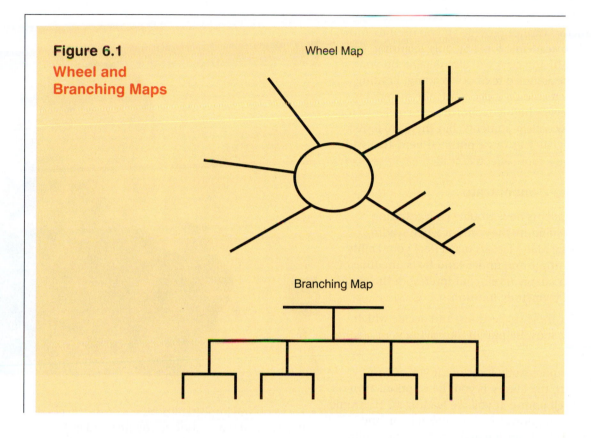

Figure 6.1

Wheel and Branching Maps

Wheel Map

Branching Map

concepts that you recorded in the lecture. Use these strategies to warm up. Ask yourself, "Why am I reading this? What do I need to learn?"

Mapping or Outlining a Chapter

Mapping a chapter as you preview it provides a visual guide for how different chapter ideas fit together. Because about 75 percent of students identify themselves as visual learners, mapping is an excellent learning tool.

How do you map a chapter? While you are previewing, draw either a wheel or a branching structure (see Figure 6.1). In the wheel structure, place the central idea of the chapter in the circle. You should find the central idea in the chapter introduction; it may also be apparent in the chapter title. For example, in this chapter it is "reading successfully." Place secondary ideas on the spokes radiating from the circle, and draw off-shoots of those ideas on the lines attached to the spokes. In the branching structure, put the main idea (most likely the title) at the top, followed by supporting ideas on the second tier, and so forth. If you prefer a more linear visual image, make an

outline of the headings and subheadings of the chapter.

Marking Your Textbook

After completing your preview and creating your map or outline, you should be able to read more quickly and with greater comprehension. Marking your textbooks is another active reading strategy that will help you concentrate on the material as you read. Be sure to finish reading a section before you decide which are the most important ideas and mark only those ideas.

However, sometimes highlighting or underlining can provide you with a false sense of security. You may have determined what information is most important, but you might not really understand the material. When you put something in your own words while taking notes, you will predict exam questions and test your understanding. These active reading strategies take more time initially, but they can save you time in the long run because they promote concentration and make it easy to review—so that you probably won't have to pull an all-nighter before an exam.

Reading to Question, Interpret, and Understand

Instructors cannot provide all you need to know about an academic topic by only lecturing. Your learning in any class will also depend on your doing the assigned textbook reading. Reading a college textbook, especially if the material is brand new or highly technical, is a challenge for most new college students, but there are tested strategies, such as those outlined here, that will make you a more effective reader.

Learn to Concentrate

Many students have trouble concentrating or understanding the content when reading textbooks. Many factors may affect your ability to concentrate and understand texts: the time of day, your energy level, your interest in the material, and your study location.

Consider these suggestions, and decide which would be most helpful in improving your reading ability:

- Find a quiet study location. If you are on campus, the library is your best option. Turn off your cell phone. If you are reading an electronic document, download the information and disconnect from the network to reduce online distractions.
- Read in blocks of time, with short breaks in between. By reading for small blocks throughout the day instead of cramming in all your reading at the end of the day, you should be able to understand and retain the material more easily.
- Set goals for your study period, such as "I will read twenty pages of my psychology text in the next 50 minutes." Reward yourself with a 10-minute break after each 50-minute study period.
- If you have trouble concentrating or staying awake, take a quick walk around the library or down the hall. Then resume studying.
- Jot study questions in the margins, take notes, or recite key ideas. Reread confusing parts of the text, and make a note to ask your instructor for clarification.

- Focus on the important portions of the text. Pay particular attention to the first and last sentences of paragraphs and to words in italics or bold print.
- Use the glossary in the text or a dictionary to define unfamiliar terms.

Understand the Purpose of the Text

As you begin reading, you can learn more about the textbook and its author by reading the front-matter of the book—the preface, introduction, and author's biographical sketch. The preface explains why the book was written and what material is covered.

Some textbooks include questions at the end of each chapter that you can use as a study guide or as a quick check of your understanding of the chapter's main points. Take time to read and respond to these questions, whether or not your instructor requires you to do so.

Textbooks must try to cover a lot of material in a fairly limited space. But a text won't necessarily tell you everything you want to know about a topic—it may omit things that would make your reading more interesting. If you find yourself fascinated by a particular topic, go to the primary sources—the original research or documents the author used in writing the text.

Because some textbooks are sold with "test banks" to aid faculty in creating quizzes and tests, your instructors may draw their examinations directly from the text. On the other hand, they may consider the textbook to be supplementary to their lectures. When in doubt, ask for a clarification of what will be covered on the test and what types of questions will be used.

Finally, not all textbooks are equal. Some are simply better designed and better written than others. If you find a particular textbook to be disorganized in its physical layout or content, or exceptionally hard to understand, let your instructor know your opinion.

Monitor Your Comprehension

An important aspect of textbook reading is monitoring your comprehension. As you read, ask yourself, "Do I understand this?" If not, stop and reread the material. Look up words that you don't know. Try to clarify the main points and their relationship to one another.

Another way to check comprehension is to recite the material aloud to yourself, a study partner, or your study group. Using a study partner or group to monitor your comprehension gives you immediate feedback and is highly motivating. One way that study group members can work together is to divide up a chapter for previewing and studying and to get together later to teach the material to one another.

Review and Preview the Key Ideas

After you have read and marked or taken notes on the key ideas from the first section of the chapter, proceed to each subsequent section until you have finished the chapter. After you have completed each section—and before you move on to the next section—ask again, "What are the key ideas? What will I see on the test?" At the end of each section, try to guess what information the author will present in the next section. Effective reading should lead you from one section to the next, with each new section adding to your understanding.

Review Daily

The final step in effective textbook reading is reviewing. Many students expect the improbable—that they will read through their text material once and be able to remember the ideas four, six, or even twelve weeks later at exam time. But realistically, you will need to include regular reviews in your study process. Here is where your notes, study questions, annotations, flash cards, visual maps, or outlines will be most useful. Your study goal should be to review the material from each chapter every week.

Consider ways to use your many senses to review. Recite aloud. Tick off each item in a list on each of your fingertips. Post diagrams, maps, or outlines around your living space so that you will see them often and will likely be able to visualize them while taking the test.

06

Reading Textbooks for Different Types of Courses

Just as all college textbooks aren't the same, you will need different reading strategies depending on the material in the text. And your instructors may also suggest that you go beyond the textbook to read other articles or "primary sources" that give you greater understanding or even different points of view.

Reading Math Textbooks

Traditional textbooks in mathematics tend to have many symbols and fewer words than textbooks in humanities or social sciences. Typically, the authors present the material through definitions, theorems, and sample problems. As you read, pay special attention to all the definitions. Learning all the terms in a new topic is the first step toward complete understanding.

Derivations of formulas and proofs of theorems are usually included to establish mathematical rigor. You must understand and be able to apply the formulas and theorems, but unless your course has an especially theoretical emphasis, you are less likely to be responsible for all the proofs. So if you get lost in the proof of a theorem, go on to the next item in the section.

When you come to a sample problem, it's time to get busy. Pick up pencil and paper and work through the problem. Then look at the solution and think through the problem on your own. Of course, the exercises that follow each text section form the heart of any math book. A large portion of the time you devote to the course will be spent completing assigned textbook exercises.

To be successful in any math or science course, it is important that you keep up with all assignments. Don't allow yourself to fall behind. Do all your homework on time, whether or not your instructor collects it. After you complete the assignment, skim through the other exercises in the problem set. Just reading the unassigned problems will deepen your understanding of the topic and its scope. Finally, talk it through to yourself. As you do, focus on understanding the problem and its solution, not on memorization. Memorizing may help you recall how to work through one problem, but it does not help you understand the steps involved so that you can apply them to solving other problems.

Reading Science Textbooks

Your approach to your science textbooks will depend somewhat on whether you are studying a math-based science such as physics or a text-based science such as biology or zoology. In either case, you need to familiarize yourself with the overall format of the book. Review the table of contents and the glossary of terms. Check the material in the appendices. There you will find lists of physical constants, unit conversions, and various charts and tables. Many physics and chemistry books also include a brief review of the math you will need in science courses.

Notice the organization of each chapter in the book, and pay special attention to the graphs, charts, and boxes. Each chapter may begin with chapter objectives and conclude with a short summary, and you may wish to study both of these useful sections before and after reading the chapter. You will usually find answers to selected problems in the back of the book. Make sure that you understand how each problem was solved. Use the answer key and/or the student solutions manual in a responsible way to promote your mastery of each chapter.

As you begin an assigned section in a science text, skim the material quickly to get a general idea of the topic. Begin to absorb the new vocabulary and technical symbols. Then skim the end-of-chapter problems so you'll know what to look for as you do a second, and more detailed, reading of the chapter. State a specific goal—for example: "I'm going to distinguish between mitosis and meiosis," or "Tonight I'll focus on the topics in this chapter that were stressed in class."

Should you underline and highlight in your science textbooks, or should you outline the material, or both? You may decide to underline or highlight in a subject such as anatomy, which involves a lot of memorization of terms. But use a highlighter with restraint; it should pull your eye only to important terms and facts. If highlighting is actually a form of procrastination for you (you are reading through the material but planning to learn it at a later date) or if you are highlighting nearly everything you read, your colorful pages of yellow, pink, or orange may be doing you more harm than good. When you reread the text before an exam, you won't be able to identify important concepts quickly if they're lost in a sea of color.

In most sciences, it is best to outline the text chapters. You can usually identify main topics, subtopics, and specific terms under each subtopic in your text by the size of the type. Headings printed in larger type will introduce major sections; smaller type is used for subtopics within these sections. To save time when you are outlining, don't write full sentences, but include clear explanations of new technical terms and symbols. Pay special attention to topics that were covered in the lecture class or in the lab. If you aren't sure whether your outlines contain too much or too little detail, compare them with those of a classmate or the members of your study group. In preparing for a test, it's a good idea to make condensed versions of your chapter outlines so that you can see how everything fits together.

Reading Social Science and Humanities Textbooks

Many of the suggestions that apply to science textbooks also apply to reading in the social sciences (sociology, psychology, anthropology, economics, political science, and history). Social science texts are filled with terms that are unique to the field of study. They also describe research and theory building and have references to many primary sources. Your social science texts may also describe differences in opinions or perspectives. Not all social scientists agree about any one issue, and you may be introduced to a number of ongoing academic debates. In fact, your reading can become more interesting if you seek out different opinions about a common issue. You may have to go beyond your textbook, and your campus library or the Internet will be good sources of various viewpoints about ongoing controversies.

Textbooks in the humanities (philosophy, religion, literature, music, and art) provide facts, examples, opinions, and original material such as stories and essays. You will often be asked to react to your reading by identifying central themes or characters.

Some professors believe that the way we structure courses and majors artificially divides human knowledge and experience. Those with this view may argue that subjects such as history, political science, and philosophy are closely linked and that studying each subject separately results in only partial understanding. These instructors will stress the connections between courses and encourage you to think in an interdisciplinary manner. You might be asked to consider how the book or story you're reading or the music you're studying reflects the political atmosphere or the prevailing culture of the period. Your art instructor may direct you to think about how a particular painting gives you a window on the painter's psychological makeup or religious beliefs.

Reading Primary Source Material

Whether or not your instructor requires you to read other material in addition to the textbook, your reading will be enriched if you track down some of the primary sources that are referenced in your text. These sources may be journal articles, research papers, dissertations (the major research papers that students write to earn a doctoral degree), laws, personal letters or diary entries, speeches, or original essays. These kinds of documents can be found in your library and increasingly on the Internet. Reading primary source material gives you a depth of detail and breadth of perspective that few textbooks provide.

Many primary sources were originally written to be read by other instructors or researchers. Therefore they often use language and refer to concepts that are familiar to other scholars but not necessarily to first-year college students. If you are reading a journal article that describes a theory or research study, one technique for easier understanding is to read from the end to the beginning. Read the article's conclusion, "discussion," and/or "abstract" section and then go back to see how the experiment was done or the ideas were formulated. In almost all scholarly journals, articles are introduced by an "abstract," a paragraph-length summary of the methods and major findings. Reading the abstract is a quick way to get the gist of a research article before you dive in. As you're reading research articles, always ask yourself, "So what?" Was the research important to what we know about the topic, or, in your opinion, was it unnecessary? If you aren't concerned about the specific method used to collect the data, you can skip over the section on methodology.

Improving Your Reading

With effort, you can improve your reading dramatically, but remember to be flexible. How you read should depend on the material. Assess the relative importance and difficulty of the assigned reading, and adjust your reading style and the time you allot accordingly. Connect one important idea to another by asking yourself, "Why am I reading this? Where does this fit in?" It takes planning to read textbooks and other assigned readings with good understanding and recall.

Developing Your Vocabulary

Textbooks are full of new terminology. In fact, one could argue that learning chemistry is largely a matter of learning the language of chemists and that mastering philosophy or history or sociology requires a firm grounding in the terminology of each particular academic discipline or field of study.

If words are such a basic and essential component of our knowledge, what is the best way to learn them? Follow the basic vocabulary-building strategies outlined here:

- During your overview of the chapter, notice and jot down unfamiliar terms. Consider making a flash card for each term or making a list of terms.

- When you encounter challenging words, consider the context. See if you can predict the meaning of an unfamiliar term by using the surrounding words.

- If context by itself is not enough, try analyzing the term to discover the root, or base part, or other meaningful parts of the word. For example, *emissary* has a root that means "to emit" or "to send forth," so we can guess that an emissary is someone sent forth with a message. Similarly, note prefixes and suffixes. For example, *anti*- means "against" and *pro*- means "for." Use the glossary in the text, a dictionary, or the online Merriam-Webster Dictionary (**http://www .merriam-webster.com/netdict.htm**) to locate the definition. Note any multiple definitions, and search for the meaning that fits the usage you are looking for.

- Take every opportunity to use these new terms in your writing and speaking. If you use a new term a few times, you'll soon know it. In addition, studying new terms on flash cards or study sheets can be handy at exam time.

Your Reading Assignments

- Make a list of all your reading assignments for your classes this week.
- On a scale of 1 (easy) to 5 (difficult), rate each of them.
- Rate their importance, using a scale of 1 (least important) to 5 (most important).
- Determine how many total hours you will devote to reading this week.
- Allocate your time, giving yourself more time to read assignments that are both important and difficult.

- As you go through the week, keep track of how much time you actually spent reading.
- At the end of the week, go back and analyze how well your original game plan for allocation of reading time worked for you. Did you spend more or less time than predicted? And with what results? How accurate was your predicted scale of reading challenge?

06

If English Is Not Your First Language

The English language is one of the most difficult languages to learn. Words are often spelled differently from the way they sound, and the language is full of idioms—phrases that are peculiar and cannot be understood from the individual meanings of the words. If you are learning English and are having trouble reading your texts, don't give up. Reading slowly and reading more than once can help you improve your comprehension. Make sure that you have two good dictionaries—one in English and one that links English with your primary language—and look up every word that you don't know. Be sure to practice thinking, writing, and speaking in English, and take advantage of your campus's helping services. Your campus may have ESL (English as a Second Language) tutoring and workshops. Ask your adviser or your first-year seminar instructor to help you locate those services.

06 Chapter Review

One-minute paper . . .

This chapter is full of suggestions for effectively reading your college textbooks. What suggestions did you find the most doable? What do you think is your biggest challenge in using these suggestions to improve your reading habits?

Applying what you've learned . . .

Now that you have read and discussed this chapter, consider how you can apply what you have learned to your academic and personal life. The following prompts will help you to reflect on chapter material and its relevance to you both now and in the future.

1. Choose a reading assignment for one of your upcoming classes. After previewing the material, begin reading until you reach a major heading or until you have read at least a page or two. Now stop and write down what you remember from the material. Go back and review what you read. Were you able to remember all of the main ideas?

2. It is easy to say that there is not enough time in the day to get everything done, especially a long reading assignment. However, your future depends on how well you do in college. Challenge yourself not to use that excuse. How can you modify your daily activities to make time for reading?

Building your portfolio . . .

The big picture

This chapter introduces a reading strategy called mapping as a visual tool for getting the "big picture" of what you are preparing to read. Mapping a textbook chapter using wheel maps or branching maps can help you quickly recognize how different concepts and terms fit together and make connections to what you already know about the subject (see the wheel map on page 83). You might also use other types of maps, such as matrixes to compare and contrast ideas or show cause and effect, a spider web to connect themes, or sketches to illustrate images, relationships, or descriptions.

1. Look through your course syllabi, and identify a reading assignment that you need to complete in the next week.

2. Begin by previewing the first chapter of the reading assignment.

3. Practice mapping the chapter by creating your own map using the drawing toolbar in Microsoft Word.

4. Save your map in your portfolio on your personal computer or flash drive.

Example:

1. Place the central idea of the chapter in the center of the wheel.

2. Place supporting ideas on the spokes of the wheel.

3. Place important details on the lines attached to the spokes.

Tip: A good place to start is with chapter headings and subheadings. Then move on to terms in bold and graphics such as charts, tables, and diagrams. Textbooks often have study questions at the end of the chapter, which can give you clues about what the author considers the most important concepts.

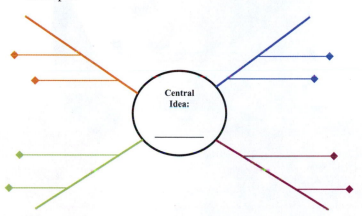

Central
Idea:

Reading a textbook efficiently and effectively requires that you develop reading strategies that will help you to make the most of your study time. Because mapping can help you organize and retain what you have read, it is a good reading and study tool. Writing, reciting, and organizing the main points, supporting ideas, and key details of the chapter will help you to recall the information on test day.

Where to go for help . . .

On Campus

Learning assistance center: Most campuses have a learning center, and reading assistance is among its specialties. The best students, good students who want to be the best students, and students with academic difficulties all use learning centers. Services are offered by both full-time professionals and highly skilled student tutors.

Fellow college students: Often the best help we can get is the closest to us. Keep an eye out in your classes, residence hall, and campus groups for the best students—those who appear to be the most serious, purposeful, and directed. Hire a tutor. Join a study group. Students who do these things are much more likely to be successful.

Online

Middle Tennessee State University: http://www.mtsu.edu/~studskl/Txtbook.html. The "Study Skills Help" web page has a link to "Advice for Getting the Most from Reading Textbooks."

Niagara University's Office for Academic Support: http://www.niagara.edu/oas/learning_center/study_reading_strategies/reading.htm. View this Web site for "21 Tips for Better Textbook Reading."

My Institution's Resources

_____

_____

_____

_____

_____

_____

_____

07 Communicating Clearly

Many people can write, but few can write really well. The same is true of speaking: Some people can speak with authority, while others seem disorganized and uncomfortable.

The ability to write and speak clearly, persuasively, and confidently makes a tremendous difference in how the rest of the world perceives you and how well you will communicate throughout your life. In almost every conceivable occupation, you will be expected to think, create, manage, lead—and communicate. That means you will have to write and speak well. In order to participate in the information age, you will need to be both a good thinker and an excellent communicator.

Most people look at writing and speaking as tasks to be mastered and then forgotten. Nothing could be further from the truth. Writing is both a process (a step-by-step method for reaching your final goal) and a product (a final paper, answers to an essay exam, or a script). Similarly, speaking is a skill that involves the mastery of several basic steps.

How Do You Measure Up?

1. I allow myself plenty of time to do a first draft and make revisions before submitting essays or major papers to my instructors.
   - ○ Always
   - ○ Occasionally
   - ○ Never

2. When preparing to write a paper, I build in time to collect the information I need before I begin to write.
   - ○ Always
   - ○ Occasionally
   - ○ Never

3. I consider my audience before deciding whether to use formal or informal language.
   - ○ Always
   - ○ Occasionally
   - ○ Never

4. Before giving a speech, I practice what I'm going to say.
   - ○ Always
   - ○ Occasionally
   - ○ Never

Review the items you marked "occasionally" or "never." Paying attention to all these aspects of your college experience can be important to your success. After reading this chapter, come back to this list and think about ways you can work on these areas.

Understanding the Basics of Writing

Hilary Braddock

First-year student in her first term

The first and best thing I learned about my Philosophy 101 course: No exams. "Your grade will depend entirely on your essay scores," said our instructor, Professor Mann. I always earned A's in papers back in high school. So when it came to our first big assignment, a paper on Plato's *Five Dialogues,* I felt pretty sure that my first draft was flawless. Professor Mann thought the opposite: He ripped it apart with negative comments. That was rough.

When I went to talk to him about my paper in his office after class, he looked over it again for a minute and said words that were hard to hear, but in the end, helpful. "I just don't see much effort here. Your paper isn't well researched, and it contains a considerable number of grammatical errors and no clear thesis statement. And your bibliography cites Wikipedia more than the actual source material," he went on.

"Oh, is that wrong?" I asked, surprised.

"Yes, that's wrong." Professor Mann studied me. "How long did you spend on this, anyway?"

"I don't know," I said. "A couple of hours at least."

"Well, most of your classmates probably spent four times that amount of time on their papers." Professor Mann's tone softened a little. "It's possible that your former teachers had a different standard. You will need to get your writing up to the level expected in college. I can help and the campus writing center can help, but the decision to put the work into improving is up to you."

Not everyone arrives at college with the same level of preparedness. What could Hilary do next to build on what she learned through this first assignment?

Few of us—even professionally published writers—say what we want to say, how we want to say it, on our first try at writing it down. But through an understanding of the writing process, practice, and more practice, you can learn to communicate your messages clearly and in the way you want.

The Exploratory/Explanatory Process

Exploratory writing helps you discover what you want to say; *explanatory* writing then allows you to transmit those ideas to others.

It is important that most or all of your exploratory writing be private, to be read only by you as a series of steps toward your finished work. Keeping your early drafts under wraps frees you to say what you mean and to mean what you say. Later, you will come back and make some adjustments, and each revision will strengthen your message. In contrast, explanatory writing is "published," meaning you have chosen to allow others (your professor, your friends, other students, the public at large) to read it.

Some writers say they gather their best thoughts through exploratory writing—by researching their topics, writing down ideas from their research, and adding their questions and reactions to what they have gathered. As they write, their minds begin to make connections between ideas. They don't attempt to organize, to find exactly the right words, or to think about structure. That might interrupt the thoughts that flow onto the paper or computer screen. They frequently get impatient with themselves for not being able to find the right words. But when they move from exploratory to explanatory writing, their preparation will help them form clear sentences, spell properly, and have their thoughts organized so that their material flows naturally from one point to the next.

The Power of Writing

William Zinsser, author of several books on writing, says, "The act of writing gives the teacher a window into the mind of the student."[1] In other words, your writing provides tangible evidence of how well you think and how well you understand concepts related to the courses you are taking. Your writing might also reveal a good sense of humor, a compassion for the less fortunate, a respect for family, and many other things. Zinsser reminds us that writing is not merely something that writers do; it is a basic skill for getting through life. He claims that far too many Americans cannot perform useful work because they never learned to express themselves.

Finding a Topic

In the book *Zen and the Art of Motorcycle Maintenance*, Robert Pirsig tells a story about teaching a first-year English class. Each week the assignment was to turn in a 500-word essay. One week, a student failed to submit her paper about the town where the college was located, explaining that she had "thought and thought, but couldn't think of anything to write about." Pirsig gave her an additional weekend to complete the assignment. As he was offering the extension, an idea flashed through his mind. "I want you to write a 500-word paper just about Main Street, not the whole town," he said.

The student stared at him angrily. How was she to narrow her thinking to just one street when she couldn't think of a single thing to write about the entire town? Monday she arrived in tears, sputtering, "I'll never learn to write." Pirsig's response: "Write a paper about one building on Main Street. The opera house. And start with the first brick on the lower left side. I want it by the next class." The student's eyes opened wide. She walked into class the next time with a 5,000-word paper on the opera house. "I don't know what happened," she exclaimed. "I sat across the street and wrote about the first brick, then the second, and all

_____

[1] William Zinsser, *On Writing Well* (New York: Harper Resource 25th Anniversary Edition, 2001).

of a sudden I couldn't stop."[2] What had Pirsig done for this frustrated student? He had helped her find a focus, a place to begin. Getting started is what blocks most students from approaching writing properly. Faced with an ultimatum, the student probably began to see the beauty of the opera house for the first time and had gone on to describe it, to find out more about it in the library, to ask others about it, and to comment on its setting among the other buildings on the block.

_____

[2] Robert Pirsig, *Zen and the Art of Motorcycle Maintenance* (New York: Bantam Books, 1974).

try it!

The Power of Focused Observation

Think about Pirsig's student who began with the first brick of the opera house and went on to write a 5,000-word paper. Find a favorite spot of yours on campus where you can sit comfortably and undisturbed. Take a good look at the entire area. Now look again, this time noticing specific parts of the area. Choose something: It might be a statue, a building, a tree, or a fence. Now look carefully at just one portion of the object you selected and start writing about it. See where the writing takes you.

Taking the Steps to Better Writing: Prewriting, Writing, and Reviewing

Most writing instructors agree that the writing process consists of these three steps:

1. **Prewriting or rehearsing.** This step includes preparing to write by filling your mind with information from other sources. It is generally considered the first stage of exploratory writing.

2. **Writing or drafting.** This step is when exploratory writing becomes a rough explanatory draft.

3. **Rewriting or revision.** This step is when you polish your work until it clearly explains what you want to communicate and is ready for your audience.

Many students skip the first and last steps and "make do" with the middle one. Perhaps the issue is a lack of time or that the student has procrastinated until the night before the paper is due. Whatever the reason, the result is often a poorly written assignment, since the best writing is usually done over an extended period of time.

Prewriting: The Idea Stage

Many writing experts, such as Donald Murray, believe that of all the steps, prewriting (or freewriting) should take the longest.[3] Prewriting is the stage when you write down all you think you need to know about a topic and then go digging for the answers. You might question things that seem illogical. You might recall what you've heard others say. This should lead you to write more, to ask yourself whether your views are more reliable than those of others, whether the topic may be too broad or too narrow, and so forth.

What constitutes an appropriate topic? When is it neither too broad nor too narrow? Test your topic by writing, "The purpose of this paper is to convince my readers that . . ." (but don't use that stilted language in your eventual paper). Pay attention to the assignment. Know the limits of your knowledge, the limitations on your time, and your ability to do the necessary research.

---

[3] Donald Murray, *Learning by Teaching: Selected Articles on Writing and Teaching* (Portsmouth, NH: Boynton/Cook, 1982).

Writing: The Beginning of Organization

Once you have completed your research and feel you have exhausted all information sources and ideas, it's time to move to the writing, or drafting, stage. It is a good idea to begin with a thesis statement and an outline so that you can put things where they logically belong. A thesis statement is a short statement that clearly defines the purpose of the paper.

Once you have a workable outline and thesis, you can begin paying attention to the flow of ideas from one sentence to the next and from one paragraph to the next, including subheadings where needed. If you have chosen the thesis carefully, it will help you to check whether each sentence relates to your main idea. When you have completed this stage, you will have the first draft of your paper in hand.

Rewriting: The Polishing Stage

Are you finished? Not by a long shot. Next comes the stage at which you take a good piece of writing and do your best to make it great. The essence of good writing is rewriting. You read. You correct.

You add smooth transitions. You slash through wordy sentences and paragraphs, removing anything that is repetitive or adds nothing of value to your paper. You substitute strong words for weak ones; sharper vocabulary for fuzzy language. You double-check spelling and grammar. Perhaps you share your work with others who give you feedback. You continue to revise until you're satisfied. You work hard to stay on deadline. And then you "publish" (turn in) your paper.

Allocating Time for Each Writing Stage

When Donald Murray was asked how long a writer should spend on each of the three stages, he offered this breakdown:

- Prewriting: 85 percent (including research, thinking, and planning)
- Writing: 1 percent (the first draft)
- Rewriting: 14 percent (revising until it's suitable for "publication")[4]

If the figures surprise you, here's a true story about a writer who was asked to create a brochure. He had other jobs to do and kept postponing the assignment. But the other work he was doing had a direct bearing on the brochure. So as he was

---

[4] Ibid.

putting off the brochure assignment, he was also "researching" material for it.

After nearly three months, he finally decided to move forward on the brochure. He sat at his computer and dashed the words off in just under 30 minutes. The more he wrote, the faster the ideas popped into his head. He actually was afraid to stop until he'd finished. He revised, sent his draft around the office, took some suggestions, and eventually the brochure was published. This writer had spent a long time prewriting (working with related information without trying to write the brochure). He went through the writing stage quickly because his mind was primed for the task. As a result, he had time to polish his work before deciding the job was done.

You can use a similar process. Begin writing the day you get the assignment, even if it's for only 10 or 15 minutes. That way, you won't be confronting a blank screen or piece of paper as the due date looms. Write something on the assignment every day; the more you write, the better you'll write. Dig for ideas. Reject nothing at first, and then revise later. Read good writing; it will help you find your own writing style. Above all, know that becoming a better thinker and writer takes hard work, but practice can make your writing nearly perfect.

07

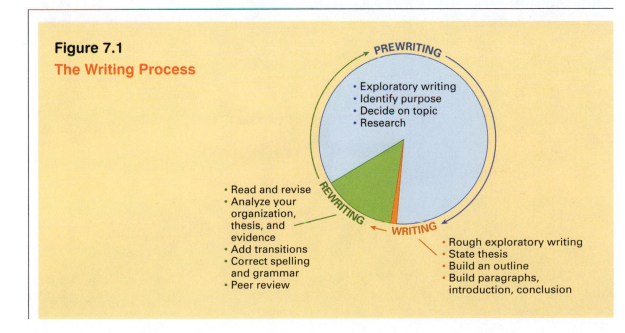

Figure 7.1
The Writing Process

PREWRITING
- Exploratory writing
- Identify purpose
- Decide on topic
- Research

REWRITING
- Read and revise
- Analyze your organization, thesis, and evidence
- Add transitions
- Correct spelling and grammar
- Peer review

WRITING
- Rough exploratory writing
- State thesis
- Build an outline
- Build paragraphs, introduction, conclusion

Choosing the Best Way to Communicate in Writing

Writing is communication. And the more you know about your audience, the easier it is to write in an appropriate and understandable manner. Consider your instructors. What kind of writing do they expect? How about your friends? How about your present or future employer?

Formal versus Informal Writing

Before you came to college, you probably spent much more time writing informally than writing formally. Think about all the time you've spent writing Facebook and blog comments, e-mails, text messages, and instant messages (IMs). Now think about all the time you've spent writing papers for school or work. Typically, writing for online communications is informal. This can be a detriment to your writing skills. The grammar and structure of e-mail and other types of electronic communication resemble a conversation instead of a formal piece of writing. Additionally, communications via IM and text messaging often use spelling and grammar conventions all their own. As a shortcut, people often condense text messages and IMs by using abbreviations such as *brb, lol, y?,* and *ttyl*. They are abbreviated for

good reason—it doesn't make sense to slave over a message for a long time, making sure that your spelling and grammar are perfect and your words are eloquent, if the point of the message is to tell your coworker that you are ready to go to lunch. The downside of these shortcuts is that they have gradually crept into our writing habits and caused many of us to become careless in our formal writing. It is important to be aware of when it's okay to be sloppy and when you have to be meticulous.

Writing Online

Electronic communication does not convey emotions as well as face-to-face or even telephone conversations do. Electronic communication lacks vocal inflection, visible gestures, and a shared environment. The person who receives your message might have difficulty telling whether you are serious or kidding, happy or sad, frustrated or euphoric. Sarcasm is particularly dangerous to use in electronic messages. Therefore, your electronic compositions will be different from both your paper compositions and your speech.

07

Being aware of the differences between formal writing and informal writing will help you build appropriate writing skills for college work. How would you write a text message to friends telling them about the volunteer work you did this past weekend? How would you write that same message as an e-mail to a potential employer who might hire you for your first job after college? Another way to improve your writing is to consider the reader's point of view. For the next week, before sending any Facebook messages, e-mails, or text messages, reread them and consider how the people who will receive them will perceive your tone. What kind of mood will they think you are in? Will they feel that you are happy to have them as a friend? In how many different ways might your message be interpreted?

Writing for class projects might be a challenge at first. Visit your institution's writing center when you are starting to work on your paper. Professional staff and trained peer consultants who work in writing centers are available to help students express their ideas clearly through writing. Ask your instructor for examples of papers that have received good grades. You might also ask your instructor to help you review your writing after you have worked with the writing center. Most important, you can practice by using a correct writing style when IMing and text messaging. You'll find that your friends won't fault you for it. (Have you ever seen an IM asking you to "pls stop using proper grammar"?) Since you spend more time with online forms of communication, it's a great way to get real-world practice in the art of academic writing.

try it!
Thinking about Facebook

Look at your own or a friend's Facebook page. If this Facebook page were part of a job application, would you alter the writing style or what you or your friend might say? What kind of information would you delete? What kinds of specific changes do you think should be made for you or your friend to have a good chance of getting the job?

07

Becoming a Better Public Speaker

The advice about writing also applies to speaking in public. The major difference, of course, is that you not only have to write the speech, but you also have to present it to an audience. Because many people believe that fear of public speaking ranks up there with the fear of death, you might be thinking: What if I plan, organize, prepare, and rehearse, but calamity strikes anyway? What if my mind goes completely blank, I drop my note cards, or I say something totally embarrassing? Remember that people in your audience have been in your position and will understand your anxiety. Just accentuate the positive, rely on your wit, and keep speaking. Your recovery is what they are most likely to recognize; your success is what they are most likely to remember. The accompanying guidelines can help you improve your speaking skills tremendously, including losing your fear of speaking publicly (see the suggestions on page 93).

Using Body Language and Your Voice

When you speak, let your hands rest comfortably at your sides, reserving them for natural, spontaneous gestures. Don't lean over or hide behind the lectern. Unless you must stay close to a fixed microphone, move comfortably about the room, without pacing nervously. Some experts suggest changing physical positions between major points to punctuate your presentation. The unconscious message is "I've finished with that point; let's shift topics." Face your audience, and move toward them while you're speaking.

Here are additional tips for successful speaking:

- Make eye contact with as many listeners as you can. This helps you to read their reactions, demonstrate confidence, and establish command.

- A smile warms up your listeners, although you should avoid smiling excessively or inappropriately. Smiling through a presentation on world hunger would send your listeners a mixed message.

- As you practice, pay attention to the pitch of your voice, your rate of speech, and your volume. Project confidence and enthusiasm by varying your pitch. Speak at a rate that mirrors normal conversation—not too fast and not too slow. Consider varying your volume for the same reasons you vary pitch and rate—to engage your listeners and to emphasize important points.

- Be aware of pronunciation and word choice. A poorly articulated word (such as *gonna* for *going to*), a mispronounced word (*nuculer* for *nuclear*), or a misused word (*anecdote* for *antidote*) can quickly erode credibility. Check meanings and pronunciations in the dictionary if you're not sure of them, and use a thesaurus for word variety. Fillers such as *um, uh, like,* and *you know* are distracting and detract from the quality of your presentation.

- Consider your appearance. Convey a look of competence, preparedness, and success by dressing professionally.

Six Steps to Better Public Speaking

Successful speaking involves six fundamental steps:

Step 1: Clarify Your Objective

Begin by identifying and clarifying what you want to accomplish. Is your goal to inform your listeners about the student government's accomplishments? Or, as a commuting student, do you want to persuade your listeners that your campus needs additional student parking? What do you want your listeners to know, believe, or do when you are finished?

Step 2: Analyze Your Audience

Understand the people you'll be talking to. Ask yourself:

• What do they already know about my topic? If you're going to give a presentation on the health risks of fast food, you'll want to determine how much your listeners already know about fast food so you won't bore them or waste their time.

• What do they want or need to know? How much interest do your classmates have in nutrition? Would they be more interested in some other aspect of college life?

• Who are my listeners? What do they have in common with me?

• What are the audience's attitudes toward me, my ideas, and my topic? How are my listeners likely to feel about the ideas I am presenting? What attitudes have they cultivated about fast food?

Step 3: Collect and Organize Your Information

Now comes the critical part of the process: building your presentation by selecting and arranging blocks of information. A useful analogy is to think of yourself as guiding your listeners through the maze of ideas they already have so that they gain the new knowledge, attitudes, and beliefs you would like them to have.

Step 4: Choose Your Visual Aids

When visual aids are added to presentations, listeners can absorb 35 percent more information—and over time they can recall 55 percent more. You may choose to prepare a chart, show a video clip, write on the board, or distribute handouts. You may also use your computer to prepare overhead transparencies or dynamic PowerPoint presentations. As you select and use your visual aids, consider these rules:

• Make visuals easy to follow. Use readable lettering, and don't crowd information.

• Explain each visual clearly.

• Allow your listeners enough time to process visuals.

• Proofread carefully. Misspelled words hurt your credibility as a speaker.

• Maintain eye contact with your listeners while you discuss visuals. Don't turn around and address the screen.

A fancy slideshow can't make up for inadequate preparation or poor delivery, but using quality visual aids can help you to organize your material and can help your listeners to understand your message. The quality of your visual aids and your skill in using them can contribute significantly to the overall effectiveness of your presentation.

Step 5: Prepare Your Notes

If you are like most speakers, having an entire written copy of your speech in front of you may tempt you to read much of your presentation. But a speech that is read word-for-word will often sound canned or artificial. A better strategy is to memorize only the introduction and conclusion and then use a minimal outline, carefully prepared, from which you can speak extemporaneously. You will rehearse thoroughly in advance. But because you are speaking from brief notes, your choice of words will be slightly different each time you give your presentation, with the result that you will sound prepared but natural. Since you're not reading, you also will be able to maintain eye contact and build rapport with your listeners. You may wish to use note cards because they are unobtrusive. (Make sure you number them, in case you accidentally drop the stack on your way to the front of the room.) After you become more experienced, you may want to let your visuals serve as notes. A handout or PowerPoint slide listing key points may also serve as your basic outline. Eventually, you may find you no longer need notes.

Step 6: Practice Your Delivery

As you rehearse, form a mental image of success rather than failure. Practice your presentation aloud several times to harness that energy-producing anxiety. Begin a few days before your target date, and continue until you're about to go on stage. Make sure you rehearse aloud, as thinking through your speech and talking through your speech have very different results. Practice before an audience—your roommate, a friend, your dog, even the mirror. Talking to someone or something helps simulate the distraction that listeners cause. Consider audiotaping or videotaping yourself to pinpoint your mistakes and to reinforce your strengths. If you ask your practice audience to critique you, you'll have some idea of what changes you might make.

07

07 Chapter Review

One-minute paper . . .

This chapter has information that you can use to improve your writing and speaking skills. Which strategies struck you as methods that you could or should put into practice? If your instructor could cover one area in more depth, what would you want it to be?

Applying what you've learned . . .

Now that you have read and discussed this chapter, consider how you can apply what you've learned to your academic and personal life. The following prompts will help you reflect on chapter material and its relevance to you both now and in the future.

1. Develop a five-slide PowerPoint presentation to introduce yourself to your classmates in a new way. You might include slides that contain points about your high school years, your hobbies, your jobs, your family, and so forth. Use the effective speaking strategies in this chapter to help you outline your presentation. In addition to text, use visuals such as photos, video clips, and art to engage your audience.

2. Before reading this chapter, had you considered the differences between writing an exam response and writing a blog post or responding to someone on Facebook? Think about the online communications you've had in the last week. Can you say for certain that you knew exactly who your audience was? Did you send anything that could be misinterpreted or end up being read by someone outside your intended audience? What advice about online communications would you give to other students?

Building your portfolio . . .

In the public eye

The media provide ample opportunities for celebrities and public figures to show off their public speaking skills. As you have probably noticed, some celebrities are much better speakers than others. However, being a good public speaker is important not only for those who are "in the public eye." Whether you want to be a movie star or a marine biologist, potential employers tend to put excellent communication skills at the top of their "must have" list.

1. Identify a public figure who, in your opinion, is a good public speaker.

2. In a Word document, explain why it is important for that person to speak well. List the specific qualities (e.g., humor, eye contact) that you think make that person a good public speaker.

3. Next, re-create the chart on page 95. Recalling the last time you gave a presentation in front of a group and using a scale of 1 to 5 (5 being excellent), rate yourself as a public speaker using the guidelines in the chart.

4. Save your responses in your portfolio on your personal computer or flash drive. The next time you make a presentation, revisit the chart and spend extra time preparing in the areas in which you rated yourself less than "good."

Public Speaking Skills

	1 Poor	2 Fair	3 Average	4 Good	5 Excellent
Level of Preparedness (well-prepared and confident, last-minute technology check)					
Professional Appearance (appropriate business attire, including proper shoes)					
Effective Vocal Presentation Style (clear and persuasive, paying attention to the pitch of your voice, rate of speech, volume, and correct grammar)					
Appropriate Behavior and Speech (no chewing gum, being careful to avoid fillers such as *um, uh, like,* and *you know*)					
Natural Body Language (good eye contact with the audience, appropriate facial expressions, relaxed posture)					

Note your lowest scores as areas you need to work on as you prepare for your next presentation.

Where to go for help . . .

On Campus

Writing center: Most campuses have a writing center—frequently, in the English Department.

Learning assistance center: Learning centers offer assistance with a wide range of learning issues, including help with writing.

Departments of speech, theater, and communications: These departments offer resources and specific courses to help develop speaking skills.

Student activities: One of the best ways to learn and practice speaking skills is to become active in student organizations, especially those such as your student government association and debate club.

Online

Writing Tips: http://www.uiowa .edu/~histwrit/website/grammar %20help.htm. The University of Iowa's History Department offers help on common writing mistakes.

Plain Language: http://www .plainlanguage.gov/howto/ guidelines/reader-friendly.com. Have you ever been confused by government gobbledygook? Here's a guide to writing user-friendly documents for federal employees.

Toastmasters International Public Speaking Tips: http://www .toastmasters.org.

My Institution's Resources

_____

_____

_____

_____

_____

08 Taking Exams & Tests

You can prepare for test taking in many ways, using your preferred learning style to determine the approach that works best for you. In this chapter you will find advice for preparing physically, emotionally, and academically. This chapter will also remind you why academic honesty and integrity are so important in college and beyond.

You'll find that most college instructors emphasize higher-level thinking skills such as analysis, synthesis, and evaluation, not just memorization. While they will expect you to remember material presented in lectures and the text, they will also frequently require you to provide the reasons, arguments, and assumptions on which a given position is based, and the evidence that confirms or discounts it. In exams as well as in other aspects of the course, instructors will want you to support your opinions and to show them how you think.

This chapter covers the following topics:

| Preparing for Tests 98 | Strategies for Under-standing, Remembering, and Studying 100 | Taking Tests and Exams 102 | Academic Honesty and Misconduct 104 |

How Do You Measure Up?

1. I am careful to maintain good eating, sleeping, and exercise habits before exams.
   - ○ Always
   - ○ Occasionally
   - ○ Never

2. I begin studying for an exam at least a week in advance.
   - ○ Always
   - ○ Occasionally
   - ○ Never

3. I read examination questions carefully so that I'm sure to give complete and precise answers.
   - ○ Always
   - ○ Occasionally
   - ○ Never

4. I understand what constitutes plagiarism and cheating in each of my classes.
   - ○ Always
   - ○ Occasionally
   - ○ Never

Review the items you marked "occasionally" or "never." Paying attention to all these aspects of your college experience can be important to your success. After reading this chapter, come back to this list and think about ways you can work on these areas.

Preparing for Tests

Ken Vonn

Third-year student

I always like to get to class a few minutes early, but that is when it starts. People ask if they can take my study outline to lunch. Or they want to copy my notes. Or they want to borrow a term paper I wrote last semester for a course they're taking now.

A lot of them aren't even my friends. They're just classmates I sit close to who know that I get good grades. Funny how many people in college are lazy and willing to cheat. And trust me: All the people who want *me* to help *them* cheat don't worry for one second that I might get caught, too. Take this morning. I'd barely sat down in my desk in the packed computer lab when this guy named Brad—someone who had only spoken to me once in the past two years—came up and said, "Did you do the calculus homework? Can I copy it?"

As usual, I tried to escape the situation: "Um, yeah. But I didn't understand it and it's probably all wrong."

To which Brad said, typically, "No, man, I don't care so long as there are numbers on it."

So there it was: I had to hand my homework over and sit there feeling weak, resentful, and nervous that someone on the Honor Council might be within earshot. Or say no and feel geeky and uptight.

What should Ken do in this situation? What does academic honesty entail?

Prepare Ahead: Three Basic Steps

You actually began preparing for tests and examinations on the first day of the term. All of your lecture notes, assigned readings, and homework are part of that preparation. As the test day nears, you should know how much additional review time you will need, what material the test will cover, and what format the test will take.

Here are three basic steps you can take to prepare for tests:

1. **Ask your instructor about the exam.** Find out about the types of questions you'll have to answer, the time you will have to complete them, and the content to be covered. Ask how the exam will be graded and whether all questions will have the same point value. But keep in mind that most instructors dislike being asked, "Is this going to be on the test?" They believe that everything that goes on in class is important enough for you to learn, whether it's "on the test" or not.

2. **Manage your time wisely.** Create a schedule that will give you time to review effectively for the exam instead of waiting until the night before.

3. **Focus your study.** Figure out what you can effectively review that is likely to be on the exam. Collaborate with other students to share information, and try to attend all test or exam review sessions offered by your instructor.

Prepare Physically

Maintain a regular sleep routine To do well on exams, you will need to be alert so that you can think clearly. And you are more likely to be alert when you are well rested. Last-minute, late-night cramming isn't an effective study strategy.

Follow a regular exercise program Walking, running, swimming, and other aerobic activities are effective stress reducers. They provide positive—and needed—breaks from intense studying and may help you think more clearly.

Eat right Avoid drinking too many caffeinated drinks and eating too much junk food. Be sure to eat breakfast before a morning exam. Ask the instructor if you can bring a bottle of water with you to the exam.

Prepare Emotionally

Know the material Study by testing yourself or by quizzing others in a study group so that you will be sure you really know the material. If you allow adequate time to review, you will enter the classroom on exam day confident that you are prepared.

Practice relaxing   If you experience an upset stomach, sweaty palms, a racing heart, or other unpleasant physical symptoms of test anxiety before an exam, see your counseling center about relaxation techniques. Practice them regularly.

Use positive self-talk   Instead of telling yourself, "I never do well on math tests" or "I'll never be able to learn all the information for my history essay exam," make positive statements such as "I have attended all the lectures, done my homework, and passed the quizzes. Now I'm ready to pass the test."

Prepare for Test Taking

Design an exam plan   Use the information about the test as you design a plan for preparing. Build that preparation into a schedule of review dates. Develop a to-do list of the major steps you need to take to be ready. Be sure you have read and learned all the material by one week before the exam. During the week before the exam, set aside one-hour blocks of time for review, and make notes on what you specifically plan to accomplish during each hour.

Join a study group   Numerous research studies have shown that joining a study group is one of the most effective strategies for preparing for exams. You can benefit from different views of your instructor's goals, objectives, and emphasis; have partners quiz you on facts and concepts; and gain the enthusiasm and friendship of others to help build and sustain your motivation.

Some professors allow class time for the formation of study groups. Otherwise, ask your instructor, adviser, or campus tutoring or learning center to help you identify interested students and decide on guidelines for the group. Study groups can meet throughout the term, or they can just review for midterms or final exams. Group members should complete their assignments before the group meets and should prepare study questions or points of discussion ahead of time. If your group decides to meet just before exams, allow enough time to share notes and ideas. Study groups are also a good way to meet new friends.

Get a tutor   Tutoring is not just for students who are failing. Often the best students seek tutorial assistance. Most campus tutoring centers offer their services for free. Ask your academic adviser or counselor or the campus learning center about arranging for tutoring. Many learning centers employ student tutors who have done well in the same courses you are taking. These students might have some good advice on how to prepare for tests given by particular instructors. Often learning centers also have computer tutorials that can help you refresh basic skills. And think about becoming a tutor yourself eventually. Serving as a tutor will greatly deepen your own learning.

Prepare for Math and Science Exams

More than in any other academic areas, your grades in math and science will be determined by your scores on major exams. To pass the course, you must perform well on timed tests. Here are suggestions for getting yourself fully prepared:

Ask about test rules and procedures   Are calculators allowed? Are formula sheets permitted? If not, will any formulas be provided? Will you be required to give definitions? Derive formulas? State and/or prove theorems?

Work as many problems as you can before the test   Practicing with sample problems is the best way to prepare for a problem-solving test.

Practice understanding the precise meaning and requirements of problems   Failure to read problems carefully and to interpret and answer what is asked is the most common mistake for students taking science and math exams.

Prepare in advance to avoid other common mistakes   Errors with parentheses (failing to use them when they are needed, failing to distribute a multiplier) and mistakes with negative signs are common in math-based courses. Pay attention in class to these details so that you don't fall into the typical traps when you are taking the exam.

Study from your outline   In a subject such as anatomy, which requires memorizing technical terms and understanding the relationships among systems, focus your preparation on your study outline.

08

Strategies for Understanding, Remembering, and Studying

The benefits of having a good memory are obvious. In college, your memory will help you retain information and ace tests. After college, the ability to recall names, procedures, presentations, and appointments will save you energy and time and will prevent a lot of embarrassment.

For many college courses, remembering concepts and ideas can be much more important than recalling details and facts. One of your important tasks as a student is to figure out what the instructor really wants you to concentrate on: the big-picture concepts and ideas, and/or the smaller individual facts and details? To embed such ideas in your mind, ask yourself these questions as you review your notes and books:

1. What is the essence of the idea?

2. Why does the idea make sense? What is the logic behind it?

3. How does this idea connect to other ideas in the material?

4. What are some possible arguments against the idea?

Specific Aids to Memory

The human mind has discovered ingenious ways to remember information. Here are some tips that you may find useful as you're trying to sort out the causes of World War I, remember the steps in a chemistry problem, or absorb the complexities of a mathematical formula.

1. **Pay attention to what you're hearing or reading.** This suggestion is perhaps the most basic and the most important. If you are sitting in class thinking about everything except what the professor is saying, your memory doesn't have a chance. If you are reading and you find that your mind is wandering, you're wasting your study time. Force yourself to focus.

2. **"Overlearn" the material.** After you know and think you understand the material you're studying, go over it again to make sure that you'll retain it for a long time. Test yourself or ask someone else to test you. Recite what you're trying to remember aloud in your own words.

3. **Use the Internet.** If you're having trouble remembering what you have learned, Google a keyword, and try to find interesting details that will engage you in learning more about the subject. Many first-year courses cover such a large amount of material that you'll overlook the more interesting information—unless you seek it out and explore it for yourself. As your interest increases, so will your memory.

4. **Be sure you have the big picture.** Whenever you begin a course, make sure that you're clear on what that course will cover. You can talk with someone who has already taken the course, or you can take a brief look at all the reading assignments. Having the big picture will help you understand and remember the details of what you're learning.

5. **Look for connections between your life and what's going on in your courses.** If you look carefully, you'll find many connections between course material and your daily life. Seeing those connections will make your course more interesting and help you remember what you're learning. For example, if you're taking a music theory course and studying chord patterns, listen for those patterns in contemporary music.

6. **Get organized.** If your desk and computer are organized, you'll spend less time trying to remember a file name or where you put a particular document. And as you rewrite your notes, put them in a logical order (either chronological or thematic) that makes sense to you so that you will more easily remember them.

7. **Try to reduce the stressors in your life.** We don't know how much worry or stress causes you to forget, but most people agree that stress can be a distraction. Healthful, stress-reducing activities such as meditating, exercising, and getting enough sleep are especially important.

Review Sheets, Mind Maps, and Other Tools

To prepare for an exam covering large amounts of material, you need to condense the volume of notes and text pages into manageable study units. Review your materials with these questions in mind. Is this one of the key ideas in the chapter or unit? Will I see this on the test? You may prefer to highlight, underline, or annotate the most important ideas, or you may create outlines, lists, or visual maps containing the key ideas.

08

Strategies for Remembering What May Be on the Test

1.	2.	3.	4.
Pay close attention to what your instructors emphasize in class. Take good notes, and learn the material well before your exam. Unless they tell you otherwise, professors are quite likely to stress in-class material on exams.	Review assigned readings before class and again after class, and note any material covered in both the reading assignments and class. You will likely see this material again— on your test.	As you reread your notes, look for repeating ideas, themes, and facts. These are likely to appear on your test.	Think and speak the key concepts and terminology of the course. The more your brain uses these ideas and words, the more you are likely to remember them.

Use your notes to develop review sheets. Make lists of key terms and ideas that you need to remember. Also, do not underestimate the value of using a recall column from your lecture notes to test yourself or others on information presented in class. A recall column is a narrow space on the left side of your notebook paper that you can use to rewrite the ideas from the lecture that you most want to remember (see Figure 5.1 on page 61). A mind map is essentially a review sheet with a visual element. Its word and visual patterns provide you with graphic clues to jog your memory. Because it is visual, the mind map approach helps many students recall information easily.

In addition to review sheets and mind maps, you may want to create flash cards. An advantage of flash cards is that you can keep them in an outside pocket of your backpack and pull them out to study anywhere. With flash cards you can make good use of precious minutes that otherwise might be wasted, such as time spent sitting on the bus or waiting for a friend.

Summaries

Writing summaries of course topics can help you prepare to be tested, especially in essay and short-answer exams. By condensing the main ideas into a concise summary, you store information in your long-term memory so that you can retrieve it to answer an essay question. Here's how to create summaries:

1. Predict a test question from your lecture notes or other resources. Look for instructor clues, such as repetition of an idea or fact.

2. Read the chapter, supplemental articles, notes, or other materials. Underline or mark main ideas as you go, make notations, or outline on a separate sheet of paper

3. Analyze and summarize. What is the purpose of the material? Does it compare, define a concept, or prove an idea? What are the main ideas? How would you explain the material to someone else?

4. Make connections between main points and key supporting details. Reread to identify each main point and supporting evidence. Create an outline to assist you in this process.

5. Select, condense, and order. Review material you have underlined, and write the ideas in your own words. Number what you have underlined or highlighted to put the material in a logical order.

6. Write your ideas precisely in a draft. In the first sentence, state the purpose of your summary. Follow this statement with each main point and its supporting ideas.

7. Review your draft. Read it over, adding missing transitions or insufficient information. Check the logic of your summary.

8. Test your memory. Put your draft away and try to recite the contents of the summary to yourself out loud, or explain it to a study partner who can provide feedback on the information you have omitted.

9. Schedule time to review your summaries, and test your memory shortly before the exam. You may want to review and test yourself with a partner, or you may prefer to review alone.

Taking Tests and Exams

Throughout your college career you will take tests in many different formats, in many subject areas, and with many different types of questions. The chart at the bottom of the page offers test-taking tips that apply to any test situation.

Essay Questions

Some college instructors have a strong preference for essay exams for a simple reason: They promote critical thinking, whereas other types of exams tend to be exercises in memorization. To succeed on essay exams, follow these guidelines.

1. **Budget your exam time.** Quickly survey the entire exam, and note the questions that are the easiest for you, along with their point values. Take a moment to weigh their values, estimate the approximate time you should allot to each question, and write the time beside each item number. Be sure you understand whether you must answer all the questions or choose among questions. Remember that writing profusely on easy questions of low value can be a costly error because it takes up precious time you may need on more important questions. Wear a watch to monitor your time, remembering to include time at the end for a quick review.

2. **Develop a very brief outline of your answer before you begin to write.** First make sure that your outline responds to all parts of the question. Then use your first paragraph to introduce the main points and subsequent paragraphs to describe each point in more depth. If you begin to lose your concentration, you will be glad to have the outline to help you regain your focus. If you find that you are running out of time and cannot complete an essay, at least provide an outline of key ideas. Instructors usually assign points based on your coverage of the main topics from the material. Thus you will usually earn more points by responding to all parts of the question briefly than by addressing just one aspect of the question in detail.

3. **Write concise, organized answers.** Read each question carefully, and pay attention to all its parts. Rather than hastily writing down everything you know on the topic, take the time to organize your thinking and to write a concise, well-structured answer. Instructors downgrade vague or rambling answers.

4. **Know the key task words in essay questions.** The following key task words appear frequently on essay tests: *analyze, compare,*

Successful Test Taking

1.	2.	3.	4.	5.	6.
Write your name on the test (unless directed not to) and on the answer sheet.	**Analyze, ask, and stay calm.** Read all the directions so that you understand what to do. Ask the instructor or exam monitor for clarification if you don't understand something. Be confident. Don't panic.	**Use your time wisely.** Quickly survey the entire test and decide how much time you will spend on each section. Be aware of the point values of different sections of the test.	**Answer the easy questions first.** Expect that you'll be puzzled by some questions. Make a note to come back to them later. If different sections consist of different types of questions (such as multiple-choice, short-answer, and essay), complete the types you are most comfortable with first. Be sure to leave enough time for any essays.	**If you feel yourself starting to panic or go blank, stop whatever you are doing.** Take a long, deep breath and slowly exhale. Remind yourself that you do know the material and can do well on this test. Then take another deep breath. If necessary, go to another section of the test and come back later to the item that triggered your anxiety.	**If you finish early, don't leave.** Stay and check your work for errors. Reread the directions one last time. If you are using a Scantron answer sheet, make sure that all your answers are filled in accurately and completely.

contrast, criticize/critique, define, describe, discuss, evaluate, explain, interpret, justify, narrate, outline, prove, review, summarize, and *trace.* Take time to learn them so that you can answer essay questions accurately and precisely.

Multiple-Choice Questions

Preparing for multiple-choice tests requires you to actively review all of the course material. Reciting from flash cards, summary sheets, mind maps, or the recall column in your lecture notes is a good way to review.

Take advantage of the many cues that multiple-choice questions contain. A careful reading of each item may reveal the correct answer. Always question choices that use absolute words such as *always, never,* and *only.* These choices are often (but not always) incorrect. Also, read carefully

for terms such as *not, except,* and *but* that are introduced before the choices. Often the answer that is the most inclusive is correct.

Some students are easily confused by multiple-choice answers that sound alike. The best way to respond to a multiple-choice question is to read the first part of the question and then predict your own answer before reading the options. Choose the letter that corresponds with the answer that best matches your prediction.

Fill-in-the-Blank Questions

In many ways preparing for fill-in-the-blank questions is similar to getting ready for multiple-choice items, but fill-in-the-blank questions can be harder because you do not have a choice of possible answers right in front of you. Not all fill-in-the-blank questions are constructed the same way. Sometimes you'll see a series of blanks to give you a clue regarding the number of words in the answer, but if just one long blank is provided you cannot assume that the answer is just one word.

True/False Questions

For the statement in a true/false question to be true, every detail of the statement must be true. As in multiple-choice tests, statements containing words such as *always, never,* and *only* tend to be false, whereas less definite terms such as *often* and *frequently* suggest the statement may be true. Read through the entire exam to see if information in one question will help you answer another. Do not second-guess what you know or doubt your answers just because a sequence of questions appears to be all true or all false.

Matching Questions

Matching questions are the hardest to answer by guessing. In one column you will find the terms; in the other, you will see the descriptions of them. Before answering any question, review all of the terms and descriptions. Match those terms you are sure of first. As you do so, cross out both the term and its description, and then use the process of elimination to assist you in answering the remaining items.

try it!

Explore Tutoring on Your Campus

Investigate your institution's options for tutoring. Share what you learn with others in your class. If you are having trouble in a particular course, consider tutoring or other options such as Supplemental Instruction, a form of free group academic support that has definitively been shown to improve student performance and is offered at many colleges and universities.

08

Academic Honesty and Misconduct

Imagine what our world would be like if researchers reported fraudulent results that were then used to develop new machines or medical treatments or to build bridges, airplanes, or subway systems. Integrity is a cornerstone of higher education, and activities that compromise that integrity damage everyone: your country, your community, your college or university, your classmates, and yourself.

Cheating

Institutions vary widely in how they define broad terms such as *lying* or *cheating*. One university defines cheating as "intentionally using or attempting to use unauthorized materials, information, notes, study aids, or other devices . . . [including] unauthorized communication of information during an academic exercise." This would apply to looking over a classmate's shoulder for an answer, using a calculator when it is not authorized, obtaining or discussing an exam (or individual questions from an exam) without permission, copying someone else's lab notes, purchasing term papers over the Internet, watching the video instead of reading the book, and duplicating computer files.

Plagiarism

Plagiarism, or taking another person's ideas or work and presenting them as your own, is especially intolerable in an academic culture. Just as taking someone else's property constitutes physical theft, taking credit for someone else's ideas constitutes intellectual theft.

On most tests, you don't have to credit specific sources. In written reports and papers, however, you must give credit any time you use (a) another person's actual words, (b) another person's ideas or theories—even if you don't quote the person directly, or (c) any other information that is not considered common knowledge.

Many schools prohibit certain other activities besides lying, cheating, unauthorized assistance, and plagiarism. Some examples of prohibited behaviors are intentionally inventing information or results, earning credit more than once for the same piece of academic work without permission, giving your work or exam answers to another student to copy during the actual exam or before that exam is given to another section, and bribing in exchange for any kind of academic advantage.

Most schools also outlaw helping or attempting to help another student commit a dishonest act.

Consequences of Cheating and Plagiarism

Although you might see some students who seem to be getting away with cheating or plagiarizing, the consequences of such behaviors can be severe and life-changing. Recent cases of cheating on examinations and plagiarizing major papers have caused some college students to be suspended or expelled and even to have their college degrees revoked. Writers and journalists whose plagiarism has been discovered, such as Jayson Blair, formerly of the *New York Times,* and Stephen Glass, formerly of the *New Republic,* have lost their jobs and their journalistic careers. Even college presidents have occasionally been guilty of using the words of others in writing and speaking. Such discoveries result not only in embarrassment and shame, but also in lawsuits and criminal actions.

Because plagiarism can be a problem on college campuses, faculty members are now using electronic systems such as **www.turnitin.com** to identify passages in student papers that have been plagiarized. Many instructors routinely check their students' papers to make sure that the writing is original. So even though the temptation to cheat or plagiarize might be strong, the chance of possibly getting a better grade isn't worth misrepresenting yourself or your knowledge and suffering the potential consequences.

08

Reducing the Likelihood of Academic Dishonesty

To avoid becoming intentionally or unintentionally involved in academic misconduct, consider the reasons why it could happen:

- **Ignorance.** In a survey at the University of South Carolina, 20 percent of students incorrectly thought that buying a term paper wasn't cheating. Forty percent thought that using a test file (a collection of actual tests from previous terms) was fair behavior. Sixty percent thought that it was acceptable to get answers from someone who had taken the exam earlier in the same or in a prior term. What do you think?

- **Cultural and campus differences.** In other countries and on some U.S. campuses, students are encouraged to review past exams as practice exercises. Some student government associations maintain test files for use by students. Make sure you know the policy on your specific campus.

- **Different policies among instructors.** Because there is no universal code that dictates such behaviors, ask your instructors for clarification. When a student is caught violating the academic code of a school or instructor, pleading ignorance of the rules is a weak defense.

- **A belief that grades are all that matter.** This might reflect our society's competitive atmosphere. It also might be the result of pressure from parents, peers, or teachers. In truth, grades are nothing if one has cheated to earn them. Even if your grades help you get a job, it is what you have actually learned that will help you keep the job and be promoted. If you haven't learned what you need to know, you won't be ready to work in your chosen field.

- **Lack of preparation or inability to manage time and activities.** If you are tempted to cheat because you are unprepared, ask an instructor to extend a deadline so that a project can be done well.

The following chart outlines some steps you can take to reduce the likelihood of problems:

Guidelines for Academic Honesty

1.	2.	3.
Know the rules. Learn the academic code for your college by going to its Web site. Also learn about any department guidelines on cheating or plagiarism. Study course syllabi. If a teacher does not clarify standards and expectations, ask exactly what they are.	**Set clear boundaries**. Refuse when others ask you to help them cheat. This might be hard to do, but you must say no. In test settings, keep your answers covered and your eyes down, and put all extraneous materials away, including cell phones. Now that cell phones enable text messaging, instructors are rightfully suspicious when they see students looking at their cell phones during an exam.	**Improve time management**. Be well prepared for all quizzes, exams, projects, and papers. This might mean unlearning habits such as procrastination.
4.	5.	6.
Seek help. Find out where you can obtain assistance with study skills, time management, and test taking. If your methods are in good shape but the content of the course is too difficult, consult your instructor, join a study group, or visit your campus learning center or tutorial service.	**Withdraw from the course**. Your institution has a policy about dropping courses and a deadline to drop without penalty. You might decide to drop only the course that's giving you trouble. Some students choose to withdraw from all classes and "stop out" of school if they find themselves in over their heads or if an unexpected emergency has caused them to fall behind. Before withdrawing, you should ask about campus policies as well as ramifications in terms of federal financial aid and other scholarship programs. See your adviser or counselor.	**Reexamine goals**. Stick to your own realistic goals instead of giving in to pressure from family members or friends to achieve impossibly high standards. You might also feel pressure to enter a particular career or profession that is of little or no interest to you. If that happens, sit down with counseling or career services professionals or your academic adviser and explore alternatives.

08 Chapter Review

One-minute paper . . .

As you were reading the tips for improving your performance on exams and tests, were you surprised to see different tips for different subjects, such as math and science, and for different kinds of tests, such as multiple-choice and essay? What did you find to be the most useful information in this chapter? What material was unclear to you?

Applying what you've learned . . .

Now that you have read and discussed this chapter, consider how you can apply what you have learned to your academic and personal life. The following prompts will help you to reflect on the material and its relevance to you both now and in the future.

1. Identify your next upcoming test or exam. What class is it for? When is it scheduled (morning, afternoon, or evening)? What type of test will it be (problem solving, computerized, etc.)? List the specific strategies described in this chapter that will help you prepare for and take this test.

2. Do you know how your institution or your different instructors define cheating or plagiarism? Look up the definition of these terms in your institution's student handbook. Also read about the penalties for students who are dishonest. Then check your syllabi for class-specific guidelines. If you still have questions about what behaviors are and are not acceptable in a particular class, check with your instructors.

Building your portfolio . . .

Promoting academic integrity

Academic integrity is a supreme value on college and university campuses. Faculty members, staff, and students are held to a strict code of academic integrity, and the consequences of breaking that code can be severe and life-changing. Create a Word document to record your responses to the following activity.

1. Imagine that your college or university has hired you to conduct a month-long academic integrity awareness campaign so that students will learn about and take seriously your campus's guidelines for academic integrity. To prepare for your "new job":

    a. Visit your institution's Web site and use the search feature to find the academic integrity code or policy. Take the time to read through the code, violations, and sanctions.

    b. Visit the judicial affairs office on your campus to learn more about the way your institution deals with violations of academic integrity policies.

    c. Research online resources from other campuses, such as information from the Center for Academic Integrity, hosted by Clemson University (**http://www.academicintegrity.org/**). This link describes the university's Fundamental Values Project.

    d. Check out several other college and university academic integrity policies and/or honor codes. How do they compare to your institution's code or policy?

2. Outline your month-long awareness campaign. Here are a few ideas to get you started:

- Plan a new theme every week. Don't forget Internet-related violations.

- Develop eye-catching posters to display around campus (check out the posters designed by students at Elizabethtown College in Pennsylvania, found at **http://www.rubberpaw.com/integrity/**).

- Consider guest speakers, debates, skits, or other presentations.

- Come up with catchy slogans or phrases.

- Send students a postcard highlighting your institution's policies or honor code.

- Consider the most effective ways to communicate your message to different groups on campus.

Academic Integrity Awareness Campaign

Events Plan

Week 1	
Week 2	
Week 3	
Week 4	

3. Consider what you have learned through your research. You might want to share your campaign ideas with other students in your class and even select the best ideas for presentation to your campus student affairs office or judicial board.

4. Save your work in your portfolio on your personal computer or flash drive.

Where to go for help . . .

On Campus

Learning assistance support center: The best students, good students who want to be the best students, and students with academic difficulties use learning centers and tutoring services. These services are offered by both full-time professionals and student tutors.

Counseling services: College and university counseling centers offer a wide array of services, often including workshops and individual or group counseling for test anxiety.

Fellow college students: Keep an eye out for the best students, those who appear to be the most serious, purposeful, and directed. Seek the help of these classmates. Or secure a tutor or join a study group.

Online

The Academic Center for Excellence, University of Illinois at Chicago: http://www.uic.edu/depts/ counselctr/ace/examprep.htm. This Web site provides a list of tips to help you prepare for exams.

Learning Centre of the University of New South Wales in Sydney, Australia: http://www.lc.unsw .edu.au/onlib/exam.html. Includes the popular SQ3R method.

My Institution's Resources

_____
_____
_____
_____
_____
_____
_____
_____
_____

09 Technology in College

Technological ability can vary significantly from person to person, especially in a college or university that brings together people with diverse experiences and ages. In your classrooms, you may be sitting next to someone on your right who created, owns, and runs an online business while the classmate on your left might have no experience in word processing, let alone using e-mail. And that's a good thing to know. It means that there is likely someone in your class who can help you learn something new, as well as someone else who can use your help. So working with technology is a natural way to be both a teacher and a learner, a way to get to know classmates and to become part of the classroom community. Therefore, you should never be afraid to ask a technology question in class, and if you see someone who looks a little stuck, don't be afraid to offer help. Whatever your technological ability at present, your college or university experience is likely to increase it, since technology plays a large role in many aspects of college life. This chapter will give you some practical ways to better understand and use technology while you are in college.

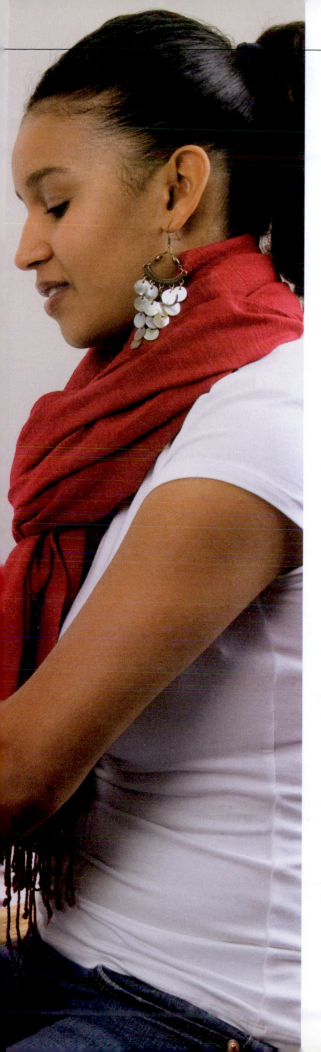

How Do You Measure Up?

1. I am comfortable with technology.
   - ○ Agree
   - ○ Don't Know
   - ○ Disagree

2. Technology has the potential to make college courses more fun and interesting.
   - ○ Agree
   - ○ Don't Know
   - ○ Disagree

3. Being information literate includes using the Internet and the campus library.
   - ○ Agree
   - ○ Don't Know
   - ○ Disagree

4. *Wikipedia* may be a good starting point for more in-depth research.
   - ○ Agree
   - ○ Don't Know
   - ○ Disagree

Review the items you marked "don't know" or "disagree." Paying attention to all these aspects of your college experience can be important to your success. After reading this chapter, come back to this list and think about ways you can work on these areas.

Some Basics of College Technology

Sarah Totten

18-year-old first-year student

On first impression, my teacher seemed to be in some kind of a techno frenzy.

"As I just said, you'll all be expected to participate in a threaded discussion and post comments—we'll use Blackboard and eCollege for that," Professor Montoya was saying. "It's important to join a couple of *Twitter* groups as well. I assume you're all on *Facebook* and use e-mail already?"

Everyone in Introduction to Media Studies nodded in agreement. I nodded, too, even though I only understood the *Facebook* and e-mail part.

"Oh, yes, and you'll need to post a video of yourself on *YouTube.*" She smiled. "You can get creative with that, of course."

I should say something, I thought. Perhaps some of the other students in the class also had some blank spots when it came to technology. As if on cue, the tall guy sitting in front of me turned his head. "Sheesh—I thought we were here to *learn* this stuff," he said. "She expects us to know it already?"

"No kidding," I whispered back. "Somebody stop her before she makes us create our own Web sites."

Before you could say "hyperdrive," Professor Montoya went on. "The whole point of this course is to gain knowledge and skills through multiple learning environments—not just from a book. So, as a final project, each of you will create an original and creative Web site!"

The tall guy turned around completely in his desk and shot me a pointed look. "We better speak up now or abandon ship," I agreed.

Students come to college with varying levels of technological expertise. How should Sarah get the help she needs to become more tech savvy?

Technology plays a vital role in almost every aspect of college. Beyond routine communication, administrative departments use technology in such tasks as admissions, course registration, financial aid, and storage of records and transcripts. Instructors use technology to deliver lectures, assign learning activities, host course discussions, and record and transmit grades. At some colleges, entire degree programs are offered completely online. This chapter presents some basics of college technology and begins with a focus on two practical areas: registering online and managing passwords.

Registering for Courses Online

If you are like most students today, you learned about your college or university through its Web site and perhaps even through forms of social media such as *Facebook*. You might have applied and paid your tuition and fees online, and you might have begun to make contact with current students through e-mail or text messages. You probably registered for your first-term courses online with the help of an academic adviser.

It might be hard to believe, but not so long ago, students used to spend the better part of a day trying to register for their courses. Before each term, students would receive a paper schedule of courses, and then they would all go to a gymnasium or auditorium on the scheduled registration day and wait in long lines to select the courses they wished to take.

Although technology has significantly streamlined the course registration process, there are still steps you have to take and deadlines you have to meet to get the courses you want and need. Before attempting to register online, be sure to talk to your academic adviser or counselor to learn exactly which courses are right for you as well as important procedures and deadlines.

If you are confident that you know where to go online, how to log in, and when to register, it is important to have a strategy. Working with your adviser, use the course schedule or catalog to develop a "plan A," a "plan B," and perhaps a "plan C" in case the classes you need are already filled. By varying the classes, days, and times in each strategy, you will create options if you run into unforeseen class closures or classes that have already been filled.

You should also make sure that you know your institution's drop/add policies. During open registration, you can add or remove courses from your schedule either online or with an adviser. But after the official drop/add deadline, policies about adding or dropping courses are more restrictive. At some institutions students may not be able to add courses after the specific deadline without an "administrative override." Conversely, students wishing to drop a course after the deadline may have to pay the total or partial cost of the course. It is important to make note of all deadlines—those related to registration as well as the drop/add period. Doing so will help you make sure you have registered on time and are able to add courses you need, remove courses you do not want, and do so without penalty.

Although course registration has come a long way from waiting in line with hundreds of other students to make your course selections, today's online systems can't work without the direct involvement of students and their advisers. The personal, face-to-face contact you have with your academic adviser or counselor will help you understand course prerequisites and options and will give you the information you need to navigate your institution's online course registration system successfully.

Managing Usernames and Passwords

As a college student, you might already have a growing collection of usernames and passwords, some of which you acquired even before orientation. If you applied for financial aid, for example, you might have created a username and password for the Free Application for Federal Student Aid (FAFSA) online application. Once on campus, you were probably given a student identification (ID)

number and password and directions for logging into the academic and administrative Web sites.

The number of times you will have to create usernames and passwords may tempt you to use the same ones for every site. But Web security experts warn against reusing this information or making it easy for others to find. Here are some tips that will help you know how to keep your personal information secure and when online security is most important.

1. The more important the information, the "stronger" your password should be. For instance, any sites on which you have financial or personal identity information, such as your social security number, should be protected by a password that has these characteristics:

   a. between eight and fourteen characters

   b. a combination of numbers, uppercase and lowercase letters, and, if the password system permits, special characters such as @ and #

2. Be sure to change the passwords to your online credit card or bank account information frequently, at least once a year.

3. You should also choose a secure password for your social networking sites and course sites where your grades might be available. Your online identity is as important as your online financial information.

4. For Web sites such as a free newspaper site that requires you to register to read articles, a simple password, such as the name of a pet or a family member, will do.

Should you keep a written record of your usernames and passwords? Online security experts warn against keeping this information in writing. But if usernames and passwords are too long or complicated to remember, you may find that you have to write them down and keep them in a secure place.

If you forget an important online password, don't panic. Often you can reset your own passwords, or you can contact a technical support person to have your password e-mailed to you.

09

Learning Management Systems

Many colleges and universities have invested in technology platforms called *course management systems* or *learning management systems* (LMSs). An LMS provides an online space and tools where students and instructors can meet and interact with each other and with course material. One of the reasons that instructors use an LMS in teaching is to enhance people's ability to connect and interact, both in class and out of class.

An LMS does several other things as well. It gives instructors a convenient way to assign and keep track of grades, and its digital drop box gives you a reliable electronic method for turning in assignments. An LMS also makes possible the following activities: online discussion forums, blogs (shared online journals), chat rooms, white boards where you can sketch ideas online that are visible to your classmates, wikis where you and classmates can co-edit written work, and video or audio recordings of lectures and speakers.

Because colleges and universities are still learning how best to integrate technology into the classroom, you might find that LMS use varies from one department or instructor to another. Sometimes the LMS is used only to deliver the syllabus or give the online exams. Other times, an instructor might use the LMS frequently as a platform for discussions, project meetings, quizzes, course readings, and lecture notes.

LMS Use in Different Types of Courses

Face-to-face classes In a traditional face-to-face class, you might use an LMS for submitting homework, doing group projects, participating in discussions, or swapping drafts of essays for review by classmates.

Hybrid or blended courses Although many college classes are still taught in a traditional face-to-face manner, your institution might be offering more hybrid or totally online courses. In a hybrid or blended course, you will have both face-to-face and online meetings supplemented by activities in the LMS. LMS use combined with class meetings will offer you multiple ways to learn and interact with your peers and the material. For example, the instructor may upload reading selections and other information for you to read before class meetings and may also assign an online discussion of readings or other topics through discussion boards instead of during a class period. Face-to-face class meetings might then be used primarily for performances, tests, or presentations on material that has been discussed online.

Online courses In a fully online course the LMS takes the place of the physical classroom, and assignments, communications, and activities are all done online via the LMS. Online courses are becoming an increasingly popular option for students with busy lifestyles who find it more convenient to take courses on their home computer rather than on campus. But you may select an online course for other reasons. Perhaps you are choosing an online course from another institution on a subject not offered at your college or university, or you may discover an online course taught by a particular instructor you have heard about. But since online courses present a number of challenges, be sure you have considered the following questions:

- Does your institution allow on-campus students to take online courses?

- Does your institution offer a self-assessment to help you determine whether an online course is right for you?

- Do you have regular access to the technologies needed for your online course, such as a computer with adequate processing speed and power, a reliable high-speed Internet connection, and the supported Web browser and plug-ins?

- Are you good at managing your time, setting schedules, and working through glitches? Keep in mind that online courses can take more time than a face-to-face course, especially at the start of the course when the system might be new to you.

- Are you comfortable reading online help manuals, directions for assignments, and talking to individuals providing technical support?

Don't leap into an online course without considering whether it is right for you at this time in your life. Be aware of the advantages and disadvantages of online instruction, and seek help from your academic adviser before making a decision.

Tips for Using an LMS

When using an LMS in any class at your college or university, here are some things to keep in mind:

- Learn how to log in. Make sure you know the login instructions and your username and password. At some institutions these are automatically issued to you. At other campuses students may be instructed to enroll in the LMS and create their own username and password. The best source for information on how to get into your LMS is your instructor for the course. Another possible place to locate your LMS login information is your institution's information technology (IT) help desk.

- Log in to your course LMS early and often. It is important to keep in mind that each LMS, instructor, and institution operates a bit differently. Don't assume that what works for one course will work for all of them. Log in the first chance you get to make sure that when it's time to do the work, you can complete it. Never postpone logging in until the day an assignment is due.

- When you are taking an online test through the LMS, ensure that you are in a quiet area that is free from distractions. If you have not already done so, take a practice test so that you are familiar with the testing interface. Many LMSs allow instructors to set their own constraints on exams. For instance, you might or might not be able to look at a prior question; you might not be able to stop, save your responses, and then resume; or you might or might not be able to copy and paste answers or to print questions as you go.

- Learn about online exam rules. Before the exam, you will want to know the exam time limit, the due date, and any navigation restrictions. Ask your instructor, or log in early to read the rules online.

Using an LMS, even with some of the challenges it might present, expands ways of learning. As you enter an LMS, do so with an open mind. Explore the system, be patient, and be prepared for some things to not go as expected or planned. All learning is an experiment and adventure. If you can enjoy the journey, even when the road is a bit rough, you will learn a lot about yourself as a learner and can apply those insights to courses you take in the future.

09

Information Literacy

During the Agricultural Age, most people farmed. Now only a tiny fraction of us work the land, yet edible goods continue to fill our silos, dairy transfer stations, feedlots, and ultimately grocery stores. During the Industrial Age, we made things. We still do, of course, but automation has made it possible for more goods to be produced by fewer people. Now we live in the Information Age, a name that was created to signify the importance of information in today's economy and our lives.

Most of the global workforce is employed in one way or another in creating, managing, or transferring information. The gross national product (GNP) of the United States is substantially information based. Library science is one of the fastest-growing career opportunities. Companies such as Google and Yahoo! have earned billions of dollars by simply offering, organizing, and selling information. Put another way, information has value: You can determine its benefits in dollars, or you can compute the cost of not having it.

The challenge is managing it all. There is more information than ever before, and it doubles at rapidly shortening intervals. Because abundance and electronic access combine to produce enormous amounts of retrievable information, people need highly developed *sorting skills* to cope. Information literacy is the premier survival skill for the modern world.

What is information literacy? Simply put, it's the ability to find, interpret, and use information to meet your needs. Information literacy has many facets, among them the following:

- **Computer literacy**. Facility with electronic tools, both for conducting inquiries and for presenting to others what you have found and analyzed.
- **Media literacy**. The ability to think critically about material distributed to a wide audience through television, film, advertising, radio, magazines, books, and the Internet.
- **Cultural literacy**. Knowing what has gone on and is going on around you. You have to understand the difference between the Civil War and the Revolutionary War, U2 and *YouTube*, Eminem and M&Ms, or you will not understand everyday conversation.

Information matters. It helps empower people to make good choices. The choices people make often determine their success in business, their happiness as friends and family members, and their well-being as citizens on this planet.

Learning to Be Information Literate

People marvel at the information explosion, paper inflation, and the Internet. Many confuse mounds of information with knowledge and conclude that they are informed or can easily become informed. But most of us are unprepared for the huge number of available sources and the unsorted, unevaluated mass of information that pours over us at the press of a button. What, then, is the antidote for information overload? To become an informed and successful user of information, keep three basic goals in mind:

1. **Know how to find the information you need**. If you are sick, you need to know where to seek medical help. If you lose your scholarship, you need to know where to get financial assistance. If you want to win a lawsuit, you need to know how to find the outcomes of similar cases. Once you have determined where to look for information, you'll need to ask

try it!

Your Sources for News and Information

Working with a small group of your classmates, list all the sources you use for news and information. Which rely on the Internet and which do not? What are the advantages or disadvantages of relying only on the Internet for gathering information?

09

good questions and to make educated searches of information systems, such as the Internet, libraries, and databases. You'll also want to cultivate relationships with information professionals, such as librarians, who can help you frame questions, broaden and narrow searches, and retrieve the information you need.

2. **Learn how to interpret the information you find**. It is very important to retrieve information. It is even more important to make sense of that information. What does the information mean? Have you selected a source you can understand? Is the information accurate? Is the source reliable?

3. **Have a purpose**. Even the best information will not do much good if you don't know what to do with it. True, sometimes you will hunt down a fact simply for your own satisfaction. More often, you will communicate what you've learned to someone else. You should know not only what form that communication will take—a research paper for a class, a proposal for your boss, a presentation at a hearing—but also what you want to accomplish. Will you use the information to make a decision, develop a new solution to a problem, influence a course of action, prove a point, or something else?

Employing Information Literacy Skills

By the time you graduate, you should have attained a level of information literacy that will carry you through your professional life. The Association of College and Research Libraries has developed the following best practices for the information-literate student. Learn how to apply them, and you'll do well no matter where your educational and career paths take you.

- **Determine the nature and extent of the information needed**. In general, this involves first defining and articulating what information you need, then identifying a variety of potential sources.

- **Access information effectively and efficiently**. Select the most appropriate research methods, use well-designed search strategies, refine those strategies along the way, and keep organized notes on what you find and where you found it.

- **Evaluate information and its sources critically**. As an information-literate person, you will be able to apply criteria for judging the usefulness and reliability of both information and its sources. You will also become skilled at summarizing the main ideas presented by others and comparing new information with what you already know.

- **Incorporate information into your knowledge base and value system**. To do this, you will determine what information is new, unique, or contradictory and consider whether it has an impact on what is important to you. You will also validate, understand, or interpret the information through talking with other people. Finally, you will combine elements of different ideas to construct new concepts of your own making.

- **Use information effectively to accomplish a specific purpose**. You will apply information to planning and creating a particular product or performance, revising the development process as necessary, and communicating the results to others.

- **Access and use information ethically and legally**. There are economic, legal, and social issues surrounding the retrieval and use of information. You will need to understand and follow laws, regulations, institutional policies, and etiquette related to copyright and intellectual property. Most important, you should acknowledge the use of information from sources in everything you write, record, or broadcast.[1]

---

[1] Adapted from *Information Literacy Competency Standards for Higher Education* (2000). http://www.ala.org/ala/acrl/acrlstandards/standards.pdf.

09

Electronic Research

To discover good information that is useful for your coursework, you will be expected to conduct research. Although students still use the library, especially to discover sources not available online, connections to the Web through search engines and online databases have made electronic research much more common for today's student. However, if not done properly, electronic research could lead you to a source that is not credible or accurate.

Electronic Resources

Online catalogs, periodical databases, and the World Wide Web allow you to locate materials in the vast universe of information. Learning how to use these resources efficiently will save you time and improve your odds of finding the information that best suits your needs.

Library catalogs   The card catalogs that were once common in libraries have been replaced by OPACs (online public access catalogs). These electronic catalogs tell you what books, magazines, newspapers, videos, and other materials are available in a particular library. They might also provide abstracts of the information presented in those materials, tables of contents for individual entries, and related search terms.

You can search the catalogs through terminals at the library or from your home computer or a laptop. The simplest way to search a catalog is by key word. You might also search by subject, author, title, date, or a combination of these elements. Be sure to spend a few minutes on the catalog's help or FAQ page, which will guide you through the options and demonstrate ways to customize your search terms. Each system has its own preferences.

Periodical databases   Periodical databases let you hunt down articles published in hundreds (even thousands) of newspapers, magazines, and scholarly journals. Some databases might provide a full text copy of the article as part of the record returned from your search; other times you'll have to use the information in the record to find a physical copy in your library or request it through interlibrary loan.

Subscription services such as EBSCOHost, Lexis-Nexis, and Gale Research compile and maintain

electronic periodical databases. These are not free to the general public and must be accessed through a library. (Ask at the circulation desk for a barcode number and PIN, which will allow you to access your library's databases from remote terminals.) Most libraries subscribe to multiple databases and subdivide them by broad general categories such as Humanities, Social Sciences, Science and Technology, Business, Health and Medicine, Government Information, or by major.

Databases have their own specialties and different strengths, so you'll want to select the best ones for your particular subject or topic. Check your library's subscription list for an overview of what's available, and don't hesitate to ask a librarian to make recommendations about which databases are most relevant to your needs.

Information in a database is usually stored in a single location or on a server that is owned by the subscription service company. Human beings, not computers, do the indexing, so you can be fairly sure the information in a database meets certain criteria for inclusion, such as accuracy, timeliness, and authoritativeness. And because most of the material indexed in a database originally appeared in print, you can be fairly certain that it was reviewed for quality by other scholars or an editorial staff.

The Web Contrary to popular belief, electronic research does not mean simply using Google. The material retrieved by Googling is an aggregation of information, opinion, and sales pitches from the vast universe of servers around the globe. Anybody can put up a Web site, which means you can't be sure of the Web site owner's credibility and reliability. The sources you find on the Web might be written by anyone—a fifth grader, a distinguished professor, a professional society, or a biased advocate.

A recent Google search on the subject "political corruption," for instance, generated over 10 million hits. The first page yielded some interesting results:

- A collection of links on politics and political corruption
- A Libertarian Party legislative program on political corruption
- Two *Amazon.com* ads
- A site that offers "research" on gambling and political corruption
- A university site offering research on political corruption in Illinois

These varied results demonstrate that one must be alert when examining Internet sources. Mixed in with credible scholarship on this topic are sales promotions, some arguments against gambling, and useful links to other sources. It isn't always easy to evaluate the quality of Internet sources.

Electronic research does not mean *Wikipedia* either. *Wiki* is a Hawaiian word for "quick," and that is exactly what *Wikipedia* is—a quick reference encyclopedia. Opinions of *Wikipedia* vary. Some scholars and professors like it and some hate it. You will likely encounter both over the course of your education. *Wikipedia*'s plethora of information can be added to by any individual connected to the Web. While today *Wikipedia* has more editors and writers correcting and analyzing user-added information, there is still the possibility of incomplete information and unidentified inaccuracies. Therefore, you might consider using *Wikipedia* as a springboard into broader electronic research, but not a one-stop-shop. Explore the reference links at the end of a *Wikipedia* article

Evaluating Electronic Sources

Although online research is becoming the norm, it is still important to be especially cautious when conducting research online. It is often difficult to tell where something on the Internet came from or who wrote it. The lack of this information can make it very difficult to judge the credibility of the source. And while an editorial board reviews most printmatter (books, articles, and so forth) for accuracy and overall quality, it's frequently difficult to confirm that the same is true for information on a Web site—with some exceptions. If you are searching through an online database such as the Human Genome Database or Eldis: The Gateway to Development Information (a poverty database), it is highly likely that documents in these collections have been reviewed. Online versions of print magazines and journals, likewise, have usually been checked out by editors. And information from academic and government Web sites (those whose URLs end in .edu or .gov, respectively) is generally—but not always—trustworthy.

try it!

Contribute to Wikipedia

Working with your classmates, create a *Wikipedia* entry on a topic you know something about. Check your entry throughout the term to see if anyone else changes, deletes, or adds to it. Discuss the advantages and disadvantages of a system like *Wikipedia*.

09

09 Chapter Review

One-minute paper . . .

Chapter 9 explores the many ways technology can be utilized on a college campus. Take a minute to think about and note what you found most helpful or meaningful in this chapter. Do you still have questions about how to use technology at your institution?

Applying what you've learned . . .

Now that you have read and discussed this chapter, consider how you can apply what you have learned to your academic and personal life. The following prompts will help you reflect on chapter material and its relevance to you both now and in the future.

1. How would you rate your own comfort level with technology? What knowledge or skills do you still need to do well in college?

2. Think about how you learn best. Do you enjoy online classes, or do you prefer a traditional classroom? What personal characteristics or learning styles might account for your preferences?

Building your portfolio . . .

The future is now

If one thing is certain, it is that changes in technology will continue to be powerful and swift. As noted in this chapter, not so long ago students were standing in line outside the college gymnasium waiting for their turn to register for classes. Now, most institutions have an online registration system. And, until recent years, professors wouldn't have dreamed of delivering a course online. But today you can take online courses from many colleges and universities around the world. Technology continually changes the way we participate in higher education opportunities. How do you think educational technology might change over the next twenty years?

1. Imagine you are in a college classroom in the year 2030. Describe the setting. Be creative and consider possibilities that seem unfathomable now. Is the classroom virtual, or is it on a college campus? Are you sitting next to other students, or are the students in your class somewhere else? How are students communicating with each other, and how is information shared? In 300 to 500 words, describe your vision of how new technology will guide educational practices in the future.

2. Discuss the potential advantages and disadvantages of the technological era you described.

3. Using one of your current social media outlets (e.g., *Facebook* or *Twitter*) or your institution's LMS, start an online discussion about how technology might change by 2030. Share your predictions with your classmates, and ask them what they think the technological landscape in colleges and universities will look like twenty years from now.

Where to go for help . . .

On Campus

The IT desk or center: Most institutions will have a special help desk or office dedicated to providing help with technology.

Your academic adviser: This person is your best source for information on course registration procedures.

Librarians: Today's college librarians are experts at helping you discover the kinds of electronic resources you need.

Student computer assistants: Many colleges and universities hire tech-savvy students to staff campus computer labs.

Your instructors: While not all instructors will be experts in technology, they will know how to get you started and where to refer you for additional help.

My Institution's Resources

_____

_____

_____

_____

_____

_____

_____

10 Managing Money

Like it or not, we can't ignore the importance of money. Money is often symbolically and realistically the key ingredient to independence and, some people conclude, even to a sense of freedom. You probably know of instances in which money divided a family or a relationship or seemed to drive someone's life in a direction that person would not have taken otherwise. Money can also affect your specific academic goals, causing you to select or reject certain academic majors or degree plans.

Although your primary goal in college should be a strong academic record, the need for money can be a significant distraction, making it more difficult to complete your degree. Educators recognize that not understanding personal finances can hinder a student's progress, and mandatory personal finance classes are now being added in high schools and are available as options at some colleges. The purpose of this chapter is to provide basic information and suggestions so that money will not be a barrier to your success in college. Think of this chapter as a summary of needed financial skills; if you want more information, consider taking a personal finance class at your college or in your community.

How Do You Measure Up?

1. My budget guides how much money I spend each month.
   - ○ Agree
   - ○ Don't Know
   - ○ Disagree

2. I know how many courses I have to take to receive or maintain financial aid.
   - ○ Agree
   - ○ Don't Know
   - ○ Disagree

3. I understand the disadvantages of working too many hours a week off campus.
   - ○ Agree
   - ○ Don't Know
   - ○ Disagree

4. I am working to build a good credit score while I'm in college.
   - ○ Agree
   - ○ Don't Know
   - ○ Disagree

Review the items you marked "don't know" or "disagree." Paying attention to all these aspects of your college experience can be important to your success. After reading this chapter, come back to this list and think about ways you can work on these areas.

Living on a Budget

Jeff Zisa

College junior

My first two years at college, it was easy to figure out my budget, so many of my expenses were fixed. But this year, I have a car and an off-campus apartment, so I decided to get off the meal plan and buy my own food.

"This is a bad idea," said my mother when I told her the plan. "What are you going to eat?"

"Stuff I cook," I said. "It'll be cheaper in the long run. All my roommates and I are taking turns."

We did take turns, for the first week or so. Sam made pizza. Nick made burritos. I made my famous spaghetti. Occasionally, we made more pizza or spaghetti. Then classes started and sports and clubs kicked in, and I guess no one really had time to go to the grocery store anymore. In fact, it was hard to even eat a bowl of cereal in the morning because we were always out of milk. It got to the point where we ate out all the time, and even the cheapest meal out costs $10. So within months, I had to call my parents and tell them I'd maxed out my credit card, drained my bank account, and run up over $200 in penalty charges—all on food.

"I know I should have kept track of what I was spending," I admitted. "It just added up so fast."

"See there?" my mother said. "You wanted a painful lesson." An ominous pause followed. "So . . . what kind of job are you planning to get?"

Why is it so important to track your spending in college? What steps could Jeff take to manage his money more carefully?

Creating a Budget

A budget will condition you to live within your means, put money into savings, and possibly invest down the road. Here are a few tips to help you get started.

Step 1. Gather basic information To create an effective budget, you need to learn more about your income and your spending behaviors.

First, determine how much money is coming in and when. Sources of income might include a job, your savings, gifts from relatives, student loans, scholarship dollars, or grants. Write them all down, making note of how often you receive each type of income (weekly paychecks, quarterly loan disbursements, one-time gifts, and so forth) and how much money you can expect each time.

To determine where your money is going and when, track your spending for a week or two (or, even better, a full month) by recording every bill you pay and every purchase you make. It might surprise you to learn how much money you spend on coffee, bagels, and other incidentals. This information will help you to better understand your spending behaviors and where you might be able to cut costs in the future.

Step 2. Build a plan Use the information you gathered in step 1 to set up three columns: one for expense categories, one for expected expenses, and one for actual expenses. Table 10.1 is an example of such a plan. Knowing when your money is coming in will help you decide how to structure your budget. For example, if most of your income comes in on a monthly basis, you'll want to create a monthly budget. If you are paid every other week, a biweekly budget might work better.

Be sure to recognize which expenses are fixed and which are variable. A *fixed expense* is one that will be the same amount every time you pay it. For example, your rent is a fixed expense because you owe your landlord the same amount each month. A *variable expense* is one that may change. Your textbooks are a variable expense because the number and amount you have to pay will be different each term.

Although you will know, more or less, how much your fixed expenses will be during each budget period, you might need to estimate your variable

Table 10.1 Sample Budget

Expense Category	Expected Expense	Actual Expense
Rent	$500	$500
Electric	$50	$47
Gas (heat)	$75	$75
Cell phone	$45	$50
Water	$15	$12
Gas	$40	$45
Groceries	$150	$135
Dining out	$50	$40
Books	$200	$170
Misc.	$100	$120
Total	**$1,225**	**$1,194**

expenses in your expected expenses column. Use past bills, checking account statements, and spending behaviors from your tracking in step 1 to create an educated guess for your expected expenses in the variable categories. When you are in doubt, it is always better to overestimate your expenses to avoid shortfalls at the end of your budget period.

Step 3. Do a test run   Use your budget plan from step 2 for a few weeks and see how things go, recording your actual expenses as you pay them. Don't be surprised to see differences between your expected and actual expense columns; budgeting is not an exact science, and you will likely never see a perfect match between these two columns. It might be wise to add a "miscellaneous" category for those unexpected and added expenses throughout the budget period.

Step 4. Make adjustments   Although your budget might never be perfect, you can strive to improve it. Are there areas in which you spent much more or much less than expected? Do you need to reallocate funds to better meet the needs of your current situation? Be realistic and thoughtful in how you spend your money, and use your budget to help meet your goals, such as planning for a trip or getting a new pair of jeans. Whatever you do, do not give up if your bottom line doesn't end up the way you expected it would.

Cutting Costs

Once you have put together a working budget, have tried it out, and have adjusted it, you're likely to discover that your expenses still exceed your income. Don't panic. Simply begin to look for ways to reduce those expenses. Here are some tips for saving money in college:

Recognize the difference between your needs and your wants   A *need* is something you must have. For example, tuition and textbooks are considered *needs*. On the other hand, your *wants* are goods, services, or experiences that you wish to purchase but could reasonably live without. For example, concert tickets and mochas are *wants*. Your budget should always provide for your *needs* first.

Share expenses   Having a roommate (or several) can be one of the easiest ways to cut costs on a regular basis. In exchange for giving up a little bit of privacy, you'll save hundreds of dollars on rent, utilities, and food. Make sure, however, that you work out a plan for sharing expenses equally and that everyone accepts his or her responsibilities.

Use low-cost transportation   If you live close to campus, consider whether or not you need a car. Take advantage of lower-cost options such as public transportation or biking to class to save money on gasoline and parking. If you live farther away, check to see whether your institution hosts a ride-sharing program for commuter students, or carpool with someone in your area.

Seek out discount entertainment options   Take advantage of discounted or free programming through your college. Most institutions use a portion of their student fees to provide affordable entertainment options such as discounted or free tickets to concerts, movie theaters, sporting events, or other special events.

Embrace secondhand goods   Use online resources such as *Craigslist* and thrift stores such as Goodwill to expand your wardrobe, purchase extras such as games and sports equipment, or furnish and decorate your room, apartment, or house.

Avoid unnecessary fees   Making late payments on credit cards and other bills can lead to expensive fees and can lower your credit score (which in turn will raise your interest rates). You might want to set up online, automatic payments to avoid making this costly mistake.

10

Getting Financial Aid

Few students can pay the costs of college tuition, fees, books, room and board, bills, and random expenses without some kind of help. Luckily, several sources of financial aid, including some you might not know about, are available to help cover your costs.

Types of Aid

Financial aid seems complex because it can come from so many different sources. Each source may have different rules about how to receive the money and how not to lose it. The financial aid staff at your college can help you find the way to get the largest amount of money that doesn't need to be repaid, the lowest interest rate on loans, and work possibilities that fit your academic program. Do not overlook this valuable campus resource. The financial aid office and its Web site are the best places to begin looking for all types of assistance. Other organizations that can help students to find the right college and money to help them attend are located across the United States. Many of these organizations are members of the National College Access Network or participate in a national effort called Know How to Go. Check their Web sites at **http://www.collegeaccess .org/accessprogramdirectory** and **http://www .knowhow2go.org**. Most students need some type of financial assistance to complete college. It is rare for students to cover all college expenses with only scholarships. The majority of students pay for college through a combination of various types of financial assistance: scholarships, grants, loans, and paid employment. Financial aid professionals refer to this combination as a "package."

While scholarships and grants are unquestionably the best forms of aid because they do not have to be repaid, the federal government, states, and colleges offer many other forms of assistance, such as loans, work-study opportunities, and cooperative education. You might also be able to obtain funds from your employer, a local organization, or a private group.

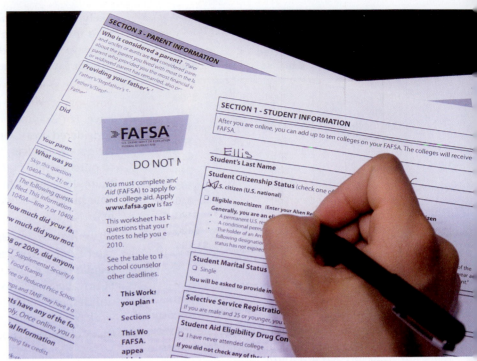

- **Need-based scholarships** are based on both a talent and financial need. "Talent" can be past accomplishments in the arts or athletics, your potential for future accomplishments, or even where you are from. Some colleges and universities want to admit students from other states or countries. "Need" in this context means the cost of college minus a federal determination of what you and your family can afford to contribute toward those costs. Your institution might provide scholarships from its own resources or from individual donors. Donors themselves sometimes stipulate the characteristics of scholarship recipients, such as age or academic major.

- **Merit scholarships** are based on talent as defined above but do not require you to demonstrate financial need. It can be challenging to match your talent with merit scholarships. Most of them come through colleges and are part of the admissions and financial aid processes, usually described on the college's Web site. Web-based scholarship search services are another good source to explore. Be certain the Web site you use is free, will keep your information confidential unless you release your name, and will send you a notice (usually through e-mail) when a new scholarship that matches your qualifications is posted. Also be sure to ask your employer, your family's employers, and social, community, or religious organizations about any available scholarships.

- **Grants** are based on financial need but, like scholarships, do not have to be repaid. Grants are awarded by the federal government and state government and by institutions themselves. Students meet academic qualifications for grants by being admitted to the college and maintaining grades that are acceptable to the grant provider.

- **Work-study** jobs are reserved for students with financial need. Students receive work-study notices as part of the overall financial aid notice and then can sign up to be interviewed for work-study jobs. Although some work-study jobs can be relatively menial, the best options provide experience related to your academic studies while allowing you to earn money for college. The salary is based on the skill required for a particular position and the hours involved. Keep in mind that you will be expected to accomplish specific tasks while on duty, although some employers might permit you to study during any down-time.

- **Cooperative (co-op) education** allows you to alternate a term of study (a semester or quarter) with a term of paid work. Engineering co-op opportunities are among the most common, and the number of co-op programs in health care fields is growing. Colleges make information about co-ops available through admissions and academic departments.

Qualifying for Aid

Most financial assistance requires some form of application. The application used most often is the Free Application for Federal Student Aid (FAFSA). All students should complete the FAFSA by the earliest deadline of the colleges they are considering. Additional forms, such as the College Board's Profile form and scholarship applications, might also be required and will be listed in colleges' financial aid or admissions materials or by organizations that offer scholarships.

The list on page 127 outlines the steps you must take to qualify for most scholarships and grants, especially those sponsored by federal or state governments. The amount of financial aid you receive will depend on the cost of your academic program and what you or your family can pay as determined by FAFSA. Cost includes average expenses for tuition and fees, books and supplies, room and board, transportation, and personal expenses. The financial aid office will subtract from the cost the amount you and your family are expected to pay. In some cases that amount can be as little as zero. Financial aid is designed to make up as much of the balance or "need" as possible.

How to Avoid Losing Your Funding

If you earn average or better grades, complete your courses each term, and finish your program or degree on time, you should have no trouble maintaining your financial aid. It's a good idea to check with the financial aid office before you drop classes to make sure you will not lose any aid.

Some types of aid, especially scholarships, require that you maintain full-time enrollment and make satisfactory academic progress. Dropping or failing a class might jeopardize all or part of your financial aid unless you are enrolled in more credits than the minimum required for financial aid. Talk with a financial aid counselor before making the decision to drop a course.

10

try it!

Saving Money

What are some ways you have found to cut costs and save money for the things you most need or want to do? Share your strategies for saving money with the other students in your class.

Remember that although the financial aid office is there to serve you, you must take the following steps to be your own advocate.

- **File for financial aid every year.** Even if you don't think you will receive aid for a certain year, you must file annually in case you become eligible in the future.

- **Meet all filing deadlines.** Students who do not meet filing deadlines risk losing aid from one year to the next.

- **Talk with a financial aid officer immediately if you or your family experiences a significant loss** (such as loss of a job or death of a parent or spouse). Don't wait for the next filing period; you might be eligible for funds for the current year.

- **Inquire every year about criteria-based aid.** Many colleges and universities have grants and scholarships for students who meet specific criteria. These might include grants for minority students, grants for students in specific academic majors, and grants for students of single parents.

- **Inquire about campus jobs throughout the year**, as these jobs are not available just at the beginning of the term. If you do not have a job and want or need to work, keep asking.

- **Consider asking for a reassessment of your eligibility for aid**. If you have reviewed your financial aid package and think that your circumstances deserve additional consideration, you can ask the financial aid office to reassess your eligibility. The office is not always required to do so, but the request might be worth your effort.

10

Steps to Qualify for Financial Aid

1.
Enroll half-time or more in a certificate or degree program at one of the more than 4,500 institutions that are certified to distribute federal financial aid. A few aid programs are available for less than half-time study; check with your department or college to see what your options are.

2.
Complete the FAFSA. The first FAFSA you file is intimidating, especially if you rush to complete it right before the deadline. Completing the FAFSA in subsequent years is easier because you only need to update items that have changed. To make the process easier, get your personal identification number (PIN) a few weeks before the deadline. This PIN will be the same one you'll use throughout your college career. Try to do the form in sections rather than tackling all of it at once. Most of the information is basic: name, address, driver's license number, and things you will know or have in your personal files and records. For many undergraduates the financial section will require your own and your parents' information from tax materials. If you are at least twenty-four years of age, married, a veteran, or have dependents of your own, your tax information and that for your spouse will be needed.

3.
If your school or award-granting organization requires it, complete the College Board Profile form. Review your college's admission information, or ask a financial aid adviser to determine if this applies to you.

4.
Identify any additional applications that are required. These are usually scholarship applications with personal statements or short essays. The organizations, including colleges, that are giving the money will provide instructions about what is required. Most have Web sites with complete information.

5.
Follow all instructions carefully, and submit each application on time. Financial aid is awarded from a fixed pool of funds. When money has been awarded, there is usually none left for those who file late.

6.
Complete the classes for which you were given financial aid with at least a minimum grade point average as defined by your academic department or college or the organization that provided you the scholarship.

10

Achieving a Balance between Working and Borrowing

After determining your budget, deciding what you can pay from savings (if any), and taking your scholarships and grants into consideration, you might still need additional income. Each term or year, you should decide how much you can work while maintaining good grades and how much you should borrow from student loans.

Advantages and Disadvantages of Working

Paid employment while you are in college can be important for reasons other than money. Having a job in a field related to your major can help you develop a credential for graduate school and make you more employable later because it shows you have the capability to manage several priorities at the same time. Work can help you determine whether a particular career is what you will really want after you complete your education. And students who work a moderate amount (15 hours per week) typically get better grades than students who do not work at all.

On the other hand, it's almost impossible to get great grades if you work full-time while trying to be a full-time student. Some students prefer not to take a job during their first year in college while they're making adjustments to a new academic environment. You might find that you're able to work some terms while you are a student but not others. And family obligations or challenging classes can sometimes make the added burden of work impractical or impossible.

The majority of students today find that a combination of working and borrowing is the best way to gain experience, finance college, and complete their educational goals on time.

While you might get lucky and find a part-time job off campus that relates to your major or career plan, those jobs are hard to come by. You will likely find that most part-time employment is unrelated to your career objectives. A better option for you might be to seek a job on campus. Students who work on campus develop relationships with instructors and staff members who can help them negotiate the academic and social sides of campus life and make plans for the future. While off-campus employers are often unwilling to allow their student employees time off for study and exam preparation, college employers will want you to put your studies and exam preparation first. The only downside to on-campus employment is that you may not make as much money as you would in an off-campus job. But if success in college is your most important objective, the advantages of working on campus may far outweigh the possible monetary disadvantage.

Student Loans

Although you should be careful not to borrow yourself into a lifetime of debt, avoiding loans altogether could delay your graduation and your progress up the career ladder. For most students, some level of borrowing is both necessary and prudent.

try it!

Working on or off Campus

Working with others in your class, investigate what on-campus jobs are available for students as well as part-time off-campus job opportunities. Rate the hourly wages of different jobs from highest to lowest and the working conditions from best to worst. Share your perspectives in class about the advantages and disadvantages of working on campus versus off campus.

The following list provides information about the most common types of student loans. The list reflects the order in which you should apply for and accept loans to get the lowest interest rates and best repayment terms.

- **Subsidized federal student loans** are backed by the government, with interest paid on your behalf while you are enrolled in undergraduate, graduate, or professional school. These loans require at least half-time enrollment and a submitted FAFSA application.

- **Unsubsidized federal student loans** may require that you make interest payments while you are enrolled. If not, the interest is added to the amount you owe, called "capitalization."

- **Parent Loan for Undergraduate Students (PLUS) loans** are applied for and owed by parents but disbursed directly to students. Interest is usually higher than that on federal student loans but lower than that on private loans. Parents who apply must provide information on the FAFSA.

- **Private student loans** are offered through banks and credit unions. Private loans often have stricter credit requirements and higher interest rates than federal loans do, and interest payments on private loans begin immediately.

Student loans are a very important source of money for college, but like paid employment, loans should be considered carefully. Loans for costs such as books and tuition are good investments. Loans for a more lavish lifestyle are likely to weigh you down in the future. As one wise person put it, if by borrowing you live like a wealthy graduate while you're a student, you'll live like a student after you graduate. Student loans can be a good way to begin using credit wisely, a skill you are likely to need throughout your life.

Plan for the Future

It's never too early to begin thinking about how you will finance your life after graduation and whether you will begin working immediately or pursue a graduate or professional degree. Your work, whether on or off campus, will help you make that decision. Here are some tips that will help you plan now for your future.

- Begin considering your next step, whether that is additional education or work. If you are working on campus, get to know faculty or staff members and seek their advice about your future plans. If you are working off campus, think carefully about whether your current job is one that you would want to continue after you graduate. If not, keep your options open and look for part-time work in a field that more closely aligns with your career plans or long-term educational objectives.

- Make sure to keep your address current with the registrar even when you have finished your degree or program and especially if you stop classes for a term. This is doubly important if you have student loans so you do not get a negative report on your credit rating because you missed information about your loan.

- Establish a savings account and add to it regularly, even if you can manage only a few dollars a month. The sooner you start, the greater your returns will be.

Your education is the most productive investment you can make for your own future and that of your family. Research shows that completion of programs or degrees after high school increases earnings, opens up career options, leads to greater satisfaction in work, results in more engaged citizenship such as voting and community service, and greatly increases the probability that your children will go on to college. Although college is a big investment of time and money, it's an investment you'll be glad you made.

10

Managing Credit Wisely

When you graduate, you will leave your institution with two significant numbers. The first is your grade point average (GPA), which represents the level of academic success you attained while in college. The second, your credit score, is a numerical representation of your fiscal responsibility. Although this second number might be less familiar to you, it could be the deciding factor that determines whether you get your dream job, regardless of your GPA. And twenty years from now, you're likely to have forgotten your GPA, while your credit score will be more important than ever.

Your credit score is derived from a credit report that contains information about accounts in your name. These accounts include credit cards, student loans, utility bills, cell phones, and car loans, to name a few. This credit score can determine whether or not you will qualify for a loan (car, home, student, etc.), what interest rates you will pay, how much your car insurance will cost, and your chances of being hired by some organizations. Even if none of these things is in your immediate future, now is the time to start thinking about your credit score.

While using credit cards responsibly is a good way to build credit, acquiring a credit card has become much more difficult for many college students. In May 2009, President Obama signed legislation that prohibits college students under the age of twenty-one from obtaining a credit card unless they can prove they are able to make the payments or the credit card application is cosigned by a parent or guardian.

Understanding Credit

Even if you can prove you have the means to repay credit card debt, it is important for you to thoroughly understand how credit cards work and how they can both help and hurt you. Simply put, a credit card allows you to buy something now and pay for it later. Each month you will receive a statement listing all purchases you made using your credit card during the previous thirty days. The statement will request a payment toward your balance and will set a payment due date. Your payment options will vary: You can pay your entire balance, pay a specified amount of the balance, or pay only a minimum payment, which may be as low as $10.

But beware: If you make only a minimum payment, the remaining balance on your card will be charged a finance fee, or interest charge, causing your balance to increase before your next bill arrives even if you don't make any more purchases. Paying the minimum payment is almost never a good strategy and can add years to your repayment time. In fact, if you continue to pay only $10 per month toward a $500 credit card balance, it will take you more than seven years to pay it off! And assuming an 18 percent interest rate, you'll pay an extra $431 in interest—almost doubling the total amount you'll pay.

Avoid making late payments. Paying your bill even one day late can result in a finance charge of up to $30; it can also raise the interest rate not only on that card but also on any other credit accounts you have. If you decide to use a credit card to build credit, you might want to set up online, automatic payments to avoid incurring expensive late fees. Remember that the payment due date is the date the payment should be received by the credit card lender, not the date you send it.

If you decide to apply for a credit card while you're in college, remember that credit cards should be used to build credit and for emergencies. They should not be used to fund a lifestyle you cannot otherwise afford or to buy wants (see

10

the section on budgeting earlier in this chapter). On the other hand, if you use your credit card just once a month and pay the balance as soon as the bill arrives, you will be on your way to a strong credit score in just a few years.

Frequently Asked Questions about Credit Cards

Here are some answers to the most common questions college students have about credit cards:

- **I have a credit card with my name on it, but it is actually my parents' account number. Is this card building credit for me?** No. You are considered an authorized user on the account, but your parents are the primary account holders. To build credit, you must be the primary account holder or at least a joint account holder.

- **I choose the "credit" option every time I use my debit card. Is this building credit for me?** No. Using the credit function of your debit card is more like an electronic check because it is still taking money directly out of your checking account. Even if your debit card has a major credit card (Visa, MasterCard, etc.) logo on it, it is not building credit for you.

- **I have a few store credit cards (Target, Best Buy, etc.). Are these accounts included on my credit report?** Yes. Although they will affect your credit score, they do not carry as much weight as major credit cards (Visa, MasterCard, etc.). It is okay to have a few store credit cards, but a major credit card will do more to help you build credit.

- **Where can I apply for a major credit card?** A good place to begin is your bank or credit union. Remember that you might have to prove your ability to make payments in order to obtain a card.

- **If one credit card will help me build credit, will several build my credit even more?** Research shows that there is no benefit to having more than two major credit cards. And even if you're able to pay the required monthly amounts, having too many accounts open can make you appear risky to the credit bureaus determining your credit score.

- **What if I forget and make a late payment? Is my credit score ruined?** Your credit report reflects at least the past seven years of activity but puts the most emphasis on the most recent two years. In other words, the farther you get from your mistakes, the less impact they will have on your credit score. There is no quick fix for improving a credit score, so beware of advertisements that say otherwise.

Debit Cards

Although you might wish to use a credit card for emergencies and to establish a good credit rating, you might also look into the possibility of applying for a debit card (also called a *checkcard*). The big advantage of a debit card is that you don't always have to carry cash and thus don't run the risk of losing it. And since the amount of your purchases will be limited to the funds in your account, a debit card is a good form of constraint on your spending. The only real disadvantage is that a debit card provides direct access to your checking account, so it's very important that you keep your card in a safe place and away from your personal identification number (PIN). The safest way to protect your account is to commit your PIN to memory. If you lose your debit card or credit card, notify your bank immediately.

10

Credit Card Dos and Don'ts				
1. **Do** use your credit card to help you build credit by making small charges and paying them off each month.	**2.** **Don't** use your credit card to bridge the gap between the lifestyle you would like to have and the one you can actually afford.	**3.** **Do** keep an eye on your credit report by visiting the free Web site **www .AnnualCreditReport .com** at least once a year.	**4.** **Do** have a credit card for emergencies if possible, even if your parents cosign for it.	**5.** **Don't** use your credit card to pay for spring break. This is not an emergency!

10 Chapter Review

One-minute paper . . .

This chapter covers a lot of information about financing your college experience and managing your money. Planning ahead is an important part of managing your finances. What did you find to be the most useful information in this chapter? Did anything that was covered leave you with more questions than answers? If so, what?

Applying what you've learned . . .

Now that you have read and discussed this chapter, consider how you can apply what you have learned to your academic and personal life. The following prompts will help you reflect on chapter material and its relevance to you both now and in the future.

1. Sometimes it is hard to plan for the future. Why not start small? Describe at least two things you can do each week to save money. For example, using public transportation when possible can help reduce the expense of owning a car.

2. Money can be a difficult subject to talk about, and sometimes it seems easier just not to worry about it. Ask yourself some hard questions. Do you spend money without much thought? Do you have a lot of debt and not much to show for it? Describe what you want your financial picture to look like.

Building your portfolio . . .

Credit cards: a slippery slope

Remember the saying "There is no free lunch"? That is a good maxim to keep in mind as you consider adding credit cards to your financial picture. College students are often targeted by credit card companies through an offer of a free T-shirt or other novelty if they sign up for a new card. While it might seem harmless at the time, signing up for multiple credit cards can put you in financial trouble—and fast!

A big factor in effectively managing your credit card debt is being aware of the terms and conditions that apply to each account you have.

1. If you already have credit cards (including gas cards and store credit cards such as a Gap or Sears card), find your most recent billing statements. If you do not have a credit card, use an Internet search engine to search for "credit cards for college students." You will find several Internet offers specifically for college students. Find the terms and conditions for one of the offers.

2. Next, to understand the fees associated with your credit accounts, create an Excel spreadsheet with the following headers (see the example at the top of page 133):

- Card Issuer and Card Type
- Credit Limit
- APR (Annual Percentage Rate)
- Default APR (A default APR may be used when you fail to make the minimum payment on your credit card account or exceed your credit limit by a certain amount. The default APR is always higher than the stated APR for the credit account.)
- Due On
- Late Fee
- Over Credit Limit Fee

3. List each credit card you have and enter the associated fees.

4. Save the file to your local computer or flash drive.

5. Update the file any time you open or close a credit account.

Understanding the terms and conditions of every credit card account you have can help you avoid paying extremely high interest rates and damaging your credit history.

Sample Credit Card Spreadsheet

Card Issuer and Card Type	Credit Limit	APR	Default APR	Due On	Late Fee	Over Credit Limit Fee
Example: Bank of America Student Visa	$500	18.25% variable	32.25%	28th day of each month	$29	$39
Card 1.						
Card 2.						
Card 3.						

Where to go for help . . .

On Campus

Your institution's financial aid office: Professionals in this office will help you understand financial aid opportunities and how to apply for scholarships.

Local United Way office: Many communities have credit counseling agencies within the local United Way.

Campus programs: Be on the lookout for special campus programs on money management. These programs are often offered in residence halls or through the division of student affairs.

Business school or college: Faculty or staff members within a school or college of business or a division of continuing education sometimes offer a course in personal finance. Check your college catalog or Web site, or call the school, college, or division office.

Counseling center: If your money problems are related to compulsive shopping or gambling, your institution's counseling center can provide help.

Online

Budget Wizard: http://www.cashcourse.org. The National Endowment for Financial Education (NEFE) offers this free, secure, budgeting tool.

Free Application for Federal Student Aid: http://www .fafsa.ed.gov. The online form allows you to set up an account, complete the application electronically, save your work, and monitor the progress of your application.

FastWeb: http://www.FastWeb.com. Register for this free scholarship search service and discover sources of educational funding you never knew existed.

Bankrate: http://www.bankrate.com. This free site provides unbiased information about the interest rates, fees, and penalties associated with major credit cards and private loans. It also provides calculators that let you determine the long-term costs of different kinds of borrowing.

Other

Knox, Susan. *Financial Basics: A Money-Management Guide for Students.* Columbus: Ohio State University Press, 2004.

My Institution's Resources

_____

_____

_____

_____

_____

_____

_____

11 Appreciating Diversity

At the core of this country's value system is the belief that the United States of America is a place where all people are welcome. This principle has created a richly diverse society that emphasizes the importance of retaining individual cultural identity while living among others. Ethnic and cultural communities throughout the United States are preserving components of their particular heritage as they join other cultures to create a nation that is more diverse than any other in the world. Throughout our history, as this country has moved toward the Constitution's goal of achieving "a more perfect union," diversity has been both a source of conflict and a national strength.

A college or university serves as a microcosm of the real world—a world that requires us all to work, live, and socialize with people from various ethnic and cultural groups. In few settings do members of ethnic and cultural groups interact in such close proximity to one another as they do on a college campus. Whether you are attending a four-year university or a community college, you will be exposed to new experiences and opportunities, all of which can enhance learning and provide a deeper sense of understanding.

Through self-assessment, discovery, and open-mindedness, you can begin to understand your perspectives on diversity. This work, although difficult at times, will intensify your educational experiences, personal growth, and development. Thinking critically about your personal values and belief systems will allow you to have a greater sense of belonging and to make a positive contribution to our multicultural society.

How Do You Measure Up?

1. I enjoy getting to know people who are different from me in terms of ethnicity, religion, or life experience.
   - ○ Agree
   - ○ Don't Know
   - ○ Disagree

2. I understand that there are many ways to think about diversity in addition to race and culture.
   - ○ Agree
   - ○ Don't Know
   - ○ Disagree

3. I am planning to take at least one course that will help me learn about other cultures.
   - ○ Agree
   - ○ Don't Know
   - ○ Disagree

4. I am willing to work with others on campus to fight discrimination, harassment, and hate crimes.
   - ○ Agree
   - ○ Don't Know
   - ○ Disagree

Review the items you marked "don't know" or "disagree." Paying attention to all these aspects of your college experience can be important to your success. After reading this chapter, come back to this list and think about ways you can work on these areas.

Understanding and Experiencing Diversity

Debra Alas

Nursing student returning to college after a 13-year break

The other students in the nursing program were about fifteen years younger than I was. They could memorize facts and work their laptops like characters in *The Matrix*. Meanwhile, I had no idea what a PDA was—much less how to get a PowerPoint off the board. Sometimes these younger students would complain. "I'm so tired." "I studied for eight hours for that test, and I can't believe I didn't get an A." "It's so unfair that they schedule all these classes and labs so close together." And here I was, working in an office, paying a mortgage, and raising my kids. I thought of it this way: The other students had more time and technological expertise. I had more life experience and writing and thinking skills. It seemed much easier to do schoolwork now than when I was in my twenties. I could focus and fit what I was learning into a larger context. Being older, I felt more comfortable talking to my professors. My degree in English literature had made me a good writer. Plus, after working as a business manager in the medical field and raising a child with developmental disorders, it turned out that I'd become a master of critical thinking.

But then we got a last-minute group assignment: an essay and PowerPoint presentation due in 90 minutes.

"There's no way," I said. But the other students were already typing furiously on their laptops and throwing flash keys at each other.

"I can't believe we got an A," said one of the boys afterwards.

"I can't believe we got it *done*," I said, smiling.

How does diversity enrich your college experience? What does it teach you about yourself? What might you learn about others?

Understanding Diversity and the Source of Our Beliefs

Diversity is the variation in social and cultural identities among people living together. Multiculturalism is the active process of acknowledging and respecting social groups, cultures, religions, races, ethnicities, attitudes, and opinions. As your journey through higher education unfolds, you will find yourself immersed in this mixture of identities. Regardless of the size of the institution, going to college brings together people who have differing backgrounds and experiences but similar goals and aspirations. Each person brings to campus a unique combination of life story, upbringing, value system, view of the world, and set of judgments. Familiarizing yourself with such differences can greatly enhance your experiences in the classes you will take, the organizations you will join, and the relationships you will cultivate. For many students, college is the first time they have been exposed to so much diversity. Learning experiences and challenges await you both in and out of the classroom. College provides opportunities to learn not only about others but also about yourself.

Many of our beliefs grow out of personal experience and reinforcement. If you have had a negative experience or endured a series of incidents involving members of a particular group, you're more likely to develop stereotypes, or negative judgments, about people in that group. Or maybe you have heard repeatedly that everyone associated with a particular group behaves in a certain way, and you might have bought into that stereotype without even thinking about it. Children who grow up in an environment in which dislike and distrust of certain types of people are openly expressed might subscribe to those very judgments even if they have had no direct interaction with those being judged.

In college you might encounter beliefs about diversity that run counter to your basic values. When your friendships with others are affected by differing values, tolerance is generally a good goal. Talking about diversity with someone else whose beliefs seem to be in conflict with your own can be very rewarding. Your goal in this kind of discussion is not to reach agreement, but to enhance your understanding of why people see diversity differently—why some seem to flee from it and others allow experiences with diversity to enrich their college experience.

Before coming to college, you might never have coexisted with most of the groups you now see on campus. Your home community might not have been very diverse, although possibly it seemed so before you reached campus. In college you have the opportunity to learn from many kinds of people. From your roommate in the residence hall to your lab partner in your biology class to the members of your sociology study group, your college experience will be enriched if you allow yourself to be open to the possibility of learning from members of all cultural groups.

Challenge Yourself to Experience Diversity

During his inaugural address, President Obama reiterated the value of diversity:

> For we know that our patchwork heritage is a strength, not a weakness. We are a nation of Christians and Muslims, Jews and Hindus—and non-believers. We are shaped by every language and culture, drawn from every end of this earth; and because we have tasted the bitter swill of civil war and segregation, and emerged from that dark chapter stronger and more united, we cannot help but believe that the old hatreds shall someday pass; that the lines of tribe shall soon dissolve; that as the world grows smaller, our common humanity shall reveal itself; and that America must play its role in ushering in a new era of peace.

Diversity enriches us all. Allowing yourself to become more culturally aware and more open to differing viewpoints will help you become a truly educated person. Understanding the value of working with others and the importance of an open mind will enhance your educational and career goals and provide gratifying experiences, both on and off campus. Making the decision to become active in your multicultural education will require you to be active and sometimes to

try it!

Lessons We Learn about Diversity

Write about any specific lessons you learned in your family about the expectations you should have of diverse groups.

step out of your comfort zone. There are many ways to become more culturally aware, including a variety of opportunities on your campus. Look into what cultural programming is being offered throughout the school year. From concerts to films, from guest speakers to information tables, you might not have to go far to gain additional insight into the value of diversity.

Challenge yourself to learn about various groups in and around your community, at both school and home. These two settings might differ ethnically and culturally, giving you an opportunity to develop the skills you need to function in and adjust to a variety of settings. Attend events and celebrations outside of your regular groups. Whether they are in the general community or on campus, this is a good way to see and hear traditions that are specific to the groups being represented. Exposing yourself to new experiences through events and celebrations can be gratifying. You can also become active in your own learning by making time for travel. Seeing the world and its people can be an uplifting experience. Finally, when in doubt, ask. If you do this in a tactful, genuine way, most people will be happy to share information about their viewpoints, traditions, and history. It is only through allowing ourselves to grow that we really learn.

11

Forms of Diversity

When you think about diversity, you might first think of differences in race or ethnicity. While it is true that those are two forms of diversity, there are many other types of diversity that you will most likely experience in college and in the workplace, including age, religion, physical ability, gender, and sexual orientation.

Ethnicity, Culture, Race, and Religion

Often, the terms *ethnicity* and *culture* are used interchangeably, although their definitions are quite distinct. Throughout this chapter we will use these two words together and in isolation. Before we start using the terms, it's a good idea to learn their definitions so that you're clear on what they actually mean.

Ethnicity refers to the identity that is assigned to a specific group of people who are historically connected by a common national origin or language. For example, let's look at one of the largest ethnic groups: Latinos. Latin America encompasses over thirty countries within North, Central, and South America, all of which share the Spanish language. A notable exception is Brazil. However, although the national language is Portuguese, Brazilians are considered Latinos (both Spanish and Portuguese are languages that evolved from Latin). The countries also share many traditions and beliefs, with some variations. However, we shouldn't generalize. Not every Latino who speaks Spanish is of Mexican descent, and not every Latino speaks Spanish. Acknowledging that differences exist within ethnic groups is a big step in becoming ethnically aware.

Culture is defined as those aspects of a group of people that are passed on and/or learned. Traditions, food, language, clothing styles, artistic expression, and beliefs are all part of culture. Certainly, ethnic groups are also cultural groups: They share a language, foods, traditions, art, and clothing that are passed from one generation to the next. But numerous other, nonethnic cultural groups can fit this concept of culture, too. Think of the hip hop community, in which a common style of dress, specific terminology, and distinct forms of musical and artistic expression also constitute a culture but not an ethnicity.

Although we don't use the term *race* much in this chapter, it's important to understand this word as it is commonly used in everyday language.

Race refers to biological characteristics that are shared by groups of people, including skin tone, hair texture and color, and facial features. Making generalizations about someone's racial group affiliation is risky. Even people who share some biological features—such as similar eye shape or dark skin—might be ethnically very distinct. For instance, people of Asian descent are not necessarily ethnically and culturally alike, since Asia is a vast region encompassing such disparate places as Mongolia, India, and Japan. Likewise, people of African descent come from very different backgrounds; the African continent is home to fifty-three countries and hundreds of different languages, and Africans are genetically very diverse. More and more individuals today, including President Obama, describe themselves as multiracial. You might meet fellow students whose families include parents, grandparents, and great-grandparents of several different racial groups.

All of us come into the world with our own unique characteristics—aspects of our physical appearance and personalities that make us who we are. But people around the world have one attribute in common: We want to be respected even if we are different from others in some ways. Whatever the color of your skin or hair, whatever your life experiences or cultural background, you will want others to treat you fairly and acknowledge and value your contribution to your communities and the world. And, of course, others will want the same from you.

Diversity of religion has been central to the American experience since our colonial origins. In fact, many settlers of the original thirteen colonies came to North America to escape religious persecution. Religious diversity might or might not have been obvious in your hometown or neighborhood, but unless you are attending an institution that enrolls only students of one religious sect, you will find religious diversity to be part of your college experience.

Religious denominations might sponsor campus centers or organizations, and students' religious affiliations might determine their dress, attitudes, or avoidance of certain behaviors. While you are in college, your openness to religious diversity will add to your understanding of the many ways in which people are different from one another.

11

Age

Although many students enter college around age eighteen, others choose to enter or return in their thirties and beyond. In the fall of 2007, almost 37 percent of American college students were twenty-five years of age or older. Age diversity in the classroom gives everyone the opportunity to learn from others who have different life experiences. All kinds of factors determine when students enter higher education for the first time or stop and then reenter. Therefore there is no such thing as "the norm" in considering the age of college students. If you are attending a college that has a large number of students who are older (or younger) than you, strive to see this as an advantage for learning. A campus where younger and older students learn together can be much more interesting than a campus where everyone is the same age.

Learning and Physical Disabilities

Although the majority of students have reasonably average learning and physical abilities, the numbers of students with physical and learning disabilities are rising on most college campuses, as are the services that are available to them. Physical disabilities can include deafness, blindness, paralysis, or a mental disorder. Also, many students have some form of learning disability that makes college work a challenge.

People who have physical and learning disabilities want to be treated just as you would treat anyone else—with respect. If a student with a disability is in your class, treat him or her as you would any student; your overzealousness to help might be seen as an expression of pity.

If you have, or think you might have, a learning disability, consult your campus learning center for a diagnosis and advice on compensating for learning problems. Most campuses have a special office to serve students with both physical and learning disabilities.

Gender

A basic example of diversity is gender. But other than the obvious physical differences, are men and women really that different? Or do we believe they are because of our own biases?

While you're in college, make friends with people of both genders, avoid stereotyping what is "appropriate" for one group or another, and don't limit your own interests. In today's world, there is almost no activity or profession that isn't open to everyone, regardless of gender. If your college or university has a Gender Studies department, consider taking a course in this area. Gender studies courses are generally interdisciplinary and look at the subject matter from the perspective of gender. Such a course could open up new ways of thinking about many aspects of your world.

Sexual Orientation

In college you will likely meet students, staff members, and professors who are homosexual or bisexual. Because most colleges and universities openly accept gay, lesbian, bisexual, or transgendered people, many individuals who were in the closet in high school will come out in the collegiate environment. The subject of sexual orientation is highly personal and often emotionally charged, but whatever your own personal sexual orientation, it is important that you respect all individuals with whom you come in contact. Most colleges and universities have campus codes or standards of behavior that do not permit acts of harassment or discrimination based on race, ethnicity, gender, or sexual orientation.

try it!

How Gender Influences Life Choices

Can you remember any time in your life when you gave up a dream because you thought it was "inappropriate" for someone of your gender? Can you remember a time when you assumed you wouldn't be good at an activity, a sport, or a course because of your gender? What advice could you give to other students about not letting their gender narrow their range of life options?

Seeking Diversity on Campus

Acknowledging the importance of diversity to education, colleges and universities have begun to take the concepts of diversity and apply them to student learning opportunities. We see this in efforts by colleges to embrace an inclusive curriculum. Today, you can find courses with a diversity focus in many departments of your college or university, such as Black Studies, Asian Studies, Latino or Hispanic Studies, Women's Studies, Gay and Lesbian Studies, and Religious Studies. Many of the courses in these departments meet graduation requirements. The college setting is ideal for promoting education about diversity because it allows students and faculty of varying backgrounds to come together for the common purpose of learning and critical thinking.

According to Gloria Ameny-Dixon, education about diversity can do the following:

- Increase problem-solving skills through different perspectives applied to reaching solutions
- Increase positive relationships through the achievement of common goals, respect, appreciation, and commitment to equality
- Decrease stereotyping and prejudice through contact and interaction with diverse individuals
- Promote the development of a more in-depth view of the world[1]

Be it religious affiliation, sexual orientation, gender, ethnicity, age, culture, or ability, your campus provides the opportunity to interact with and learn alongside a kaleidoscope of individuals.

The Curriculum

College students have led the movement for a curriculum that reflects disenfranchised groups such as women, people of color, the elderly, the disabled, gays, lesbians, bisexuals, and the transgendered. By protesting, walking out of classes, and staging sit-ins at the offices of campus officials, students have demanded the hiring of more faculty members from different ethnic groups, the creation of Ethnic Studies departments, and a variety of initiatives designed to support diverse students academically and socially. These initiatives have increased academic access for students from ethnic and cultural groups and have helped them stay in school. They exist today in the form of multicultural centers, women's resource centers, enabling services, and numerous academic support programs. The movement for multiculturalism in education has continued to gain momentum since it began during the civil rights era of the 1960s. By expressing their discontent over the lack of access and representation in many of society's niches, including higher education, ethnic and cultural groups have achieved acknowledgment of their presence on campus.

In almost all colleges and universities, you will be required to take some general education courses. The purpose of these courses is to expose you to a wide range of topics and issues so that you can develop and learn to express your own views. We hope you will include a course or two with a multicultural basis in your schedule. Such courses can provide you with new perspectives and an understanding of issues that affect your fellow students and community members—and affect you too, possibly in ways you had not considered. And just as your college or university campus is diverse, so, too, is the workforce you will be entering. A multicultural education can improve the quality of your entire life.

Student-Run Organizations

Student-run organizations can provide multiple avenues to express ideas, pursue interests, and cultivate relationships. According to our definition of culture, all student-run organizations are culturally based and provide an outlet for the promotion and celebration of a culture. Let's take, for instance, two very different student groups, a Muslim Student Union and an Animation Club, and apply the components of culture to them. Both groups promote a belief system that is common among their members: The first is based on religious beliefs, and the second is based on ideas about what constitutes animation as an art form. Both have aspects that can be taught and passed on: the teachings of the Muslim faith and the rules and techniques used in drawing. Both groups utilize language that is specific to the belief system of the group. Most campus organizations bring like-minded students together and are open to anyone who wants to become involved.

[1] Gloria M. Ameny-Dixon, "Why Multicultural Education Is More Important in Higher Education Now Than Ever: A Global Perspective." McNeese State University (http://www.nationalforum.com).

To promote learning and discovery not only inside the classroom but outside as well, colleges and universities provide programming that highlights ethnic and cultural celebrations, such as Chinese New Year and Kwanzaa; gender-related topics, such as Take Back the Night; and a broad range of entertainment, including concerts and art exhibits. These events expose you to new and exciting ideas and viewpoints, enhancing your education and challenging your current views.

Most college students, especially first-year students, are seeking their own niche and their own identity. Many have found that becoming involved in campus organizations eases the transition and helps them make connections with their fellow students.

Fraternities and Sororities

Fraternities and sororities provide a quick connection to a large number of individuals—a link to the social pipeline, camaraderie, and support. Fraternities and sororities differ in their philosophies and commitment to philanthropy. Some are committed to community service; others are more socially oriented. Fraternities and sororities created by and for specific ethnic groups have existed for years and were developed by students of color who felt the need for campus groups that allowed them to connect to their communities and cultures. Nu Alpha Kappa Fraternity, Alpha Rho Lambda Sorority, Omega Psi Phi Fraternity, Alpha Kappa Alpha Sorority, Lambda Phi Epsilon Fraternity, and Sigma Omicron Pi Sorority are just some of the many ethnically based fraternities and sororities that exist across the country. Such organizations have provided many students with a means to become familiar with their campus and to gain friendships and support while promoting their culture and ethnicity.

Career/Major Groups

You can explore diversity through your major and career interests as well. Groups that focus on a specific field of study can be great assets as you explore your interests. Are you interested in helping minority and majority groups interact more effectively?

Consider majoring in sociology or social work. Do you want to learn more about human behavior? Study psychology. If you join a club that is affiliated with the major that interests you, not only will you find out more about the major, but you can also make contacts in the field that could lead to career options. Many of these clubs participate in challenges and contests with similar groups from other colleges and contribute to campus activities through exhibitions and events. The Psychology Club; the Math, Engineering, and Science Association; and the Association of Student Filmmakers are examples of such groups.

Political/Activist Organizations

Adding to the diversity mix on campuses are organizations devoted to specific political affiliations and causes. Campus Republicans, Young Democrats, Amnesty International, Native Students in Social Action, and other groups provide students with a platform to express their political views and share their causes with others. Contributing to the diversity of ideas, organizations provide debating events and forums to address current issues and events.

Special-Interest Groups

Perhaps the largest subgroup of student organizations is the special-interest category, which encompasses everything from recreational interests to hobbies. On your campus you might find special-interest clubs such as the Brazilian Jujitsu Club, the Kite Flyers' Club, the Flamenco Club, and the Video Gamers' Society. Students can cultivate an interest in bird watching or indulge their curiosity about ballroom dance without ever leaving campus. Many of these clubs will sponsor campus events highlighting their specific interests and talents so that you can check them out. If a club for your special interest is not available, create one yourself.

11

Discrimination, Prejudice, and Insensitivity on College Campuses

You might feel uncomfortable when asked about your views of diversity. We all have biases against certain groups or value systems. Yet it is what we do with our individual beliefs that separates the average person from the racist, the bigot, and the extremist.

Unfortunately, some individuals opt not to seek education for the common good but instead respond negatively to groups that differ from their own. Documented acts of discrimination and prejudice on campuses span the country. You might be shocked to hear that these acts of violence, intimidation, and stupidity occur on campuses, when the assumption is that college students are "supposed to be above that."

Raising Awareness

At a midwestern university, students arrived on campus to find racial slurs and demeaning images aimed at various ethnic groups spray-painted on the walls of the Multicultural Center. In the wake of the terrorist attack on the World Trade Center and the Pentagon in September 2001, many students of Middle Eastern descent were subjected to both violence and intimidation because of their ancestry.

While actions like these are deliberate and hateful, others occur out of a lack of common sense. Consider a campus party to celebrate Cinco de Mayo. Party organizers asked everyone to wear sombreros. On arrival, guests encountered a mock-up of a border patrol station on the front lawn and were required to crawl under or climb over a section of chain-link fencing. Student groups voiced their disapproval over such insensitivity, which resulted in campus probationary measures for the organization that had thrown the party. At a Halloween party at a large university, members of a campus organization decided to dress in Ku Klux Klan outfits while other members dressed as slaves and wore black shoe polish on their faces. The group then simulated slave hangings during the party. When photos of the events surfaced, the university suspended the group from campus, and the community demanded that the group be banned indefinitely.

For a number of years, stereotypes that are used to identify school sports teams and

their supporters have disturbed ethnic and cultural groups such as Native Americans. Mascots that incorporate a bow and arrow, a tomahawk, feathers, and war paint have raised awareness about the promotion and acceptance of stereotypes associated with the concept of the "savage Indian." Some schools have responded by altering the images while retaining the mascot. Other schools have changed their mascots altogether.

Colleges and universities are working to ensure that a welcoming and inclusive campus environment awaits all students, both current and prospective. Campus resources and centers focus on providing acknowledgment of and support to the diverse student population. Campus administrations have established policies against any and all forms of discriminatory actions, racism, and insensitivity, and many campuses have adopted zero-tolerance policies that prohibit verbal and nonverbal harassment, intimidation, and violence. Find out what resources are available on your campus to protect you and other students from discriminatory and racist behavior and what

try it!

Combating Harassment and Hate on Campus

Have you ever witnessed or been a victim of harassment because of your gender, race, regional identity, religion, or ethnic group? What can colleges and universities do to reduce the incidence of harassment?

steps your college or university takes to promote the understanding of diversity and multiculturalism. If you have been a victim of a racist, insensitive, or discriminatory act, report it to the proper authorities.

What You Can Do to Fight Hate on Campus

Hate crimes, regardless of where they occur, should be taken very seriously. A hate crime is any prejudicial activity and can include physical assault, vandalism, and intimidation. One of the most common hate crimes on campus is graffiti that expresses racial, ethnic, and cultural slurs.

Whatever form these crimes might take on your campus, it is important to examine your thoughts and feelings about their occurrence. The most important question to ask yourself is: Will you do something about it, or do you think it is someone else's problem? If you or a group to which you belong is the target of the hate crime, you might feel compelled to take a stand and speak out against the incident. But what if the target is not a group you associate with? Will you feel strongly enough to express your discontent with the actions that are taken? Or will you feel that it is the problem only of the targeted group?

Many students, whether or not they were directly targeted in a hate crime, find strength in unity, forming action committees and making it clear that hate crimes will not be ignored or tolerated. In most cases, instead of dividing students, hate crimes bring students together to work toward denouncing hate. It is important not to respond to prejudice and hate crimes with violence. It is more effective to unite with fellow students, faculty, staff, campus police, and administrators to address the issue and educate the greater campus community.

How can you get involved? Work with existing campus services such as the campus police and the Multicultural Center as well as the faculty

and administration to plan and host educational opportunities, such as training sessions, workshops, and symposiums centered on diversity, sensitivity, and multiculturalism. Organize an antidiscrimination event on campus in which campus and community leaders address the issues and provide solutions. Join prevention programs to come up with ideas to battle hate crimes on campus or in the community. Finally, look into the antidiscrimination measures your college is employing and decide whether you think they need updating or revising.

Just because you or your particular group has not been targeted in a hate crime doesn't mean that you should do nothing. Commit to becoming involved in making your campus a safe place for students with diverse views, lifestyles, languages, politics, religions, and interests to come together and learn. If nothing happens to make it clear that hate crimes on campus will not be tolerated, it's anyone's guess as to who will be the next target.

11

11 Chapter Review

One-minute paper . . .

One aspect of a liberal arts education is learning about differences in cultures, races, and other groups. Were there any ideas in this chapter that influenced your personal opinions, viewpoints, or values? Was there anything that you disagreed with or found unsettling?

Applying what you've learned . . .

Now that you have read and discussed this chapter, consider how you can apply what you have learned to your academic and personal life. The following prompts will help you reflect on chapter material and its relevance to you both now and in the future.

1. Use your print or online campus course catalog to identify courses that focus on topics of multiculturalism and diversity. Why do you think academic departments have included these issues in the curriculum? How would studying diversity and multiculturalism help you prepare for different academic fields?

2. Reflecting on our personal identities and values is a way to increase self-awareness. Read and answer the following questions to the best of your ability: How do you identify yourself ethnically and culturally? How do you express yourself according to this identity? Are there practices or beliefs in your culture to which you have difficulty subscribing? If so, what are they? Why do you have difficulty accepting these beliefs? What aspects of your identity do you truly enjoy?

Building your portfolio . . .

It's a small world after all!

The concepts of diversity, ethnicity, culture, and multiculturalism have been explored in this chapter. Reading about these controversial topics is one thing, but really stepping into someone else's shoes is another. Study abroad and student exchange programs are excellent (and enjoyable) ways of adding new perspectives to your college experience. What better way of learning about other parts of the world than by immersing yourself in a foreign culture, language, and people?

Consider the possibilities:

1. Visit your institution's International Programs/Study Abroad office, or, if you are at a college that does not have a study abroad program, search for study abroad opportunities on the Web. Tip: Look for the Center for Global Education (**http://www.lmu.edu/globaled/index.html**), the Council on International Education Exchange (**http://www.ciee.org/study.aspx**), or the International Partnership for Service Learning (**http://www.ispl.org**).

Using a major or career that you have selected or are interested in, think about how you would like to spend a summer, semester, or year abroad to learn more about or gain experience in your major field.

2. On the basis of your research, create a PowerPoint presentation to share with your class, outlining the opportunities to study abroad or participate in an exchange program.

- Describe the steps students need to take at your campus to include a study abroad trip in their college plan (e.g., whom to contact, financial aid, the best time to study abroad, how to earn course credit).
- Describe the benefits of study abroad (e.g., observing different cultures, building a good résumé).
- Include photos of the country or countries you would like to visit.
- Include information about your current or intended major and career and how a study abroad or exchange trip would fit into your plans.
- Reference Web links you found useful in preparing your presentation.

3. Save your presentation in your portfolio on your personal computer or flash drive.

Where to go for help . . .

On Campus

Most colleges and university campuses take an active role in promoting diversity. In the effort to ensure a welcoming and supportive environment for all students, institutions have established offices, centers, and resources to provide students with educational opportunities, academic guidance, and support networks. Look into the availability of the following resources on your campus, and visit one or more: Office of Student Affairs; Office of Diversity; Multicultural Centers; Women's and Men's Centers; Lesbian, Gay, Bisexual, and Trans-gendered Student Alliances; Centers for Students with Disabilities; and academic support programs for under-represented groups.

Online

Student Now Diversity Resources: http://www .studentnow.com/collegelist/diversity.html. A list of campus diversity resources.

Diversity Web: http://www.diversityweb.org. More resources related to diversity on campus.

Tolerance.org: http://www.tolerance.org. This Web site, a project of the Southern Poverty Law Center, provides numerous resources for dealing with discrimination and prejudice both on and off campus.

My Institution's Resources

12 Majors & Career Choices

You don't have to be sure about your academic and career goals as you begin or return to college. Rather, you can use your first classes, and even your first year, to explore your interests and see how they might connect to various academic programs. You may discover interests and opportunities you never imagined.

Depending on your academic strengths, you can major in almost anything. As this chapter will emphasize, it is how you integrate classes with extracurricular pursuits and work experience that prepares you for a first career—or, if you have been in the labor force for some time, for advancement in your current job or even a new career. Try a major you think you will like or that you feel drawn toward, and see what develops. But keep an open mind, and don't pin all your hopes on finding a career in that major alone. Your selection of a major and a career ultimately has to fit with your overall life goals, purposes, values, and beliefs.

How Do You Measure Up?

1. I understand how the world economy is changing and how those changes might affect my job prospects.
   - ○ Agree
   - ○ Don't Know
   - ○ Disagree

2. I have clear goals for attending college.
   - ○ Agree
   - ○ Don't Know
   - ○ Disagree

3. I know my own strengths and how they might influence my career choice.
   - ○ Agree
   - ○ Don't Know
   - ○ Disagree

4. I am aware of the advantages and disadvantages of working while I'm in college.
   - ○ Agree
   - ○ Don't Know
   - ○ Disagree

Review the items you marked "don't know" or "disagree." Paying attention to all these aspects of your college experience can be important to your success. After reading this chapter, come back to this list and think about ways you can work on these areas.

Careers and the New Economy

Brett Kossick

First-year student near the end of his first term

"Well, I really admire your focus," said Dr. Woloshyn, my academic adviser, when I dropped by his office early to talk about my course schedule. Many people study a whole gamut of things until they settle on a major and don't specialize until graduate school. That's so not me.

"I've wanted to be an engineer for as long as I can remember," I said. "Which is why I'm here. I got your e-mail with the courses you suggested, and I'm confused. *Business Writing and Communication*? *Team Skills and Critical Thinking*? I plan to work in robotics," I said, "not marketing."

"Oh, really?" Dr. Woloshyn nodded. Then he leaned forward on his desk and made a tent with his hands. "Brett, didn't you tell me that you have an internship with a leading technology corporation this summer? Did anyone tell you what you would be doing there?"

"Not really," I said. "They just said I'd be helping out in different divisions of the company, depending on what they need."

"Right," said Dr. Woloshyn. "And is there a chance you might like to work there after you graduate?"

"Yes, are you kidding? That would be my dream job."

"Good. So, let's think about it: Some divisions of the company might be working on new business proposals and will value a gifted writer. Some might be working on projects involving media companies, investment bankers, schools, or even foreign governments. They will need someone who is great at teamwork. Some divisions might be working on new apps or software applications, which means—"

"Critical thinking," I cut in. We grinned at each other as I stood up. "Thanks, Professor. I guess I'll go register now."

What kinds of skills do you need to develop as a college student? How can an expertise in writing, critical thinking, and teamwork help you achieve your goals?

In your lifetime, companies have restructured to remain competitive. As a result, major changes have taken place in how we work, where we work, and the ways we prepare for work while in college. In many ways the following characteristics define today's economy:

Global   Increasingly, industries have become multinational, not only moving into overseas markets but also seeking cheaper labor, capital, and resources abroad. Around the world, factories built to similar standards can turn out essentially the same products. Your career is bound to be affected by the global economy, even if you never leave the United States. For example, when you call an 800 number for customer service, the person who talks to you might be answering your call in Iowa, Ireland, or India. College graduates in the United States are now competing for jobs with others around the world who are often willing to work longer hours for less money than American workers.

Unstable   In 2008 and 2009 the world economy suffered a series of events that led to downturns in stock markets, bankruptcies, foreclosures, failing businesses, and lost jobs. Scandals within the highest ranks of major companies and constant mergers and acquisitions of companies have destabilized the workforce. Depending on how long it takes to stabilize the economy in the United States and the rest of the world, your career goals might have to be refocused. Because the global economic situation is changing continuously, it's important to keep up-to-date on the economic situation as it relates to your prospective major and career.

Innovative   The economy depends on creativity in new products and services to generate consumer interest around the world. Especially in times of economic instability, the flexibility and responsiveness of companies to the changing economic climate will affect their ability to survive.

Boundaryless   Teams of workers within an organization need to understand the missions of other teams because they most likely will have to work together. You might be an accountant and find yourself working with the public relations division of your company, or you might be a human resources manager who does training for a number of different divisions in a number of different countries.

Customized   More and more, consumers are demanding products and services tailored to their specific needs. You have probably noticed the seemingly endless varieties of a single brand of shampoo or cereal crowding store shelves. Such market segmentation requires a constant adaptation of ideas to identify new products and services as new customer demands emerge.

Fast   When computers became popular, people rejoiced because they believed the new technology would reduce their workloads. Actually, the reverse happened. Whereas secretaries and other support workers once performed many tasks for executives, now executives design their own PowerPoint presentations and format their own documents. For better or worse, "We need it now" is the cry in the workplace, with product and service delivery time cut to a minimum (the "just-in-time" policy). Being fast requires constant thinking outside the lines to identify new approaches to designing and delivering products.

According to *Fast Company* magazine, the new economy has changed many of the rules about work. Leaders are now expected to teach and encourage others as well as to head up their divisions. Careers frequently zigzag into other areas. People who can anticipate the needs of the marketplace are in demand. Change has become the norm. Workers are being urged to continue their learning, and companies are volunteering to play a critical role in the welfare of all people through sponsorship of worthy causes. As the lines between work and the rest of life continue to blur, workers need to find a healthy balance in their lives. Bringing work home may be inevitable at times, but it shouldn't be the rule.

Essential Qualities and Skills for the New Economy

In addition to being well educated and savvy about the realities of the twenty-first-century economy, you'll also need a wide range of qualities and skills to succeed in your career, such as:

try it!

Thinking about a Career Choice

List your personal interests, preferences, characteristics, strengths, and skills. Match your list to what you believe to be the skills and interests of successful people in a field that interests you. Note other influences that may be drawing you to that career (such as your parents' preferences). Share the notes you have prepared with a career counselor, and get feedback on how you and your career interests mesh.

- Communication skills that demonstrate strong oral and listening abilities, in addition to a good foundation in the basic skill of writing

- Presentation skills, including the ability to justify and persuade as well as to respond to questions and serious critiques of your presentation material

- Leadership skills and the ability to take charge or relinquish control, according to the needs of the organization

- Team skills—the ability to work cooperatively and collaboratively with different people while maintaining autonomous control over some assignments

- Interpersonal abilities that allow you to relate to others, inspire others to participate, and resolve conflict between people

- Positive personal traits, including initiative and motivation, adaptability to change, a work ethic, reliability, honesty, and integrity

- Critical thinking and problem solving—the ability to identify problems and their solutions by integrating information from a variety of sources and effectively weighing alternatives

- A willingness to learn quickly and continuously from those with whom you work and others around the world

12

Aligning Your Sense of Purpose and Your Career

As you begin the process of choosing or confirming a major and career path, you will first want to consider why you decided to go to college and why you chose this particular institution. Ask yourself:

- Am I here to find out who I am and study a subject I'm truly passionate about, regardless of whether it leads to a career?

- Am I here to engage in an academic program that provides an array of possibilities when I graduate?

- Am I here to prepare myself for a graduate program or immediate employment?

- Am I here to obtain specific training in a field that I'm committed to?

- Am I here to gain specific skills for a job I already have?

Remember the following six simple, one-word questions. They can help you to prepare for a career and obtain that important first job:

- **Why?** Why do you want to be a _____? Knowing your goals and values will help you pursue your career with passion and an understanding of what motivates you.

- **Who?** Who at your college or university or in your community can help you make career decisions? Network with people who can help you find out what you want to do. Right now those people might be instructors in your major, an academic adviser, or someone at your campus career center. Later, network with others who can help you attain your goal.

- **How?** How will you develop the technical and communications skills required to work effectively? Don't be a technophobe. Learn how to do PowerPoint presentations, build Web pages, and create Excel spreadsheets. Take a speech course. Improve your writing skills. Even if you think your future job doesn't require these skills, you'll be more marketable with them.

- **What?** What opportunities are available in your preferred career fields? Be aware of the range of job options an employer presents, as well as such potential threats as outsourcing—a company's hiring of outside businesses to perform particular functions at a lower cost. Understand the employment requirements for the career field you have chosen. Know what

training you will need to remain and move up in your chosen profession.

- **Where?** Where will your career path take you? Will you be required to travel or live in a certain part of the country or the world? Or will job success require that you stay in one location? Although job requirements may change over the course of your lifetime, try to achieve a balance between your personal values and preferences and the predictable requirements of the field you are pursuing.

- **When?** When will you need to start looking for your first job? Certain professions, such as teaching, tend to hire employees at certain times of the year.

Connecting Your Major and Your Interests with Your Career

Some students are sure about their major when they enter college, but many others are at a loss. Either way, it's okay. At some point you might ask yourself: Why am I in college? Although it sounds like an easy question to answer, it's not. Many students would immediately respond, "So I can get a good job or an education for a specific career." Yet most majors do not lead to a specific career path or job. You actually can enter most career paths from any number of academic majors. Marketing, a common undergraduate business major, is a field that recruits from a wide variety of majors, including advertising, communications, and psychology. Sociology majors find jobs in law enforcement, teaching, and public service.

Today, English majors are designing Web pages, and history majors are sales representatives and business managers. You do not have to major in

try it!

Thinking about Your Major

Would you describe your major as something you're really passionate about? Why or why not? If your answer is no, why are you pursuing this particular major?

science to gain admittance to medical school. Of course, you do have to take the required science and math courses, but medical schools seek applicants with diverse backgrounds. Only a few technical or professional fields, such as accounting, nursing, and engineering, are tied to specific majors.

Exploring your interests is the best way to choose an academic major. If you're still not sure, take the advice of Patrick Coombs, author of *Major in Success,* who recommends that you major in a subject about which you are really passionate. Most advisers would agree.

You can major in almost anything. As this chapter emphasizes, it is how you integrate your classes with your extracurricular activities and work experience that prepares you for a successful transition to your career. Try a major you think you'll like, and see what develops. But keep an open mind, and don't pin all your hopes on finding a career in that major alone. Your major and your career ultimately have to fit your overall life goals, purposes, values, and beliefs.

Career Choice as a Process of Discovery

Students frequently encounter bumps along the road toward planning and achieving their career goals. Choosing a career is a process of discovery, involving a willingness to remain open to new ideas and experiences. Why should you begin thinking about your career early in your college experience? Because many of the decisions you make during your first year will have an impact on where you end up in the workplace.

As you think about your career, also consider that:

- **You are, more or less, solely responsible for your career.** At one time, organizations provided structured "ladders" that employees could climb to advance to higher professional levels. In most cases, such ladders have disappeared. Companies may assist you with assessments and information on available positions in the industry, but the ultimate task of engineering a career path is yours.

- **To advance your career, you must accept the risks that accompany employment and plan for the future.** Organizations continually restructure, merge, and either grow or downsize in response to economic conditions.

As a result, positions may be cut. Because you can be unexpectedly unemployed, keep other career options in mind as you take courses.

- **A college degree does not guarantee employment.** As a college graduate, you'll be able to pursue opportunities that are more rewarding, financially and otherwise, than if you did not have a degree. But simply wanting to work in a certain field or for a certain organization doesn't mean there will always be a job for you there. Be flexible when exploring your career options; you may have to begin your work life in a job that is not exactly in line with your major or career goals.

- **A commitment to lifelong learning will help keep you employable.** In your college courses you are learning a vital skill: how to learn. Actually, much of your learning will begin when you receive your diploma.

Now the good news: Thousands of graduates find jobs every year. Some may have to work longer to get where they want to be, but persistence pays off. If you start now, you'll have time to build a portfolio of academic and co-curricular experiences that will add substance to your career profile.

12

Exploring Your Interests

John Holland, a psychologist at Johns Hopkins University, developed a number of tools and concepts that can help you organize the various dimensions of yourself so that you can identify potential career choices and choose your major. Holland separates people into six general categories on the basis of differences in their interests, skills, values, and personality characteristics—in short, their preferred approaches to life.[1] Holland's system organizes career fields into the same six categories. Career fields are grouped according to what a particular career field requires of a person (skills and personality characteristics most commonly associated with success in those fields) and what rewards those fields provide (interests and values most commonly associated with satisfaction).

The Holland Model: Personality Characteristics

Realistic (R) These people describe themselves as concrete, down-to-earth, and practical doers. They exhibit competitive and assertive behavior and show interest in activities that require motor coordination, skill, and physical strength. They tend to be interested in scientific or mechanical areas rather than the arts. Examples of career fields in this category include agricultural engineer, electrical contractor, industrial arts teacher, navy officer, fitness director, packaging engineer, electronics technician, and computer graphics technician.

Investigative (I) These people describe themselves as analytical, rational, and logical problem solvers. They value intellectual stimulation and intellectual achievement and prefer to think rather than to act, to organize and understand rather than to persuade. They usually have a strong interest in physical, biological, or social sciences. They are less apt to be people oriented. Examples of career fields in this category include urban planner, chemical engineer, bacteriologist, flight engineer, genealogist, and college professor.

Artistic (A) These people describe themselves as creative, innovative, and independent. They value self-expression and relating with others through artistic expression and are also emotionally expressive. Examples of career fields in this category include architect, film editor/director, actor, cartoonist, interior decorator, and reporter.

Social (S) These people describe themselves as kind, caring, helpful, and understanding of others. They value helping and making a contribution. They satisfy their needs in one-on-one or small-group interaction using strong speaking skills to teach, counsel, or advise. Examples of career fields in this category include nurse, teacher, social worker, genetic counselor, marriage counselor, rehabilitation counselor, and convention planner.

Enterprising (E) These people describe themselves as assertive, risk-taking, and persuasive. They value prestige, power, and status and are more inclined than other types to pursue it. Examples of career fields in this category include banker, city manager, FBI agent, health administrator, judge, labor arbitrator, salary and wage administrator, and marketing specialist.

Conventional (C) These people describe themselves as neat, orderly, detail oriented, and persistent. They value order, structure, prestige, and status and possess a high degree of self-control. Examples of career fields in this category include accountant, statistician, database manager, and abstractor/indexer.

Your career choices ultimately will involve a complex assessment of the factors most important to you. To display the relationship between career fields and the potential conflicts people face as they consider them, Holland's model is commonly presented in a hexagonal shape (see Figure 12.1). The closer the types, the closer the relationships among the career fields; the farther apart the types, the more conflict between the career fields.

Holland's model can help you address the problem of career choice in two ways. First, you can begin to identify many career fields that are consistent with what you know about yourself. Once you've identified potential fields, you can use the career center at your college to get more information about those fields, such as daily activities for specific jobs, interests and abilities

[1] Reproduced by special permission of the publisher, Psychological Assessment Resource, Inc., 16204 North Florida Ave., Lutz, FL 33549. Adapted from *The Self-Directed Search: Professional User's Guide*, by John L. Holland, Ph.D. Copyright © 1985, 1987, 1994, 1997. Further reproduction is prohibited without permission from PAR, Inc.

12

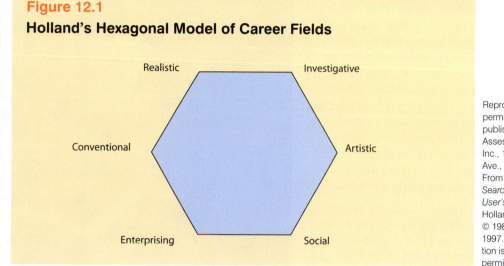

Figure 12.1

Holland's Hexagonal Model of Career Fields

required, preparation required for entry, working conditions, salary and benefits, and employment outlook. Second, you can begin to identify the harmony or conflicts in your career choices.

Never feel you have to make a decision based on the results of only one assessment. Career choices are complex and involve many factors; furthermore, these decisions are reversible. Take time to talk your interests over with a career counselor. Another helpful approach is to shadow an individual in the occupation that interests you, to obtain a better understanding of what the occupation entails in terms of skills, commitment, and opportunity.

Factors That Affect Career Choices

Some people have a definite self-image when they enter college, but most of us are still in the process of defining (or redefining) ourselves throughout life. We can look at ourselves in several useful ways with respect to possible careers:

- **Values.** Today, more than ever, knowing your core values (your most important beliefs) will be important in shaping your career path. In a faltering and unpredictable economy, having a strong rudder will help you steer through the turbulent times.

- **Interests.** Your interests will develop from your experiences and beliefs and can continue to develop and change throughout life. You

may be interested in writing for the college newspaper because you wrote for your high school paper. It's not unusual to enter Psych 101 with a great interest in psychology and realize halfway through the course that psychology is not what you imagined.

- **Skills.** You may be aware of skills you currently have or skills you want to develop while you're in college. Almost always, the ability to do something well can be improved with practice.

- **Aptitudes.** Your inherent strengths, or aptitudes, are often part of your biological heritage or the result of early training. Each of us has aptitudes we can build on.

- **Personality.** Your personality makes you who you are and can't be ignored when you make career decisions. The quiet, orderly, calm, detail-oriented person probably will make a different work choice than the aggressive, outgoing, argumentative person will.

- **Life goals and work values.** Each of us defines success and satisfaction in our own way. The process is complex and very personal. Two factors influence our conclusions about success and happiness: knowing that we are achieving the life goals we've set for ourselves, and finding that we gain satisfaction from what we're receiving from our work. If your values conflict with the organizational values where you work, you might be in for trouble.

12

Working While in College

It's a fact that most students work, and there are pluses and minuses to working in college. Work can support you in attaining your college goals, provide you with the financial means to complete college, and help you structure your time so that you are a much better time manager. It can help you meet people who will later serve as important references for graduate school and/or employment. However, working too much can interfere with your college success, your ability to attend class, your homework, and your participation in many other valuable parts of college life, such as group study, foreign study and travel, and group activities.

If you have to work in order to pay for your tuition and/or your living expenses, take some time to determine how much you need to work, and stay within reasonable limits. Many college students work too many hours just to support a lifestyle and acquire things they want. It's important to keep a reasonable balance between work and study. Don't fall into the trap of thinking "I can do it all." Too many college students have found that "doing it all" means they don't do anything very well.

On-Campus Jobs

If you want or need to work, explore on-campus opportunities as soon as (or even before) you arrive. Even if a campus job pays less than you could earn off campus, there are real advantages to on-campus employment. Generally, on-campus supervisors will be much more flexible than off-campus employers in helping you balance your study demands and your work schedule. And the relationships you'll develop with influential people who really care about your success in college and who will write those all-important reference letters will make the smaller paycheck well worth it.

Your career center can tell you how to access your college's employment system. You may have to register in person or online, but the process is easy, especially if you have a résumé or a draft of one. College employment systems generally channel all jobs collected through faculty, advisers, and career counselors into one database, so it is convenient for you to identify jobs you are looking for.

Many campuses offer an on-campus job fair early in the fall term. Even if you might not be interested at the time, a visit to the job fair will give you a great idea of the range and types of jobs available on campus. You might be pleasantly surprised to learn that there are more opportunities than washing dishes in the cafeteria. Job fairs usually include off-campus community employers, in part because your institution must spend some of the federal college work-study funds it receives supporting off-campus work by students.

It is a good idea to pursue job opportunities that are related to your major or your career. For example, if you are a pre-med major, you might be able to find on-campus work in a biology or chemistry lab. That work would help you to gain knowledge and experience and to make connections with faculty experts in these fields. In fact, getting an on-campus job is one of the best ways to develop relationships with instructors and administrators on your campus.

Off-Campus Jobs

The best places to start looking for off-campus jobs are your campus career center and financial aid office. They might well have listings or Web sites with off-campus employment opportunities. Don't hesitate to speak to a career counselor for suggestions. You can also use the following job search strategies:

- Learn the names of the major employers in your college's geographic area: manufacturers, service industries, resorts, and so on. Once you know who the major employers are, check them out, visit their Web sites, and learn the details.

- Check out the Web site for the agency in your state that collects and disseminates information about available employment opportunities. Find out whether this agency has an office in the community where you are attending college.

- Visit employment agencies, particularly those that seek part-time temporary workers. This is a convenient, low-risk (for both you and the employer) way to "shop" for a job and to obtain flexible, short-term, low-commitment employment.

- Visit online job boards, and look at the classified ads in the local newspaper, in print or online. Don't forget the classifieds in the national press. Some national firms will have jobs that can be done part-time in your area or even from your own living space.

- Check your campus student newspaper. Employers who favor hiring college students often advertise there.

- Be aware that many jobs are never posted. Employers find it easier to hire people recommended to them by current employees, friends, or the person vacating the position. Faculty members often hire students for their research labs on the basis of performance in the classroom.

- Realize that who you know is important. Your friends who already work on campus or who have had an internship can be the best people to help you when you are ready to search for your job. In fact, nearly 50 percent of all student jobs are found through family and friends.

Internships

Your academic department or the campus career center can provide information on off-campus internships that may be available. Internships offer valuable hands-on experience in a career you may want to pursue. Through an internship, you'll learn not only about the nature of the industry and the daily work routine but also about employment in an organization. You'll work with people who can be instrumental in helping you find a job when your studies are done. And adding the experience of having been an intern to your résumé will make it all the stronger when the time comes for a job search.

try it!
College Jobs and Your Career

At this point in your college experience, you probably have at least tentative plans about the major and/or the career you will pursue. If you must take a job while going to school, think about what jobs may be available on campus and in the outside community that might provide valuable experience with respect to your goals. Make two lists—one for on-campus jobs and the other for off-campus jobs—that identify jobs related to your career interests, and look into the availability of such work.

Co-op Programs

Some colleges and universities have "co-op programs," in which you spend some terms in class and other terms in temporary job settings in your field. Although they usually prolong your education somewhat, co-op programs have many advantages. They offer an excellent preview of what work in your chosen field is like and give you valuable experience and contacts that you can tap into to get a job when you finish college; in fact, many firms offer successful co-op students permanent jobs when they graduate. Alternating work and school terms may be a more agreeable schedule for you than eight or ten straight terms of classes would be, and the work/academics balance may help you keep your ultimate goal in mind. Co-op programs can help you pay for college, too; during their co-op terms, some co-op students, especially in technical fields, make almost as much as their professors do!

The bottom line is to try to limit the number of hours you work while you're in college. Research finds that full-time students who work more than fifteen or twenty hours a week have a lower chance of finishing college. And students who work off campus, as opposed to on campus, are also less likely to be successful in college unless their work is directly connected with their major.

12

12 Chapter Review

One-minute paper . . .

Making the right choices when it comes to picking a major and a career can be intimidating. What did you learn in this chapter that will help you prepare for declaring a major? Of the topics covered in this chapter, which would you like to learn more about?

Applying what you've learned . . .

Now that you have read and discussed this chapter, consider how you can apply what you have learned to your academic and personal life. The following prompts will help you reflect on chapter material and its relevance to you both now and in the future.

1. Sometimes the best way to learn about a career is to talk to someone who is working or teaching in that field. Set up an appointment to talk with a professor who teaches in the area in which you are interested. Find out as much as possible about the education required for a specific career in the field.

2. Choosing a major is a big decision and should include consideration of your personal learning style, your personality, and your goals and values. Review what you learned in Chapter 3 about your emotional intelligence and preferred ways of learning. How will those insights guide your exploration of majors and careers?

Building your portfolio . . .

Investigating occupations

How can you select a major if you are not sure what you want to do when you graduate? College classes, out-of-class activities, and part-time jobs will help you narrow your choices and make decisions about a major and a potential career.

1. Create a Word document and list at least two majors that you are considering right now or that you would like to know more about. Why do you find these majors interesting?

2. Name two or more careers you think you might be interested in after you graduate. Explain your choice.

3. The U.S. Bureau of Labor Statistics publishes the online *Occupational Outlook Handbook,* which provides details about hundreds of jobs. You can find in-depth information on any job in which you might have an interest.

   a. Visit the *Occupational Outlook Handbook* online at **http://www.bls.gov/oco/**; in the search field, enter one or two of the careers you listed above.

   b. Create a chart like the one below. Note the training or degree required, describe the job outlook, and list the median earnings for each career. Look through the other descriptions to learn more about the careers.

	Example	Career 1	Career 2
Career	Computer software engineer		
Training Required	Bachelor's degree, computer science/software engineering		
Job Outlook	One of the fastest-growing occupations from 2004 to 2014		
Median Annual Earnings	About $74,980		

4. Save your findings in your portfolio on your personal computer or flash drive. Even in your first college year it is important that you begin to think about what you are going to do after graduation. The more you investigate different types of careers, the easier it will be for you to identify a major or decide what kind of internship, part-time job, or service learning opportunity you want to experience while you are still in college.

Where to go for help . . .

On Campus

Your college Web site: Search your campus career resources. Larger campuses might have specialized career service centers for specific professional schools and clusters of majors. Often student professional organizations, academic advisers, and departments will provide relevant career information on their Web sites.

Career center: Almost every college campus has a career center where you can obtain free counseling and information on careers. A career professional will work with you to help you define your interests, interpret the results of any assessment you complete, coach you on interview techniques, and critique your résumé. It's important to schedule an appointment. By the end of your first year you should be familiar with the career center, where it is located, and the counselor who is responsible for your academic major or interests. You might also find opportunities for internships and interview practice there.

Academic advising: More and more advisers have been trained in what is known as "developmental advising," or helping you see beyond individual classes and working to help you initiate a career search. Talking to your adviser is often the best place to start. If you have not declared a major—which is true of many first-year students—your adviser might be able to help you with that decision as well.

Faculty: On many campuses, faculty members take an active role in helping students connect academic interests to careers. A faculty member can recommend specific courses that relate to a particular career. Faculty members in professional curricula, such as business and other applied fields, often have direct contact with companies and serve as contacts for internships. If you have an interest in attending graduate school, faculty sponsorship is critical to admission. Developing a relationship with a faculty mentor can open a number of important doors.

Library: Some campuses have a separate library in the career center staffed by librarians whose job is to help you locate career-related information resources. Of course, all campuses have a main library that contains a wealth of information on careers. The reference librarian at the main desk will be glad to help you. If you are a student on a large university campus, you might find additional libraries that are specific to certain professional schools and colleges within the university, such as business, education, law, medicine, music, and engineering; these are also excellent sources for career information.

Upperclass students: Ask whether more experienced students can help you navigate courses and find important resources. Upperclass students might also have practical experience gained from internships and volunteering. Since they have tested the waters, they can alert you to potential pitfalls or inform you of opportunities.

Student organizations: Professional student organizations that focus on specific career interests meet regularly throughout the year. Join them now. Not only will they put you in contact with upperclass students, but also their programs often include employer representatives, helpful discussions on searching for internships or jobs, and exposure to current conditions in the workplace.

Online

Career center: Go to your campus career center's home page, and check its resources, such as links to useful pages.

Occupational Information Network: http://www.online.onetcenter.org. This federal government site has information on occupations, skill sets, and links to professional sites for selected occupations. This is a great place to get started thinking about your interests.

Mapping Your Future: http://www.mappingyourfuture.org. This comprehensive site provides support for those who are just starting to explore careers.

The Riley Guide: http://www.rileyguide.com. One of the best sites for interviewing, job search strategies, and other critical career tips.

My Institution's Resources

_____

_____

_____

_____

_____

_____

_____

13 Staying Healthy

College provides countless opportunities to exercise your mind and expand your horizons. Unfortunately, while college students exercise their minds, many neglect to exercise their bodies. Sometimes they also experiment with a variety of risky behaviors. While most students find healthy ways to cope with the transition to college, some become so stressed that their anxiety overwhelms them. Others ignore the consequences of their sexual decisions and end up getting a sexually transmitted infection or facing an unplanned pregnancy. Some students drink too much, smoke, or abuse drugs. If you fail to take care of your mind and body while you're in college, you can seriously compromise your health, well-being, academic performance, and future.

This chapter explores the topic of *wellness*, which is a catchall term for taking care of your mind, body, and spirit. Wellness means making healthy choices and achieving balance. It includes reducing stress in positive ways, keeping fit, maintaining good sexual health, and taking a sensible approach to alcohol and other drugs.

How Do You Measure Up?

1. When I feel overwhelmed, I deal with my stress in healthy ways, like taking a walk or exercising.
   - ○ Agree
   - ○ Don't Know
   - ○ Disagree

2. I exercise regularly and manage my weight to stay fit.
   - ○ Agree
   - ○ Don't Know
   - ○ Disagree

3. I have adequate information about sex and contraception.
   - ○ Agree
   - ○ Don't Know
   - ○ Disagree

4. I know the difference between responsible and irresponsible alcohol use.
   - ○ Agree
   - ○ Don't Know
   - ○ Disagree

Review the items you marked "don't know" or "disagree." Paying attention to all these aspects of your college experience can be important to your success. After reading this chapter, come back to this list and think about ways you can work on these areas.

Managing Stress

Christie Sarlin

First-year student

Week 5 at college: My roommate Brooke Chappell slips on a pair of elegant heels with the air of a movie heroine. To look at perfectly manicured Brooke, you would never guess at her complex life — taking fifteen credits, playing on the field-hockey team, and working part-time in the math department, all while maintaining a 3.8 GPA.

"Why so haunted-looking, Sarlin?" she says. "C'mon, get dressed."

Brooke and I share a major in business administration. We both have part-time academic jobs. Sadly, the similarities end there.

"God, how do you always manage to channel Heidi Klum?" I ask her. "Look at me: I'm like someone who's been hiding in a Pepperidge Farm warehouse." It's not much of an exaggeration: I'm so stressed out by school and work that I've embraced every brownie I can get my hands on. I no longer fit into anything in my wardrobe that doesn't involve an elastic waist. The weight gain then makes me more stressed. I can't sleep. I feel totally disorganized.

Brooke shifts a basket of dirty laundry from my bed and sits down beside me. "Don't be silly," she says sympathetically.

"I just don't know how you get everything done and stay so Zen," I tell her. "I feel like I'm running as fast as I can just to keep up."

What can Christie learn from Brooke? What steps could she take to better manage the way she is responding to stress? Why is it important for students to eat properly, get regular exercise, and keep a detailed schedule?

In the fall of 2007, according to a survey conducted by the American College Health Association, about one-third of college students reported that stress had negatively affected either an exam grade or a course grade.[1] When you are stressed, your body undergoes rapid physiological, behavioral, and emotional changes. Your rate of breathing can become more rapid and shallow. Your heart rate begins to speed up, and the muscles in your shoulders, forehead, the back of your neck, and perhaps across your chest begin to tighten. Your hands may become cold or sweaty. You may experience gastrointestinal symptoms such as an upset stomach. Your mouth and lips may feel dry and hot, and you might notice that your hands and knees begin to shake or tremble. Your voice may quiver or even go up an octave.

A number of psychological changes also occur when you are under stress. You might experience changes in your ability to think, such as confusion, trouble concentrating, inability to remember things, and poor problem solving. Emotions such as fear, anxiety, depression, irritability, anger, and frustration are common, and you might have trouble getting to sleep at night or wake up too early and not be able to go back to sleep.

The best starting point for handling stress is to be in good physical and mental shape. When your body and mind are healthy, it's like inoculating yourself against stress. This means you need to pay attention to your diet, exercise, sleep, and mental health.

Diet and Exercise

There is a clear connection between what you eat and drink, your overall health and well-being, and stress. Eating a lot of junk food will add pounds to your body and reduce your energy level. And when you can't keep up with your work because you're sluggish or tired, you might experience more stress. One dietary substance that can be directly linked to higher stress levels is caffeine.

In moderate amounts (50–200 milligrams per day), caffeine increases alertness and reduces feel-

[1] http://www.acha-ncha.org/docs/ACHA-NCHA_Reference_Group_Report_Fall2007.pdf.

ings of fatigue. But even at this low dosage, it can make you perkier during part of the day and more tired later. Consumed in larger quantities, caffeine can cause nervousness, headaches, irritability, stomach irritation, and insomnia—all symptoms of stress. If the amount of caffeine you consume is excessive, consider drinking water, or choose decaf coffee or tea. Be aware that even a small, five-ounce cup of regular coffee contains 65–115 milligrams of caffeine.

Exercise is an excellent stress management technique, the best way to stay fit, and a critical part of weight loss. While any kind of recreation benefits your body and spirit, aerobic exercise is the best for both stress management and weight management. In aerobic exercise, you work until your pulse is in a "target zone," and you keep it in this zone for at least 30 minutes. You can reach your target heart rate through a variety of exercises: walking, jogging, running, swimming, biking, and using a stair climber. Choose activities that you enjoy so you will look forward to your exercise time. That way, it's more likely to become a regular part of your routine.

Sleep

Getting adequate sleep is another way to protect yourself from stress. According to the National Sleep Foundation, 63 percent of American adults do not get the recommended eight hours of sleep per night. Lack of sleep can lead to anxiety, depression, and academic struggles such as an

inability to focus and concentrate. Try the following suggestions to establish better sleep habits:

- If you can't sleep, get up and do something boring.
- Get your clothes and school materials together before you go to bed.
- Read or listen to a relaxation tape before going to bed.
- Get exercise during the day.
- Sleep in the same room and bed every night.
- Set a regular schedule for going to bed and getting up.

Relaxation Techniques

Relaxation techniques such as visualization and deep breathing can help you reduce stress. Learning these skills is just like learning any new skill. You need knowledge and practice. Check your course catalog, college counseling center, health clinic, student newspaper, and fitness center for classes that teach relaxation. You'll also find books as well as CDs and DVDs that guide you through relaxation techniques.

Here are several additional things you can do to improve your level of stress and your mental health:

- Reward yourself on a regular basis when you achieve small goals.
- Remember that there is a reason you are in a particular situation. Keep the payoff in mind.
- Laugh. A good laugh will almost always make you feel better.
- Pray or meditate.
- Do yoga.
- Practice a hobby.
- Get a massage.
- Practice deep breathing.

Getting Help for Stress

Most campuses have counseling centers that offer one-on-one sessions as well as support groups for their students. Remember that there is no shame attached to being stressed or anxious and that you are not alone in feeling this way. Proper counseling and medical attention when needed can help you deal more effectively with high levels of stress.

13

Nutrition and Weight Management

"You are what you eat" is more than a catchphrase; it's an important reminder of the vital role diet plays in our lives. You've probably read news stories about how there are more and more obese young people than ever before in our history. The Centers for Disease Control (CDC) reports that the rates of obesity have more than doubled in the United States since 1990: In 1990 an estimated 11.6 percent of U.S. citizens were obese; in 2007 an estimated 25.6 percent were classified as obese. One expert, Dr. James Hill, director of human nutrition at the University of Colorado, predicts, "If obesity is left unchecked, almost all Americans will be obese by 2050." Many people attribute this situation to the explosion of fast-food restaurants, which place flavor and low prices before health. A Tufts University researcher found that 60 percent of college students eat too much saturated fat, which increases the risk for heart disease. Also, most of us do not consume enough fiber and whole grains. As a result, we are more likely to have long-term health problems, such as diabetes, heart disease, and cancer.

Healthy Eating

So what can you do about your eating habits? It's not easy at first, but if you commit to a new eating regimen, you will not only feel better, you'll be healthier and probably happier. Your campus health center might have a registered dietitian to help you make healthy changes in your diet. Meanwhile, here are some suggestions:

- Restrict your intake of red meat, butter, white rice, white bread, and sweets. "White foods" are made with refined flour, which has few nutrients. Instead, go for fish, poultry, soy products, and whole wheat or multigrain breads. Remember that brown bread is not necessarily whole wheat. Check the label.

- Eat plenty of vegetables and fruits daily. These are important building blocks for a balanced diet, and they contain lots of fiber (to help fight off cancer and heart disease). Instead of fruit juices, which contain concentrated amounts of sugar, opt for the actual fruit. When you sit down to eat any meal (including breakfast), make sure you have at least one fruit or vegetable on your plate.

- Avoid fried foods—french fries, fried chicken, and so forth. Choose grilled or broiled meats instead. Avoid foods with large amounts of fat and sugar, such as doughnuts.

- Keep your room stocked with healthy snacks, such as fruit, vegetables, yogurt, pretzels, and graham crackers.

- Eat a sensible amount of nuts and all the legumes (beans) you want to round out your fiber intake.

- Watch your portion size. Avoid "supersized" fast-food items and all-you-can-eat buffets.

- Eat breakfast! Your brain will function more efficiently if you eat a power-packed meal first thing in the morning. Eating breakfast can also jump-start your metabolism. If you are not normally a breakfast eater, try eating just a piece of fruit or half a bagel. You will notice a big difference in your energy level during your early morning classes. Avoid sugar-coated cereals. Go for healthier options that are loaded with fiber.

- Always read the government-required nutrition label on all packaged foods. Check the sodium content (sodium will make you retain fluids and increase your weight and possibly your blood pressure) and the number of grams of fat. Strive for a diet with only 20 percent fat.

Figure 13.1 shows the Healthy Eating Pyramid, designed by Walter Willett, chairman of the Department of Nutrition at Harvard's School of Public Health. The Healthy Eating Pyramid puts exercise and weight control at the base, recommends eating whole-grain foods at most meals, and encourages eating vegetables "in abundance." This pyramid emphasizes eating lots of plant oils, such as olive, canola, and soy, and gives fish and poultry a higher profile than red meat, which you should eat sparingly.

Obesity

People have been joking about the "freshman 15" forever, but it's no joke that new college students tend to gain weight during their first term. Nutrition experts at Tufts University reported that the average weight gain is 6 pounds for men and about 4.5 pounds for women during the first year of college. Increased stress, lifestyle changes, new food choices, changes in physical activity, and alcohol consumption can all cause weight gain. Try eating smaller meals more often, getting regular exercise, keeping a food journal (to keep track

13

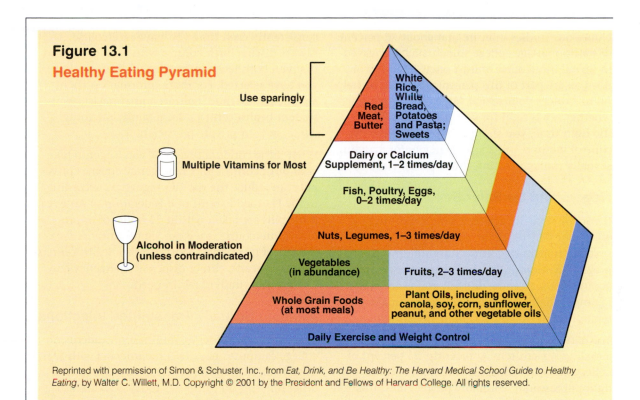

Figure 13.1

Healthy Eating Pyramid

Use sparingly

White Rice, White Bread, Potatoes and Pasta; Sweets

Red Meat, Butter

Multiple Vitamins for Most

Dairy or Calcium Supplement, 1–2 times/day

Fish, Poultry, Eggs, 0–2 times/day

Nuts, Legumes, 1–3 times/day

Alcohol in Moderation (unless contraindicated)

Vegetables (in abundance)

Fruits, 2–3 times/day

Whole Grain Foods (at most meals)

Plant Oils, including olive, canola, soy, corn, sunflower, peanut, and other vegetable oils

Daily Exercise and Weight Control

of what you are actually consuming), and being realistic about dieting.

Eating Disorders

An increasing number of college students are obsessed with their bodies and food intake. This can lead to conditions such as anorexia, bulimia, or binge eating disorder, all of which affect women disproportionately more than men. Anorexia is characterized by self-induced starvation, extreme preoccupation with food, and a body weight less than 85 percent of a healthy weight. Bulimia is characterized by cycles of bingeing (eating large amounts of food) and purging by vomiting, abusing laxatives and/or diuretics, exercising excessively, and fasting. People with a binge eating disorder do not purge the calories after the binge. Individuals with binge eating disorder tend to eat secretively and are often clinically obese.

Some of the signs and symptoms of an eating disorder are as follows:

- Intense fear of gaining weight
- Restricting types of food, such as those containing any kind of fat
- Weighing less than 85 percent of recommended body weight based on height, or failure to make appropriate weight gain during a period of growth
- Stopping or never getting a monthly menstrual period
- Seeing one's body as fat, even though it is underweight
- Overexercising
- Secrecy about food and denial of a problem with eating

Anyone who is struggling with an eating disorder should seek medical attention. Eating disorders can be life-threatening if they are not treated by a health care professional. Many colleges and universities have eating disorder case management teams to help individuals on campus. Contact your student health center for more information, or contact the National Eating Disorder Association (**http://www.nationaleatingdisorders .org** or 1-800-931-2237) to find a professional in your area who specializes in the treatment of eating disorders.

13

Sexual Health

Numerous studies indicate that about 75 percent of traditional-age college students have engaged in sexual intercourse at least once. Whether or not you are part of this percentage, it can be helpful to explore your sexual values and to consider whether sex is right for you at this time. If it is the right time, you should choose a good birth control method and adopt strategies for avoiding sexually transmitted infections (STIs).

Negotiating for Safer Sex

If you are sexually active, it's important to talk with your partner about ways to protect against sexually transmitted infections and unwanted pregnancy. Communicating with your partner about safer sex can be difficult and even embarrassing initially, but this dialogue can make your relationship stronger and more meaningful.

You can avoid STIs and unwanted pregnancies by avoiding sex entirely. Apparently, 25 percent of college students choose this option, according to national research. For many people, masturbation is a reasonable alternative to sex with a partner.

If you're in the remaining 75 percent, you'll be safer (in terms of STIs) if you have only one partner. Yet you might feel that you're at a point in your life where you would prefer to have multiple relationships simultaneously. Whether you're monogamous or not, you should always protect yourself by using a condom or being sure your partner uses one.

In addition to being a contraceptive, a condom can help prevent the spread of STIs, including HIV. A condom's effectiveness against disease holds true for anal, vaginal, and oral intercourse. The most current research indicates that the rate of protection provided by a condom against STIs is similar to its rate of protection against pregnancy (90–99 percent) when used correctly and consistently for every act of intercourse or oral sex. Note that only latex rubber condoms and polyurethane condoms—not lambskin or other types of natural membrane condoms—provide this protection.

Birth Control

Sexually active heterosexual students have to take steps to prevent unwanted pregnancy. Planning is the key. What is the best method of contraception? It is any method that you use correctly and consistently each time you have intercourse. Always discuss birth control with your partner so that you both feel comfortable with the option you have selected. For more information about a particular method, consult a pharmacist, your student health center, a local family planning clinic, or your private physician.

What if the condom breaks or you forget to take your birth control pill? Emergency contraceptive pills can reduce the risk of pregnancy. According to the Planned Parenthood Federation of America, if the pills are taken within 72 hours of unprotected intercourse, they can significantly reduce the risk of pregnancy. Most campus health centers and local health clinics dispense emergency contraception to individuals in need.

Avoiding Sexually Transmitted Infections

In recent years epidemic numbers of students on college campuses have become infected with STIs. In general, STIs continue to increase faster than other illnesses on campuses today. STIs are usually spread through genital contact. Sometimes, however, these infections can be transmitted mouth-to-mouth. There are more than twenty known types of STIs; seven are most common on college campuses.

Chlamydia   The most common STI in the United States, chlamydia is particularly threatening to women because only about 30 percent of those infected have symptoms. When symptoms are present in women, they include a burning sensation during urination, painful intercourse, rectal pain or discharge, and vaginal discharge. If left untreated, the infection can progress to pelvic inflammatory disease (PID), thought to be the main cause of infertility in women. Men with chlamydia are often asymptomatic but may have urinary burning and discharge or testicular and rectal pain.

Human Papilloma Virus (HPV)   The leading STI affecting college students, HPV causes warts on the outer genitals and in the rectum of those who practice anal-receptive intercourse. If undetected, HPV can lead to cervical cancer in women. Gardasil, a vaccine that became available in 2006, provides protection against four types of HPV that cause 70 percent of cervical cancer cases. For more information about this vaccine or to receive the three-injection series, contact your college or university health services or local health care provider.

Gonorrhea   A bacterial infection with symptoms similar to chlamydia, gonorrhea usually causes pain and burning with urination and possible discharge in men, while women are often asymptomatic.

Herpes   The herpes virus affects men and women, and the infection can be both oral and genital. Symptoms include blisters, and currently there is no cure. Infected individuals are most contagious just before or after the blisters erupt.

Hepatitis B   Symptoms include yellowing of the skin and eyes and an upset stomach. Some infected people recover completely, while others remain carriers for life. A small percentage will experience permanent liver damage, and in some patients this disease is fatal. There is no cure or medical treatment for hepatitis B, although it can be prevented with a vaccine.

Hepatitis C   Like hepatitis B, hepatitis C is a long-term infection caused by a virus (HCV), but there is no known vaccine for prevention. The disease spreads through blood or bodily fluids and may advance to liver disease.

HIV/AIDS   The number of people infected with AIDS and the virus that causes it, HIV, continues to increase. Anyone can contract the disease if exposed to the virus, and heterosexual women are one of the groups at increased risk. Having other STIs may predispose a person to contracting HIV more readily upon exposure.

Protecting against Sexual Assault

Anyone is at risk for being raped, but the majority of victims are women. By the time they graduate from college, an estimated one out of four college women will be the victim of attempted rape, and one out of six will be raped. Most women will be raped by someone they know—a date or an acquaintance—and most will not report the crime. Alcohol is a factor in nearly three-fourths of the incidents. Whether raped by a date or a stranger, a victim can suffer long-term traumatic effects.

Tricia Phaup of the University of South Carolina offers this advice on avoiding sexual assault:

- Know what you want and do not want sexually.
- Go to social gatherings with friends, and leave with them.

try it!

What's Your Decision?

Although you might know the strategies to keep yourself from contracting an STI, knowledge doesn't always translate into behavior. List all the reasons you can think of that people wouldn't practice prevention strategies of abstinence, monogamy, or condom use. Then review your list and consider whether each barrier would apply to you ("Yes," "No," or "Maybe"). In this way, you can evaluate where you stand on the issue of safer sex and determine what areas you may need to work on to ensure that you always protect yourself.

- Avoid being alone with people you don't know very well.
- Trust your intuition.
- Be alert to subtle and unconscious messages you may be sending and receiving.
- Be aware of how much alcohol you drink, if any.

If you are ever tempted to force another person to have sex:

- Realize that it is never okay to force sex on someone.
- Don't assume that you know what your date wants.
- If you're getting mixed messages, ask.
- Be aware of the effects of alcohol.
- Remember that rape is morally and legally wrong.

If you have been raped, regardless of whether you choose to report the rape to the police or get a medical exam, it is very helpful to seek counseling by contacting resources such as a campus sexual assault coordinator, local rape crisis center, campus police department, student health services, women's student services, local hospital emergency rooms, and campus chaplains.

13

Substance Abuse

In this section our purpose is not to make judgments, but to warn you about irresponsible use of some substances that can have a major negative impact on your college experience and your life: alcohol, tobacco, prescription drugs, and illegal drugs. While you're in college, you will likely be exposed to the reckless use of one or more of these substances. We hope that this information will help you think twice and avoid the trouble that can come from substance abuse.

Making Decisions about Alcohol

Even if you don't drink, you should read this information because 50 percent of college students reported helping a drunken friend, classmate, or study partner in the past year.

Alcohol can turn even people who don't drink into victims, such as people who are killed by drunk drivers or family members who suffer from the behavior of an alcoholic. Over the course of one year, about 20 to 30 percent of students report serious problems related to excessive alcohol use. You might have heard news reports about college students who died or were seriously or permanently injured as a result of excessive drinking. Just one occasion of heavy or high-risk drinking can lead to problems.

How alcohol affects behavior depends on the dose of alcohol, which is best measured by blood alcohol content, or BAC. Most of the pleasurable effects of alcoholic beverages are experienced at lower BAC levels, when alcohol acts as a behavioral stimulant. For most people, the stimulant level is around one drink per hour. Usually, problems begin at an intake higher than .05, when alcohol acts as a sedative and begins to slow down areas of the brain. Most people who have more than four or five drinks at one occasion feel "buzzed," show signs of impairment, and are likely to be at higher risk for alcohol-related problems. However, significant impairment at lower doses can occur.

How fast you drink makes a difference, too. Your body gets rid of alcohol at a rate of about one drink an hour. Drinking more than one drink an hour may cause a rise in BAC because the body is absorbing alcohol faster than it can eliminate it.

At BAC levels of .025 to .05, a drinker tends to feel animated and energized. At a BAC level of around .05, a drinker may feel rowdy or boisterous. This is where most people report feeling a buzz from alcohol. At a BAC level between .05 and .08, alcohol starts to act as a depressant. So as soon as you feel that buzz, remember that you are on the brink of losing coordination, clear thinking, and judgment.

Driving is measurably impaired even at BAC levels lower than the legal limit of .08. In fact, an accurate safe level for most people may be half the legal limit (.04). As BAC levels climb past .08, you will become progressively less coordinated and less able to make good decisions. Most people become severely uncoordinated with BAC levels higher than .08 and might begin falling asleep, falling down, or slurring their speech.

Most people pass out or fall asleep when their BAC is above .25. Unfortunately, even after you pass out and stop drinking, your BAC can continue to rise as alcohol in your stomach is released to the intestine and absorbed into the bloodstream. Your body may try to get rid of alcohol by vomiting, but you can choke if you are unconscious, semi-conscious, or severely uncoordinated.

Worse yet, at BAC levels higher than .30, most people will show signs of severe alcohol poisoning, such as an inability to wake up, slowed breathing, a fast but weak pulse, cool or damp skin, and pale or bluish skin. Anyone exhibiting these symptoms needs medical assistance immediately. If you find someone in such a state, keep the person on his or her side with the head lower than the rest of the body. Check to see that the airway is clear, especially if the person is vomiting or if the tongue is blocking the back of the throat.

Heavy Drinking: The Danger Zone

We know that many students have been subjected to what they might regard as exaggerated scare tactics by well-intentioned educators. However, there are many compelling warning indicators related to heavy drinking. Think about the following statistics and their possible application to you and your friends. The effects of heavy drinking are nothing less than a tragedy for many college students:

- 1,700 college students between the ages of eighteen and twenty-four die each year from alcohol-related unintentional injuries, including motor vehicle crashes.

13

- 599,000 students between the ages of eighteen and twenty-four are unintentionally injured each year while under the influence of alcohol.

- More than 696,000 students between the ages of eighteen and twenty-four are assaulted each year by another student who has been drinking.[2]

Heavy drinking, sometimes called binge drinking, is commonly defined as five or more drinks for males and four or more drinks for females on a single occasion. For a very large person who drinks slowly over a long period of time (several hours), four or five drinks may not lead to a BAC associated with impairment. However, research suggests that in many cases the BAC of heavy drinkers exceeds the legal limit for impairment (.08).

The academic, medical, and social consequences of heavy drinking can seriously endanger the quality of life. Research based on surveys conducted by the Core Institute at Southern Illinois University (**http://www.siuc.edu/~coreinst**) provides substantial evidence that heavy drinkers have a significantly greater risk of adverse outcomes, including increased risk of poor test performance, missed classes, unlawful behavior, violence, memory loss, drunk driving, regretful behavior, and vandalism, compared with all drinkers and all students. At the same time, college health centers nationwide are reporting increasing occurrences of serious medical conditions—even death—resulting from excessive alcohol use. These medical problems include alcohol poisoning, leading to coma and shock; respiratory depression, choking, and respiratory arrest; head trauma and brain injury; lacerations and fractures; and unwanted or unsafe sexual activity causing STIs and pregnancies.

If you engage in heavy drinking so long that your body can tolerate large amounts of alcohol, you might become an alcoholic. Fortunately, most college students do not advance to alcoholism. However, if you or someone you know shows signs of becoming an alcoholic, you should contact a source on campus that can help. The student health center is a good starting place, but an instructor, a minister, or an academic adviser can also counsel you on where to seek help.

Tobacco—The Other Legal Drug

Tobacco use is clearly the cause of many serious medical conditions, including heart disease, some forms of cancer, and lung ailments. Over the years, tobacco has led to the deaths of hundreds of thousands of individuals, and, unfortunately, many college students smoke. The University of Michigan's Monitoring the Future Survey published by the National Institute on Drug Abuse estimates that rates of smoking have declined among college students and were at 20 percent as of 2007.[3] But one concern is "social smoking." This term describes smoking by students who do so only when hanging out with friends, drinking, or partying. Most college students feel they will be able to give up their social smoking habit once they graduate, but after four years of college, some find that they are addicted to cigarettes.

try it!

Sharing and Comparing Experiences

List five ways that the quality of life of you or a friend has been influenced by others' drinking or smoking. In small groups, share some or all of these with others. What did you find out when you compared your experiences with theirs? Did you handle the situation in a healthy manner in comparison to other members of your group? What would you do differently in the future?

[2] R. Hingson et al., "Magnitude of Alcohol-Related Mortality and Morbidity among U.S. College Students Ages 18–24: Changes from 1998–2001." *Annual Review of Public Health* 26 (2005): 259–79.

[3] L.D. Johnston, P.M. O'Malley, J.G. Bachman, and J.E. Schulenberg, *Monitoring the Future: National Survey Results on Drug Use, 1975–2007.* Volume II: *College Students and Adults Ages 19–45* (NIH Publication No. 08-6418B). Bethesda, MD: National Institute on Drug Abuse, 2008.

13

The chemicals in tobacco are so highly addictive that they make it hard to quit. Although young people may not worry about long-term effects such as lung cancer and emphysema, increased respiratory infections, worsening of asthma, bad breath, stained teeth, and the huge expense should be motivations to not start smoking. Many institutions and local hospitals offer smoking cessation programs to help people quit smoking. If you smoke, contact your campus health center for more information about how to quit.

Prescription Drug Abuse and Addiction

Researchers at the University of Michigan reported in 2008 that 11.2 percent of college students have used prescription stimulants for nonmedical purposes at some point, 6.9 percent in the past year. Three classes of prescription drugs are the most commonly abused: opioids, central nervous system depressants, and stimulants.

Opioids include morphine, codeine, and such branded drugs as OxyContin, Darvon, Vicodin, Demerol, and Dilaudid. Opioids work by blocking the transmission of pain messages to the brain. Chronic use can result in addiction. Taking a large single dose of an opioid can cause a severe reduction in your breathing rate that can lead to death.

Taken under a doctor's care, central nervous system depressants, such as Valium, Librium, Xanax, and Halcion, can be useful in the treatment of anxiety and sleep disorders. The flip side is that exceeding the recommended dosage can create a drug tolerance, and the user will need larger doses to achieve the same result. If the user stops taking the drug, the brain's activity can rebound and race out of control, possibly leading to seizures and other harmful consequences.

Stimulants, such as ephedrine, Ritalin, and Dexadrine, enhance brain activity, causing an increase in alertness, attention, and energy accompanied by elevated blood pressure and increased heart rate. Legal use of stimulants to treat obesity, asthma, and other problems has dropped off as their potential for abuse and addiction has become apparent.[4]

Ritalin is prescribed for a condition called ADHD (attention deficit/hyperactivity disorder) but is gaining recognition on college campuses as a "cramming drug." This prescription drug costs only about 50¢ per tablet but sells on the street for as much as $15. College students are using Ritalin to stay awake for long periods of time to study for exams. Many students think that since it is a prescribed drug, it must be harmless. The U.S. Department of Education's Higher Education Center for Alcohol and Other Drug Abuse and Violence Prevention lists the following as possible adverse effects from abusing Ritalin: nervousness, vomiting, changes in heart rate and blood pressure, dependency, fevers, convulsions, headaches, paranoia, hallucinations, and delusions.

Another class of drugs that is of concern in the college setting is anabolic steroids. When most people think of steroids, they think about collegiate and professional athletes. But it is important for all college students to know and understand the dangers of these synthetic substances.

According to the National Institute on Drug Abuse, steroids are taken orally or injected into the body in cycles that last weeks or months. Steroid abuse has many major side effects, including liver tumors, cancer, jaundice, fluid retention, high blood pressure, kidney tumors, and severe acne. Most anabolic steroid users are male and therefore have gender-specific side effects, including shrinking of the testicles, reduced sperm count, infertility, baldness, development of breasts, and increased risk for prostate cancer. Abusers also put themselves at risk for contracting HIV or other blood-borne viruses from using or sharing infected needles.

The abuse rate for steroids is fairly low among the general population. The 2007 Monitoring the Future Survey found that 1.9 percent of young adults ages nineteen to twenty-eight reported using steroids at least once during their lifetimes. Just over half a percent (0.6 percent) reported using steroids at least once in the past year, and 0.3 percent reported using steroids in the past month.[5]

[5] L.D. Johnston, P.M. O'Malley, J.G. Bachman, and J.E. Schulenberg, *Monitoring the Future: National Survey Results on Drug Use, 1975–2007.* Volume II: *College Students and Adults Ages 19–45* (NIH Publication No. 08-6418B). Bethesda, MD: National Institute on Drug Abuse, 2008.

[4] Adapted from *Prescription Drugs: Abuse and Addiction.* Bethesda, MD: National Institute on Drug Abuse, part of the National Institutes of Health, a division of the U.S. Department of Health and Human Services, 2009.

13

Illegal Drugs

Athletic departments, potential employers, and government agencies routinely screen for many commonly used illegal drugs. Future employability, athletic scholarships, and insurability may be compromised if you have a positive drug test for any of these substances.

Marijuana   The effects of marijuana can linger for three to seven days, depending on the smoker and the potency of the drug. Chronic use of marijuana can lead to a lethargic state in which users may forget about current responsibilities (such as going to class). Long-term use carries the same risks of lung infections and cancer that are associated with smoking tobacco.

Ecstasy   MDMA, commonly known as ecstasy, is a synthetic (human-made) drug. While many young people believe that MDMA is safe and offers nothing but a pleasant high for the $25 cost of a single tablet, the reality is far different. When MDMA is taken orally, its effects last approximately 4 to 6 hours. Many people will take a second dose when the initial dose begins to fade. Some tablets contain not only MDMA but also other drugs, including amphetamine, caffeine, dextromethorphan, ephedrine, and cocaine. MDMA significantly depletes serotonin, a substance in the brain that helps regulate mood, sleep, pain, emotion, appetite, and other behaviors. It takes the brain time to rebuild the serotonin needed to perform important physiological and psychological functions. Of great concern is MDMA's adverse effect on the pumping efficiency of the heart. Heavy users can experience obsessive traits, anxiety, paranoia, and sleep disturbance. One study indicates that MDMA can have long-lasting effects on memory.[6]

Heroin   Numerous reports have suggested a rise in heroin use among college students. A highly addictive drug with the potential to be more damaging and fatal than other opioids, heroin is the most abused and most rapidly acting of this group. One of the most significant—and surest—effects of heroin use is addiction. The human

body begins to develop tolerance to the drug on first use. Once this happens, the abuser must use more of the drug to achieve a high of the same intensity. Heroin can be injected, smoked, or snorted. Injection is the most efficient way to administer low-purity heroin. However, the availability of high-purity heroin and the fear of infection by sharing needles have made snorting and smoking the drug more common. Some users believe that snorting or smoking heroin will not lead to addiction. They are 100 percent wrong.

Chronic users may develop collapsed veins, infection of the heart lining and valves, abscesses, and liver disease. Users are also at risk for pulmonary complications, including various types of pneumonia. In addition to the effects of the drug itself, users who inject heroin or share needles also put themselves at risk for contracting HIV, hepatitis B and C, and other blood-borne viruses. A heroin overdose is known to cause slow and shallow breathing, convulsions, coma, and possibly death.

Cocaine   Cocaine produces an intense experience that heightens senses. A cocaine high lasts only a short time; then the good feelings are gone. During the crash, the user may feel tired and unmotivated and find it impossible to sleep. Cocaine is highly addictive. In some instances, users have died of cardiac arrest while taking the drug.

Methamphetamine   Methamphetamine, often abbreviated to "meth," is particularly dangerous because it costs so little and is so easy to make. Much of it is produced in makeshift labs in homes or college residences, which means not only that the quality varies from batch to batch but also that it's virtually impossible to know what else is in the mixture. The drug can initially produce euphoria, enhanced wakefulness, increased physical activity, and decreased appetite. Prolonged use can lead to binges, during which users take more meth every few hours for several days until they run out or become too disorganized to continue. Chronic abuse can lead to psychotic behavior characterized by intense paranoia, visual and auditory hallucinations, and out-of-control rages that can be coupled with extremely violent behavior.

---

[6] Excerpted from *Ecstasy: What We Know and Don't Know about MDMA: A Scientific Review*. Bethesda, MD: National Institute on Drug Abuse, part of the National Institutes of Health (NIH), a division of the U.S. Department of Health and Human Services, 2001.

13

13 Chapter Review

One-minute paper . . .

This chapter provides a lot of tips and strategies for staying mentally and physically healthy. What was the most surprising or unexpected point made in this chapter? What interesting questions remain unanswered about these topics?

Applying what you've learned . . .

Now that you have read and discussed this chapter, consider how you can apply what you have learned to your academic and personal life. The following prompts will help you reflect on chapter material and its relevance to you both now and in the future.

1. Identify one area in your life in which you need to make changes to become healthier. How do you think becoming healthier will improve your performance in college? What are the challenges you face in becoming healthier?

2. If you could make only three recommendations to an incoming first-year college student about managing stress in college, what would they be? Use your personal experience and what you have learned in this chapter to make your recommendations.

Building your portfolio . . .

Are you "technostressed"?

Ever-changing, ever-improving technology is a wonderful part of our modern world, but it can also be an additional stressor in our everyday lives. It seems the list of hot, new gadgets grows longer every day. How do being constantly accessible, being a multitasking marvel, having constant reminders of what you haven't done yet, and sorting an overload of information

affect your stress level? Do you occasionally find yourself overwhelmed or even a bit lonely when you are face to face with your computer instead of your friends, families, or coworkers?

How are you "plugged in"? Create a Word document in your portfolio and re-create the table below.

1. Describe all the ways in which your life is affected by technology. How are your health and well-being affected, both positively and negatively, by the things you list? Tip: Think of how you use technology for entertainment and for class or work.

My Gadgets and Gizmos	Positive Aspects	Negative Aspects
Instant Messenger	Ability to communicate anywhere in the world, in a matter of seconds, 24/7	Staying up late, talking to my friends = No Sleep!

Sometimes it seems as if all of the technology that is supposed to make our lives easier actually adds to the balancing act. Here are a few tips for reducing your stress level and avoiding a "technology takeover":

- Schedule some down-time offline for yourself.
- Don't become a text message junkie.
- Don't try to multitask 24/7! Take advantage of time to exercise, eat, or just take a break without the demands of e-mail and cell phones.
- Recognize the warning signs of Internet addiction—for example, using the Internet to escape from problems or responsibilities; missing class, work, or appointments to spend time online; and always allowing the Internet to substitute for face-to-face interaction with others.

2. Save your reflections in your portfolio on your personal computer or flash drive. The next time you're feeling stressed out, revisit this activity and evaluate the role technology is playing in your life.

Where to go for help . . .

On Campus

Counseling center: Professionals here will offer individual and group assistance and lots of information. Remember that their support is confidential, and you will not be judged.

Health center/infirmary: On most campuses the professionals who staff the health center are especially interested in educational outreach and practicing prevention. You should be able to receive treatment as well.

Health education and wellness programs: College campuses assume and recognize that, for many students, problems and challenges with alcohol, other drugs, and sexual decision making and the consequences are part of the college universe. Student peer health educators who are trained and supervised by professionals can provide support. Taking part in such peer leadership is also a great way to develop and practice your own communication skills.

Campus support groups: Many campuses provide student support groups led by professionals for students dealing with problems related to excessive alcohol and drug use, abusive sexual relationships, and other issues.

Online

Advice about College Student Health Issues: http://www.goaskalice.com. This Web site, sponsored by Columbia University, has answers to many health questions.

Dealing with Stress: http://www.stress.org. Want to combat stress? Find out how at the American Institute of Stress Web site.

Advice from the American Dietetic Association: http://www.eatright.org. This Web site provides information on healthy eating and nutrition.

How Tobacco Affects Your Health: http://www.cancer.org. To learn more about the health effects of tobacco, visit the American Cancer Society.

The Center for Young Women's Health: http://www.youngwomenshealth.org/collegehealth10.html. This Web site has helpful advice on sexual health as well as other issues.

National Clearinghouse for Alcohol and Drug Information: http://www.ncadi.samhsa.gov/. This organization provides up-to-date information about the effects of alcohol and drug use.

DrugHelp: http://www.drughelp.org. This is a private, nonprofit referral service for drug treatment.

Methamphetamine Addiction: http://www.methamphetamineaddiction.com. Learn more about the dangers of methamphetamine at this Web site.

The Centers for Disease Control and Prevention: http://www.cdc.gov. This Web site is an excellent resource for all of the topics in this chapter.

Other Valuable Resources

National Eating Disorders Association: http://www.nationaleatingdisorders.org

U.S. Government's Nutrition Information: http://www.nutrition.gov

Shape Up America: http://www.shapeup.org

National Health Information Center: http://www.healthfinder.org

Planned Parenthood Federation of America: http://www.plannedparenthood.org

U.S. Food and Drug Administration: http//www.fda.gov

My Institution's Resources

_____

_____

_____

_____

_____

_____

_____

_____

_____

_____

_____

_____

_____

Index

N

National Clearinghouse for Alcohol and Drug Information, 171
National College Access Network, 124
National Eating Disorders Association, 163, 171
National Endowment for Financial Education, 133
National Health Information Center, 171
National Institute on Drug Abuse, 167, 168
National Institutes of Mental Health, 42
Need-based scholarships, 124
Needs *versus* wants, in budgeting, 123
Networking, 150
  social, 9, 10–11, 111
New Economy, career choices and characteristics of, 148–149
  essential qualities and skills for, 149
Newspaper classifieds, 155
Niagra University's Office for Academic Support, 83
Note taking, 32
  comparing notes, 68–69
  listening and, 58–60
  in nonlecture courses, 66
  paper *versus* electronic, 67b
  for public speaking, 93
  recall column in, 61, 66, 69b, 101
  reviewing, 68–69
  services for, 69
  systems for, 61–62, 62i, 63i
  techniques for, 62–63
Nutrition, 162

O

Obama, Barack, 130, 137, 138
Obesity, 162–163
Occupational Information Network, 157
Off-campus employment, 154–155
Online, social networking sites for, 9, 111
Online, writing, 90–91, 91b
Online courses, 112–113
Online degree programs, 110
Online payment, 130
Online public access catalogs (OPACs), 116
Online resources
  See also Web sites
  career choices, 157
  critical thinking, 57
  dictionaries, 80
  diversity, 145
  health, 171
  job boards, 155
  learning management systems and, 112–113
  learning support, 45
  public speaking, 71
  reading, 83

registering for courses, 110–111
  for speaking, 95
  time management, 27
  for writing, 95
Online security, 111
Open-mindedness, 49, 134
  in critical listening, 64–65
  diversity and, 134, 137
Opioids, 168
Optimism, 39
Organization, personal, 14, 100
  daily, 22–23
  for note-taking, 64
  public speaking and, 93
Outline (note-taking) format, 61, 62i
Outlining
  in chapters, 79
  prewriting and, 88
Overextension, 4, 23
Overhead transparencies, 62
Overlearning, 100

P

Paragraph (note-taking) format, 62
Parent Loan for Undergraduate Students (PLUS), 129
Parents, 4, 8
  See also Family
Partners, 8
Passwords, managing, 111, 113
Paul, Richard, 48
Peers (fellow students)
  assistance from, 27, 71, 83, 91
Periodical databases, 116
Personal attacks, in arguments, 50
Personal finance classes, 120
  See also Money management
Personal influences, 56
Personality characteristics, career and, 152–153
Personal values. *See* Values
Phaup, Patricia, 165
Phone numbers, 69
  cell phones, 76
Physical activity, 21
  exercise program, 98, 161
Physical disabilities, 139
PIN (personal identification number), 116, 127, 131
Pirsig, Robert, 87
Plagiarism, 104
Planned Parenthood Federation of America, 171
Planner, 18, 19
Planning, 40
  schedules, 18
Point of view, 137
  in critical thinking, 46, 49, 52, 55
  of reader, 91
  study groups and, 99

Politeness, rules of, 24–25
Political organizations, 11, 141
Portfolio, building
  academic integrity and, 105–106
  credit cards and, 132
  investigating occupations, 156
  mapping strategies and, 82–83
  personal influences and, 56
  PowerPoint presentation, 70
  public speaking skills, 94–95
  self-assessment and, 44
  skills matrix and, 12, 13
  study abroad programs and, 144
  technological change and, 118, 170
  time management and career, 26, 27t
Positive competition, 31
Positive personal traits, 149
Positive self-talk, 99
Positive thinking, 92
PowerPoint presentations, 63, 70, 93, 94
Prejudice, 142–143
Prescription drug abuse, 168–169
Presentation skills, 148
Primary source material, 77, 79
  scholarly journals, 55, 79
Problem solving, 46, 49, 149
  note-taking and, 66
  study groups and, 32–33
Procrastination, 14, 24, 26
  highlighting and, 78
Professional organizations, 157
Professional school, 25
Professors. *See* Instructors
Pronunciation, 92
Public speaking. *See* Speaking
Punctuality, 14, 25
  See also Time management

Q

Quantitative courses, taking notes in, 66–67
Questionnaires
  emotional intelligence, 39b
  VARK, 34–37
Questions, 32
  about technology, 108
  in class, 65
  for critical thinking, 49
  in reading, 76–77
  for study groups, 69
  in tests, 102–103

R

Race, 138
Racial slurs, 142
Rape, protection against, 165
Rating instructors, 48